THE TIMELINE OF WORLD WAR II

WORLD HISTORY TIMELINE

THE TIMELINE OF WORLD WAR II

THE ULTIMATE GUIDE TO THE BIGGEST CONFLICT OF THE TWENTIETH CENTURY

David Jordan

THUNDER BAY
P·R·E·S·S

San Diego, California

Thunder Bay Press
An imprint of the Advantage Publishers Group
5880 Oberlin Drive, San Diego, CA 92121-4794
www.thunderbaybooks.com

ISBN-13: 978-1-59223-721-0
ISBN-10: 1-59223-721-5

Project Editor: Sarah Uttridge
Picture Research: Terry Forshaw
Design: Zoë Mellors

Printed in China

1 2 3 4 5 11 10 09 08 07

PICTURE CREDITS

Art-Tech/Aerospace: 5, 7–11, 14, 16–19, 21, 23, 24, 29–33, 35–39, 45–47, 49, 53, 58–60, 62, 63, 72, 74, 77, 86–88, 91, 92, 95(right), 97, 104, 108, 110(right), 113, 114, 115(right), 126(left), 127, 129, 130(right), 132(left), 133, 137, 138(left), 141, 145(right), 146(left), 147, 151, 154, 168–170, 179, 181(right), 188, 199, 200, 202–205, 209–212, 214–216, 221; Art-Tech/MARS: 12, 40, 41, 43, 48, 50(right), 61, 73, 75, 78–81, 83–85, 89, 93, 95(left), 96, 98–103, 105, 120–123, 130(left), 131, 132(right), 134, 142, 143,146(right), 150, 153, 155, 156, 158, 159, 164–167, 171–178, 180, 181(left), 182–187, 189, 190, 191(left), 192–194, 196–198, 201, 206, 207, 217, 218, 219(right); Corbis: 15, 22, 28, 64, 66, 46(right), 160(left); Defense Visual Information Center: 6, 25(right), 27, 50(left), 51, 52, 55, 56, 90, 94, 135, 136, 138(right), 139, 140, 144, 145(left), 152, 160(right), 161, 162, 163, 191(right), 195, 208, 213, 219(left), 220; Getty Images: 20, 25(left), 34, 42, 57, 65, 107, 119, 124, 128, 157, 191(right); Private Collection: 82; TopFoto: 13; TRH Pictures: 26, 44, 54, 125; Ukrainian State Archive: 67–71, 76, 106, 109, 110(left), 111, 112, 115(left), 116–118, 126(right), 148, 149, 162, 163.

Contents

Introduction

At 11 a.m. on 11 November 1918, the guns fell silent along the Western Front, bringing an end to more than four years of bitter fighting. Yet despite the hopes of the victorious powers, the peace settlements brought only a temporary calm to Europe.

Against a background of economic collapse, the next two decades brought chaos, despair and bitterness at the increasingly unsatisfactory legacy of the war – and laid the foundations for dictatorship. Less than 25 years after 'the war to end all wars', the world found itself in the midst of conflict once more.

The seeds of World War II were sown within six months of the end of World War I. The Paris peace conferences were severe to Germany, the

Left: Delegates gather in the Hall of Mirrors at the Palace of Versailles in 1919 to witness the signing of the peace treaty that ended World War I.
Right: Hitler inspects his supporters in Berlin, 1932.

infamous 'war guilt' clause of the Treaty of Versailles blaming the country for the conflict. Nor was this all. The French, having suffered two invasions from German territory in less than half a century, wished to ensure that they would never be threatened by Germany again.

It must be said, too, that the French (and to a lesser extent, the British) considered the peace settlement to be a useful means of punishing Germany. Depriving Germany of its colonies and redrawing the country's boundaries to give a third of its original territory to other nations, the peace settlements also saddled the German nation with crippling reparations.

German resentment at this was considerable, not least because many Germans felt that they had not truly lost the war. Their army had not been completely defeated in the field, and no Allied soldiers had entered German territory. How, the German population asked, did this

constitute a defeat so total that the victorious Allies could dictate peace terms? True, this question that did not take account of the military realities pertaining in November 1918, but the facts did not matter: it was the perception that counted.

The new republic seemed weak and a poor replacement for the Kaiser, who had abdicated and was now living in the Netherlands. Attempted Communist uprisings, most notably in Berlin, meant that the new republic began life in the small town of Weimar, the parliament choosing to meet there until it was safe to return to Berlin. The chaotic birth of the Weimar Republic, as it came to be known, did not augur well for Germany. And the impact of the peace treaties forced upon the new, uncertain government simply added to the nation's woes.

The Germans were not at all comforted by the fact that others were suffering similar depredations in the aftermath of the war. The Austro-Hungarian Empire had collapsed, and the redrawing of European boundaries gave birth to Czechoslovakia, Poland and Yugoslavia, leaving the rump of the once-great empire divided into two separate nations: Austria and Hungary. Austria presented something of a problem for the peacemakers, in that President Woodrow Wilson's principle of self-determination meant

Mussolini's 'Black Shirts' guard the General Post Office in Milan in the build-up to the Fascist 'March on Rome'.

1919

JUNE

June Treaty of Versailles. Germany accepts that German aggression had caused the war and is forced to pay high reparations. The League of Nations is established.

1920

MARCH

March Poland concludes a successful campaign to retain its independance from Soviet Russia by the signing of the Treaty of Riga.

1921

MAY

May In Italy, Benito Mussolini's Fascist Party wins 35 seats in the national elections.

SEPTEMBER

September Mussolini's Fascists seize control of Ravenna's public utilities, thus effectively controlling the town.

that its Germanic population could have demanded to unify with Germany. As a result, the peace treaties specifically barred Austro-German unification, which was seen by many Germans as rather hypocritical.

A further blow to national pride came with the imposition of strict conditions on the German armed forces. The Versailles settlement limited the size of the German Army to 100,000 men, forbade the existence of an air force, and prevented the German Navy from owning submarines. For a country that had been inordinately proud of its military might, this was a bitter pill.

The German Crisis

Not surprisingly, a resentful Germany soon emerged, to become the greatest problem facing Europe. By 1922, the German Government could not afford to pay reparations, at which the French and Belgians occupied the Ruhr to seize them directly from German industry. Anger was considerable, and a general strike was called throughout the country, forcing the occupiers to bring in their own workforces to run the mines and factories.

Mussolini rides in state with King Victor Emmanuel. The king and the dictator could barely tolerate each other.

The effect on the German economy was disastrous. Already operating under great strain, it now collapsed, leading to hyperinflation. Recent historical research suggests that the effect of hyperinflation has been treated in too simplistic a manner until recently, but the fact remains that it added to the resentment felt by Germany. It encouraged political extremism, as the population sought solutions from groups other than the mainstream political parties. Indeed, the aftermath of the crisis brought an abortive coup attempt in Munich by the Nationalist Socialist German Workers' Party, better known as the Nazis. The party leader, a little-known firebrand called Adolf Hitler, was imprisoned for his part in the *putsch*. His sentence was lenient, and in light of the experience he vowed that he would use legal means to gain power in Germany.

The Allied powers did now recognize the fact that the Germans simply could not meet the reparation payments demanded of them by the Versailles settlement, and attempts were made to modify these terms. The resulting Dawes Plan laid down a more reasonable rate of repayment, and also encouraged large-scale

1922

JANUARY

January France and Belgium occupy Germany's Ruhr area to seize directly from German industry the reparations that the country is unable to pay.

FEBRUARY

February The London Naval Treaty is signed. The USA and UK agree to limit the size of their fleets, with Japan, France and Italy all agreeing on smaller fleets.

MAY

May Italian Fascists seize control of Bologna and Ferrara.

investment in Germany from the United States. The extreme political parties in Germany suffered a setback, and the country entered a period of stability and prosperity. It was not to last.

Italy

Italy, despite being one of the victorious powers in the war, suffered from political instability in its aftermath. This encouraged extremist political thinking, most notably from the Fascist Party. It was headed by a former socialist leader, Benito Mussolini, who had grand visions of making Italy a great power.

In May 1921, the party won 35 seats in the national elections, success that encouraged it to seek control of the whole nation. In September, a band of Fascist supporters entered Ravenna and seized control of all the public utilities, giving them effective control of the town. The success of this tactic proven, the Fascists repeated it in May 1922, taking over both Ferrara and Bologna. When the Socialists declared a general strike in September, the Fascists broke the strike by taking over the rail network and trams.

The momentum gained by the party now prompted Mussolini to seek power. The Fascists occupied public buildings throughout northern and southern Italy, and bands of Fascist supporters began to converge on Rome. The Government tried to impose a state of emergency to deal with this attempted coup, but King Victor Emmanuel refused to sign the necessary proclamation. Mussolini arrived in triumph on 30 October 1922, and the king now offered him the premiership. Mussolini accepted, and Italy fell under Fascist control.

Opposition parties were permitted, but the Fascists thought nothing of using violence to break up political meetings, of rigging elections and of generally behaving in an antidemocratic manner. Mussolini's ambitions for Italy were grand, including the acquisition of colonies. However, for the first years of his regime, he concentrated predominantly on domestic issues and upon establishing his power base. His change of focus in the mid-1930s would create serious problems within Europe.

Adolf Hitler leaves Landsberg Prison at the completion of his sentence for organizing the failed Munich Putsch.

1922

OCTOBER

October King Victor Emmanuel of Italy offers Mussolini the premiership of the country.

1923

NOVEMBER

November Hyperinflation in Germany reaches its peak with an exchange rate of 130 billion marks to the dollar.

November Munich Putsch – Adolf Hitler, leader of the National Socialist German Workers' Party, fails in a coup attempt.

Nazi Party supporters crowd into the rear of a lorry during the failed 'Beer Hall Putsch' of 1923.

The Soviet Union, Japan and Other Problems

Russia, meanwhile, had been in a state of chaos since the Bolshevik Revolution, and had plunged into a state of civil war. The

Western allies had intervened, attempting to overthrow the new Communist government – a step that ensured the Soviet leadership was inclined to mistrust the West for many years, well beyond even the second global conflict. The civil war also meant that the newly created Soviet Union (USSR) played no part in the peace settlement. Then in 1920, to add insult to injury, the newly formed state of Poland attempted to gain territory it felt should have been granted to it under the peace settlement.

The redistribution of territory that followed the war satisfied few. It was questioned not just by the Poles and those Germans who found themselves citizens of newly created states, but also by Italy and Japan. During the war, the Italian Government had carefully weighed up the possible benefits of joining the Allies or the Central Powers before siding with the

1924
AUGUST

August After Germany has proved unable to pay the high reparations demanded by the Versailles settlement, a revised arrangement is agreed under the Dawes Plan.

1925
DECEMBER

December Germany recognizes its western frontiers and renounces war as an instrument of policy in the Locarno Treaty.

1926
SEPTEMBER

September Germany joins the League of Nations.

Polish armoured units equipped with French FT17 light tanks, during the Russo-Polish War over disputed territories in Ukraine.

....

Volunteers parade in Warsaw during the summer of 1920, during the height of the Russo-Polish War.

country had been a staunch ally of Britain since the naval treaty of 1902 – the terms of which were extended to provide ships for convoy escort in 1917 – and it had been quick to declare war against Germany in 1914 (albeit with a view to seizing German possessions in the Far East).

Collective Security – the Flawed Ideal

As a consequence of the war, the United States, Britain and France moved towards the notion of creating a collective security organization to

Allies, so it was angered when the Dalmatian Coast was placed under Yugoslav control, rather than handed to Italy, as the Nationalists wished. Equally, the Japanese felt that they had been held in contempt by the Western allies, as their territorial ambitions in the Far East went largely ignored. Given that only two Japanese citizens died on the Western Front during the entire conflict, it is perhaps unsurprising that the Japanese contribution to the war was not widely recognized in Europe. The government in Tokyo, however, felt that it deserved a peace settlement that brought it greater rewards. The

1929

OCTOBER

October Wall Street Crash – prices on the New York Stock Exchange collapse and a world economic depression begins.

1930

APRIL

April The 2nd London Naval Treaty continues the ban on new battleships until 1937 and sets new limits for smaller battleships.

1931

SEPTEMBER

September Japan seizes the Chinese territory of Manchuria.

ensure that the world could not be plunged into conflict again. This culminated in the formation of the League of Nations. The cherished creation of President Wilson, this was designed to be the forum that would promote international harmony. Sadly for Wilson, he could not command the support of the American Congress, which refused to ratify American involvement in the League. Since the League was intended to serve as a 'world policeman', the task of keeping international peace fell upon Britain and France, who were both war-weary, financially stretched, and generally unwilling to assume the mantle of leaders of the international community. Without the Americans, the League was far weaker than it might have been, and as time progressed, it became clear that the League was viewed by the nations as little more than an inconvenience and that it lacked the will to enforce collective security upon the world.

The Rise of Dictatorship: Hitler

The years after the implementation of the Dawes Plan were successful for Germany. The economy improved, and by the Locarno Treaty of 1925, Germany recognized its western frontiers and renounced war as an instrument of policy. Foreign relations were generally improved, partly because it eased French complaints about the country's military, which maintained a General Staff and was training sufficient reservists so that the size of the army exceeded the figure of 100,000 men allowed by the Treaty of Versailles.

Within four years, however, Germany had been thrown into chaos once more. A further attempt to alleviate reparation payments, the Young Plan, was overshadowed by the Wall Street Crash of October 1929. The Crash led to further economic collapse – and this time there was no respite. Once again, the German electorate turned to the extremist parties, benefiting the Nazis in particular. Their share of the vote declined in elections in November 1932, but the political situation was such that Hitler was able to demand the position of chancellor, as part of a coalition between the Nazis and the Nationalist Party. The

Diplomats gather for the camera before a meeting of the League of Nations.

1932

JUNE

June German elections leave the Nazis the largest party in the Reichstag.

1933

JANUARY

January Hitler becomes Chancellor of Germany.

FEBRUARY

February Burning of the Reichstag in Berlin. Allegedly the work of an arsonist, Hitler uses the attack to suspend political and civil liberties.

OCTOBER

October Hitler takes Germany out of the League of Nations, ostensibly because other nations had failed to disarm to the German level.

Nationalists foolishly thought that they could control Hitler – a gross misjudgement.

On 30 January 1933, Hindenburg, the German president, appointed Hitler as chancellor. Hitler now controlled state apparatus, and by purging the police and replacing senior officers with Nazi supporters, he was able to sabotage the opposition parties campaigning for the election scheduled for early March. On 27 February, the Reichstag burned to the ground, allegedly as a result of an arson attack by a Dutch Communist. Hitler used the attack to rally middle-class support, and convinced Hindenburg to grant him extraordinary powers, enabling him to suspend political and civil liberties. When the votes were counted after the 6 March elections, the Nazis had 43.9 per cent of the vote, and 288 seats in parliament. With the support of the Nationalists, who now understood that their notions of 'controlling' Hitler were misplaced, he enjoyed a clear majority in the Reichstag.

Nazi Party members celebrate outside party headquarters, acknowledging Hitler's appointment as chancellor.

1934

JUNE

June Hitler has a large number of potential enemies killed in what becomes known as the 'Night of the Long Knives'.

AUGUST

August Hitler becomes sole ruler of Germany after President Hindenburg dies.

DECEMBER

December The Japanese break from the 1930 London Naval Treaty.

Hitler secured his position on 23 March 1933, with the passing of an Enabling Act, which gave Hitler the power to take whatever action he deemed necessary for effective government in Germany for the next four years. Reichstag deputies seemed unwilling to ponder the fact that this might include the extension of the Enabling Act. The Nazi seizure of power was near complete, and when Hindenburg died on 2 August 1934, Hitler assumed complete control.

A third potent dictatorship was now added to the ranks of European states, alongside Italy and the Soviet Union. Worse still for Europe, Hitler was determined to overturn the Versailles settlement and restore Germany to prominence: he was prepared to use force if necessary, and therefore embarked upon a secret rearmament programme, contrary to the peace agreement, as soon as he was in power. The consequences of this step were to prove far-reaching, ultimately plunging the world into a new, bloodier conflict that would completely reshape the map of the world once again.

The Reichstag burns out of control in 1938. The fire was allegedly started by a communist sympathizer.

1935

MARCH

March Germany introduces compulsory military service and announces the existence of a German air force, both contravening the Treaty of Versailles.

APRIL

April The US Neutrality Act prevents the Government giving financial assistance to any country involved in war.

OCTOBER

October Italy invades Abyssinia.

PART 1:

The European Theatre 1939–1945

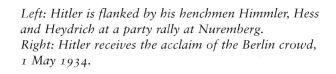

Left: Hitler is flanked by his henchmen Himmler, Hess and Heydrich at a party rally at Nuremberg.
Right: Hitler receives the acclaim of the Berlin crowd, 1 May 1934.

The Build-Up to War

His power now total, Hitler set about fulfilling his aim of returning the country to the first rank of powers. Creating 'Lebensraum' ('living space') in central and eastern Europe would enable him to build a new Reich that would last a thousand years.

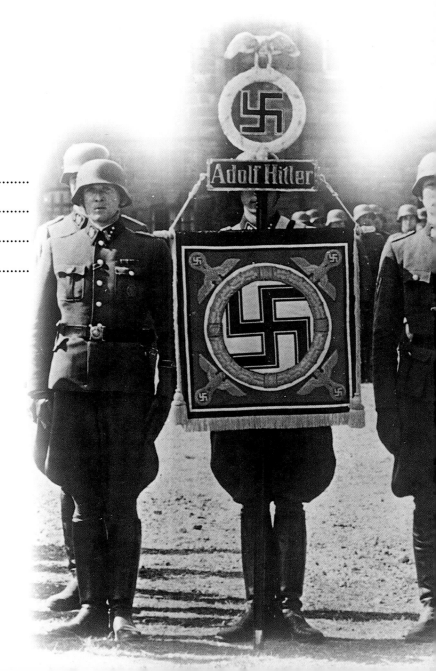

Hitler now sought to renegotiate the terms of the peace settlements. He first made a bid to increase the size of the country's armed forces to bring them to parity with their neighbours. This was rejected by the League of Nations, at which point Germany withdrew from the organization. Unless Britain and France, the two principal members of the League, were prepared to act, there was little to prevent Germany from abrogating its commitments.

Left: Luftwaffe aircraft overfly the Nuremberg rally. Hitler covertly put together a large air force.
Right: Members of the SS-Leibstandarte Adolf Hitler parade with the unit's standard.

On 26 January 1934, Hitler signed a 10-year non-aggression pact with Poland. This was a piece of deceitful diplomacy, intended to disguise his true intentions and to draw the country away from an alliance with France. Less than a month later, Hitler ordered that the German Army be increased in size to 300,000 men – in contravention of the Versailles accords – and that it should be ready to take offensive action by 1942.

Hitler's aggressive approach to foreign policy was revealed when Austrian Nazis murdered Chancellor Engelbert Dollfuss. Dollfuss had been governing without reference to parliament since 1932, in response to the threat of both left- and right-wing political extremism. The Austrian Nazis made little secret of their view that the country should be unified with Germany, and the assassination was part of a coup, covertly

Chancellor Engelbert Dollfuss of Austria lies in state after his assassination by Nazi sympathizers in 1934.

supported by Hitler. The coup failed, however, and the Government retained control, led by Kurt von Schuschnigg. The new chancellor was encouraged by the fact that Mussolini sent troops to the Brenner Pass, indicating his opposition to the Nazi coup. At this point, Hitler did not have the military might to ignore Italy, and he was forced to withdraw. Though his support for the coup was widely recognized across Europe, the consequences for him were limited.

Fortune continued to favour Hitler. In January 1935, the scheduled plebiscite in the Saarland voted overwhelmingly in favour of returning to German control; it had been under French control since 1920. Hitler was now able to exploit the fact that ethnic Germans wished to be reunited with their 'true' homeland, and on 1 March he sent members of his personal bodyguard, the SS Liebstandarte Adolf Hitler, into the Saar. Just eight days later, on 9 March, he revealed that he had created an air force, the *Luftwaffe*, and then, on 16 March, he announced that Germany would increase the size of its army to 36 divisions. Both Britain and France protested – for what that was worth.

The British Government was particularly concerned by the creation of the *Luftwaffe*, and set about reinforcing the Royal Air Force (RAF). It also feared the possibility of a naval race breaking out between Britain and Germany, and to this it was quick to react. On 18 June 1935, it signed a naval treaty, the terms of which restricted the German surface fleet to 35 per cent of the size of the Royal Navy and established parity for its submarine fleet.

The French were understandably outraged by Hitler's action. Not only did this overturn the Versailles condition forbidding Germany to have submarines, it also gave legitimacy to the notion that the terms of the postwar settlement could be altered. The British view was that these had already been altered under the Dawes and Young Plans, and that it was much better to reach agreement with Hitler and thus bind him to some conditions rather than to simply sit back and watch him breach the Versailles accords anyway. The possibility that the French and British could take military action to ensure that Hitler did not stray from the terms of the peace accords was not given serious consideration in either London or Paris.

1936

MARCH

7 March Germany reoccupies the Rhineland, in contravention of the Versailles settlement.

NOVEMBER

1 November Mussolini and Hitler sign the Berlin–Rome Axis.

1937

JANUARY

2 January An informal agreement is reached between Britain and Italy to maintain the status quo in the Mediterranean.

The Role of Italy

The British and French Governments now decided to seek some form of accommodation with Mussolini. In part, this was because they recognized that the Italian dictator had prevented the Austrian Nazi coup from having a chance of success, but perhaps their principal concern was that an alliance between two right-wing dictators would obviously be a disaster for their diplomacy.

However, reaching an accommodation would prove difficult. Mussolini was determined to increase Italy's international prestige, and the acquisition of colonies was the means to achieve this. He now looked to Africa, where there was a clear candidate for colonial subjugation. The Italians had attempted to seize Abyssinia in 1896, but suffered a humiliating defeat at Adowa – an embarrassment that continued to be felt. Mussolini initially contented himself with trying to exert influence over Abyssinia, and supported the country's application to join the League of Nations in 1923. He also signed a treaty of friendship with the Abyssinian Emperor Haile Selassie in 1928. Selassie, though, was determined that Abyssinia should not fall under Italian domination, and sought relations with other countries. Mussolini's response was to conclude that Italian influence could be achieved only through force.

The first clash between Italian and Abyssinian troops came at the Wal Wal oasis on 5 December 1934. Mussolini now determined on war. On 30 December, he gave instructions that an invasion was to take place later in 1935, after the end of the rainy season. The Abyssinians, alarmed by events at Wal Wal, sought arbitration with the Italians, and when

Emperor Haile Selassie of Abyssinia at a field headquarters during the Battle of Lake Ashang in April 1936.

1938

MARCH

13 March *Anschluss* ('union') between Austria and Germany is announced.

MAY

20 May Czechoslovakia mobilizes its army following German threats over the Sudetenland.

SEPTEMBER

12 September British prime minister Neville Chamberlain flies to Germany to negotiate with Hitler over the Sudeten crisis.

29 September The Munich Pact is signed. The Czechs are forced to cede Sudetenland to Germany.

this failed, appealed to the League of Nations. Mussolini agreed to arbitration, but increased the number of troops in Eritrea. Further armed clashes led to a second Abyssinian appeal to the League on 17 March. However, this was just one day after Hitler announced the increase in size of the German Army, which made the concerns of Abyssinia seem of much less importance.

On 11 and 14 April 1935, a conference was held at Stresa to discuss the problem of rearmament. Britain, France and Italy presented a united front – at the expense of the Abyssinians. Privately, the French made it known that they would do nothing to stop Italian aspirations, and the British studiously avoided any mention of Abyssinia. By June, however, the British had begun to doubt the wisdom of their approach. If Italy embarked on a war of aggression that would remove the right of self-determination from the Abyssinian people, the covenant of the League of Nations would be broken. Foreign Secretary Anthony Eden tried to dissuade Mussolini from action, but his efforts were rejected. On 11 September, the British Foreign Secretary, Sir Samuel Hoare, declared that Britain would stand by the principle of collective

Left to right: Foreign Minister Pierre Laval of France, Prime Minister Benito Mussolini of Italy and Prime Minister Ramsay MacDonald of Great Britain at the Stresa Conference in 1935.

1938

OCTOBER

28 October Hitler insists that the Poles restore Danzig to Germany.

1939

MARCH

15 March Czechoslovakia is broken up by the Germans: Bohemia and Moravia are annexed by Germany, Slovakia made a protectorate, and Ruthenia given to Hungary.

21 March Hitler repeats his demands for Poland to restore Danzig to German control.

23 March German troops occupy Memel on the East Prussian/Lithuanian border. Poland warns Germany that a similar attempt to seize Danzig will lead to war.

31 March France and Britain guarantee that they will support Poland.

Italian troops parade in Mogadishu, Italian Somaliland, before the start of operations against Abyssinia in late 1935. Within seven months the area had been annexed by Mussolini's forces.

action against aggression – but it was a speech made for show. The Italians invaded Abyssinia on 3 October, and the League was remarkable only for its hesitation. Britain and France oversaw the imposition of sanctions, but these were extremely limited in scope. They did not apply to coal or oil, and states that were not members of the League were not obliged to abide by the sanctions. Its only result was to create a breach between Mussolini and the French and British. On 9 May 1936, Mussolini announced that Abyssinia had been annexed by Italy. The League had failed again – and for the second time in just three months.

This encouraged Hitler to take another step, bolder than any he had taken before. On 7 March 1936, he sent troops into the Rhineland. They were welcomed with acclaim by the local population – and still the French and British failed to respond. What made this particularly unfortunate was that Hitler privately acknowledged that a response would force him to back down. When none came, he took the view that France and Britian would do almost anything to avoid war – a fact he intended to exploit to the full.

APRIL

7 April Mussolini invades Albania.

15 April President Roosevelt seeks assurances from Germany and Italy that they will not attack any European nations.

18 April Stalin proposes a 10-year alliance with France and Britain.

28 April Hitler repudiates the 1934 non-aggression pact with Poland and reiterates demands for Danzig.

Civil War in Spain

Civil war broke out in Spain on 17 July 1936, giving Hitler and Mussolini the chance to act against a left-leaning government in Madrid. German aircraft transported General Francisco Franco's forces from Spanish Morocco to the mainland on 28 July, and the Italians joined in two days later. Attempts by Britain and France to prevent the intervention of foreign powers foundered, and by October it was clear that the Germans and Italians were supporting the Nationalists, who had appointed Franco as head of state at the end of September. The Soviet Union now intervened to support the Republican government, and then, in November, Germany and Italy recognized Franco's regime. Both dictators made it clear that they would not withdraw their 'volunteer' forces until victory was achieved.

The pace of the war increased, and on 26 April 1937, the town of Guernica was bombed by aircraft from the German Condor Legion. The attack killed an estimated 6000 civilians, demonstrating that a future war would bring huge civilian casualties, lost to air raids. This added impetus to Franco-British efforts to

Reichsmarshal Hermann Goering reviews a parade of German volunteers recently returned from fighting in Spain.

1939

MAY

22 May The Pact of Steel – Italy and Germany guarantee to support each other in any future war.

AUGUST

23 August A German–Soviet non-aggression pact is signed.

25 August Britain enters a formal alliance with Poland.

maintain peace, although both governments now found themselves accused of seeking 'peace at any price'. Franco's regime was endorsed by the Spanish bishops on 1 July, and on 28 August, the Vatican recognized Franco's legitimacy as head of state. He formed his first ministry on 30 January 1938, but the war still had over a year to run.

Attention turned away from Spain on 13 March, when the Union of Austria and Germany was proclaimed. In 1936, Chancellor Schuschnigg

A dog wanders through the wreckage of the Spanish town of Guernica after it was bombed in April 1937.

German troops march into Austria following Hitler's decision to unify the country with Germany in 1938.

SEPTEMBER

1 September German forces invade Poland.

2 September Britain and France issue an ultimatum demanding that Germany withdraw from Poland within 12 hours.

3 September Britain and France declare war on Germany. The liner SS *Athenia* is sunk by a U-boat.

4 September The RAF undertakes bombing raids against shipping in Schilling Roads and the Kiel Canal, but more than 20 per cent of the attacking force is lost.

5 September The USA declares its neutrality.

Prime Minister Neville Chamberlain addresses eager crowds prior to his departure for the Munich summit, at which he believed he would secure 'peace for our time'.

1939

SEPTEMBER

6 September South Africa declares war on Germany.

7 September French forces cross into German territory in Saarland.

9 September The 4th Panzer Division reaches the outskirts of Warsaw. The first elements of the British Expeditionary Force (BEF) cross the Channel to France.

10 September Canada declares war on Germany.

12 September Major battle between German forces and the Poznan Army.

14 September German forces enter Gdynia.

had secured an agreement with Hitler that Germany would not interfere in Austrian affairs, but another Nazi plot was uncovered in January 1938, and Schuschnigg sought a meeting with Hitler, intending to protest. Instead, when the two met on 12 February, he was lectured about his treatment of Austrian Nazis. The situation was such that he was forced to announce a plebiscite on the issue of uniting with Germany. This was scheduled for 13 March 1938, but Hitler sent troops over the border the day before. The troops were welcomed by the supporters of *Anschluss* (union), and Hitler declared that this made plain the desire of the Austrian people.

Czechoslovakia and the Sudetenland

Hitler now sought to reunite the Czechoslovakian territory of Sudetenland with Germany. This had been awarded to the newly formed Czechoslovakia at Versailles, since it was the only way of ensuring that the Czechs had an enforcible border with Germany. However, the territory was home to a sizeable ethnic German minority, so this appeared to contravene the principle of self-determination. Hitler now chose to exploit the supposedly disadvantageous treatment of the Sudeten Germans and encouraged them to protest, intimating that he would support them militarily. President Hacha was not intimidated, and mobilized the Czech Army. This served as a sufficient

A woman weeps as German troops enter the Sudentenland.

deterrent, even though Hitler considered it unlikely that France or Britain would go to Czechoslovakia's aid.

Hitler's assumption was correct. Alarmed by a summer filled with predictions of a European war over the Sudetenland, both governments sought to mediate between the two parties. On 12 September 1938, the British prime minister, Neville Chamberlain, flew to Germany for a meeting with Hitler, and was assured that the Sudetenland represented the last of Germany's territorial demands. Chamberlain persuaded the French that appeasing him would avert war, and the French then informed the Czechs that they would withdraw support unless the German areas of Sudetenland were surrendered. At a summit meeting in Munich, Hitler demanded all of Sudetenland, and the British and French agreed. On 29 September 1938, a formal agreement was signed without reference to the Czechs. Chamberlain flew back to London, where he was welcomed by ecstatic crowds convinced that war had been averted. Waving a copy of the agreement, he told the crowds that it meant 'peace for our time' – words that he would regret within a year.

15 September German troops surround Warsaw and demand its surrender.

16 September Warsaw is subjected to German artillery and air attacks.

17 September Soviet troops enter Poland; Stalin declares that Poland no longer exists as an independent state. A U-29 sinks the British aircraft carrier HMS *Courageous*.

19 September German and Soviet troops meet at Brest-Litovsk.

22 September Soviet troops reach Lvov.

27 September Warsaw capitulates. The German pocket battleships *Deutschland* and *Graf Spee* are ordered to begin attacks on British shipping in the Atlantic.

German workers, known as the 'Shovel Brigade'.

An Eye on Poland

German troops entered the Sudetenland on 1 October. Shortly after, any hopes that this was Hitler's last territorial demand evaporated. On 28 October, he demanded that the Poles restore Danzig to Germany and permit the establishment of road and rail links to East Prussia through the Polish Corridor. The Poles refused, but to what end?

On 15 March 1939, the Germans dismembered Czechoslovakia into its component states. Slovakia became a German protectorate, Ruthenia was given to Hungary, and Bohemia and Moravia were incorporated into Germany. Attitudes towards Germany in both Britain and France now began to change, particularly in Britain. Chamberlain came under pressure to declare that Britain would support Poland against German aggression. Hitler reiterated his demands to the Poles on 21 March, and was rebuffed again. Two days later, German troops occupied the town of Memel on the border of East Prussia and Lithuania, an act that was seen to imply that the German Army could do the same to Danzig. The Poles warned that any attempt to seize Danzig would mean war. And on 31 March 1939, Britain and France declared that they would support the country should this occur.

On 15 April, in the wake of Mussolini's annexation of Albania just a week earlier, President Roosevelt sought assurances that the Germans and Italians would not attack other European states. Both Hitler and Mussolini ignored him, knowing that the Neutrality Acts of 1935–37 prevented the United States from intervening in a European war. Three days later, Stalin proposed a 10-year alliance with Britain and France. Had this been agreed, it is possible

1939

SEPTEMBER

28 September The Modlin garrison surrenders, leaving Hel naval base as the final area of organized Polish resistance against the Germans.

29 September German and Soviet foreign ministers Ribbentrop and Molotov meet in Moscow.

30 September A Polish government-in-exile forms in Paris. The *Graf Spee* begins a run of successes against British shipping.

that subsequent events might have been very different. However, negotiations proved difficult as a result of Soviet–Polish antagonism dating back to the 1920 war. Poland had no wish to be linked to two powers that were allied to a neighbour it mistrusted – and the same was true for the Soviet Union.

Hitler renounced the 1934 non-aggression pact with the Poles on 28 April 1939, and repeated his demand for Danzig. This was followed on 22 May by the 'Pact of Steel', under which Italy and Germany promised to support each other in any future war. To make matters worse, the Soviets and Germans shocked observers by signing a non-aggression pact on 23 August. The pact included clauses that agreed to divide Poland between Germany and the USSR, and allowed the Soviets a free hand in the Baltic states. Perhaps more importantly, it meant that Germany no longer faced the prospect of fighting a war on two fronts – a serious blow to the Western allies, who realized that Hitler would be free to attack Poland. On 25 August,

Italian alpine troops are inspected on their return from Albania, following the Italian annexation of the country.

Britain signed a treaty allying itself with Poland. Hitler had already issued orders for an invasion to take place on the following day, but Britain's action caused him to delay.

Concluding, however, that there was nothing that either Britain or France could do to prevent victory in Poland, he issued a new order to invade on 1 September.

OCTOBER

1 October Hel garrison surrenders. French troops begin to withdraw from Saarland. The USSR signs a 'mutual assistance' treaty with Estonia, effectively ending Estonian independence.

2 October The RAF makes its first night raid on Berlin, dropping propaganda leaflets.

5 October A Soviet–Latvian mutual assistance treaty is signed, allowing Soviet troops to establish military bases in Latvia.

6 October The last of the Polish resistance ends. Hitler proposes peace with France and Britain.

The Blitzkrieg on Poland

Early in the morning of 1 September 1939, Polish airbases came under attack from German bombers. The *Luftwaffe*'s plan was to inflict as much damage as possible on the Polish Air Force, to ensure that it could not interfere with the ground invasion that would follow. At 0445, the lead elements of the invasion force crossed the Polish border.

The Poles were caught by surprise. The mobilization of forces ordered just two days previously was nowhere near complete. Some of the reserve units were at, or near, full strength and waiting to move to their designated positions when the invasion began, but many others were still waiting for most of their personnel to arrive, and were therefore in no position to head for the front. This meant that the Germans faced an opposition that was somewhat under strength when first encountered, towards the end of the afternoon of 1 September.

The lead German formations from Army Group North benefited from the fact that their advance was conducted under the cover of an autumn mist. There were one or two incidents

Polish cavalry ford a stream while on exercise shortly before the outbreak of war.

1939

OCTOBER

9 October Following the rejection of a peace proposal, Hitler orders planning for an attack in the West to begin.

10 October A Soviet–Lithuanian mutual-assistance pact is signed, marking end of independence for the Baltic states.

12 October Territorial negotiations begin between the USSR and Finland.

14 October The battleship HMS *Royal Oak* is sunk by U-47 while at anchor in Scapa Flow.

16 October First German air raid on Britain as bombers attack shipping in the Firth of Forth.

of German units mistaking one another for Poles in the poor visibility, which led to the occasional exchange of fire, but these were not serious. The Germans quickly secured Danzig,

the Third and Fourth Armies moving to cut off the Polish Corridor before the Third Army diverted its effort towards Warsaw. Opposition proved to be relatively light, with only those

Polish positions along the Baltic coast being able to put up notable resistance.

The day also saw the birth of the myth of the gallant Polish cavalry attacking tanks. The 18th Lancer Regiment was indeed called upon to deliver a cavalry charge against German infantry, and even seemed to hold its own. But some German armoured cars succeeded in outflanking the Poles, and the Lancers suffered heavy casualties from the armoured cars' guns, forcing them to retreat.

The situation looked bleak for the Polish defenders as they struggled to put their defensive plans into operation. The guarantee of support from France and Britain looked particularly hollow, since it had not prevented the invasion, and there seemed to be little that either of the powers could do to assist their ally with sufficient speed.

On the second morning of the invasion, the Germans anticipated more serious opposition as they reached the River Brade. This, they assumed, would form the base for the Polish mainline of resistance. However, the Poles were not sufficiently prepared, and air attacks on transport targets had been effective, meaning

German SS troops, supported by an armoured car, advance through the streets of Danzig.

NOVEMBER

1 November Germany formally annexes western Poland, Danzig and the Polish Corridor.

7 November Offers by Dutch, Belgian and Romanian monarchs to act as mediators in the peace negotiations are rejected.

8 November An assassination attempt against Hitler fails.

14 November General Sikorski, head of the Polish government-in-exile, arrives in London.

A pair of Junkers Ju-87B Stukas on patrol. The Ju-87 became famed during the Blitzkrieg, *providing accurate air support for the* Wehrmacht.

that the river was crossed with ease, despite the best efforts of the resisting units.

The main difficulties for the Germans came when some of XIX Panzer Corps' tanks ran out of fuel because they had outrun their supply lines. This was a taste of things to come during the war, since the German Army relied heavily upon horse-drawn transport. As a result, supplies were not always available at the critical moment.

By this time, the Polish Air Force had sustained heavy losses. The surprise of the initial attack meant that there were few aircraft in the air to resist, and although a few pilots did take off, they could not affect the outcome. The Polish pilots were well trained and capable, but their aircraft were largely outclassed. This was particularly true of the Polish fighter aircraft, which were a generation behind the *Luftwaffe*'s Messerschmitt Bf-109s – more commonly, but incorrectly, referred to as the Me-109. Nonetheless, the air force continued to operate. Fighter patrols in defence of Warsaw put up stiff resistance while they could, but by 3 September the *Luftwaffe* had gained almost complete air superiority over the whole country, enabling German air power to play a major part in support of the land battle.

This, however, did not mean that the *Luftwaffe* spent all its time over the battlefield. One of the key aims of using air attack in support of the rapid, mobile warfare that came to be known as *Blitzkrieg* was to confuse and demoralize the enemy by attacking communications targets and administrative and industrial centres. Warsaw was bombed on the first day, and the Polish troops attempting to reach the front line found their journeys interrupted by a series of air attacks against

1939

NOVEMBER

21 November German battlecruisers *Scharnhorst* and *Gneisenau* set sail to begin attacks on British shipping.

23 November *Scharnhorst* and *Gneisenau* sink the British merchant cruiser *Rawlpindi*.

24 November Germany warns neutral shipping to avoid British and French waters or risk being sunk.

29 November The Soviet Union breaks off relations with Finland.

30 November The Soviet Union invades Finland.

roads, bridges and railways. Furthermore, pockets of Polish resistance were subjected to bombardment from the air, most notably by the soon-to-be infamous Junkers Ju-87 dive-bomber, better known as the Stuka.

A Wider War

With the dawn of 3 September 1939, the Germans were in a favourable position. The Poles had still not been able to put up concentrated resistance while attempting to mass their forces in the face of the German assault. And the Third and Fourth Armies were on the verge of linking up, thus cutting off the Polish Corridor completely. As the morning developed, the Germans ran into difficulties in the vicinity of Graudenz, the Poles putting up a stiff defence. Further north, the bridge over the Vistula at Dirschau was demolished by Polish engineers. This did not, however, prevent the Germans crossing the river, by establishing a pontoon bridge at Meve. The Third and Fourth Armies continued to advance, and met at Neuenberg, cutting off Polish forces in the north of the Corridor. The remnants of the Polish Pomorze Army fell back on the city of Bromberg, where

the sizeable ethnic German population promptly launched an uprising. The Polish citizens came to the aid of the army to suppress it, and the German community suffered a considerable number of casualties. This was exploited by German propagandists, who publicized the incident in newsreels.

Perhaps the most significant events of 3 September occurred outside Poland.

When news of the invasion first reached London and Paris, the reaction of the two governments was rather different. The British realized that war was now inevitable, the French still hoped that conflict could be averted through

The bridge at Dirschau, seen on 5 September 1939 after its demolition by Polish engineers in a fruitless attempt to prevent the Germans from crossing the Vistula. German troops built a temporary bridge at Meve instead.

DECEMBER

1 December A Finnish 'government' is formed in Moscow under Otto Kuusinen.

3 December The Finns withdraw to defensive positions along the Mannerheim Line.

6 December Soviet attacks on the Mannerheim Line end in failure.

13 December A Royal Navy task force sent to hunt down German pocket battleships engages the *Graf Spee* at Battle of the River Plate.

diplomacy. Two days of negotiations between London and Paris ended with the British view prevailing: Hitler must be issued with an ultimatum to withdraw from Poland.

At 9 a.m. on 3 September, Sir Neville Henderson, the British ambassador to Berlin, delivered the ultimatum to Hitler. If hostilities did not end by 11 a.m., and if the Germans did not then withdraw from Poland, both Britain and France would declare war.

Hitler may have hoped the Anglo-French alliance would continue to appease him, despite the assault on Poland, but he was to be disappointed. Nonetheless, he paid no heed to the ultimatum. The deadline came and went, just as the Allies had expected.

The consequence was inevitable: Britain and France declared war. The British public sat around their wireless sets to hear the strained tones of Neville Chamberlain announce that the Germans had failed to respond to the ultimatum, and that as a result Britain was now at war. Within minutes of the broadcast ending, air-raid sirens sounded in London. Fears that this was the 'knockout blow' from German strategic bombers were swiftly assuaged when it became

Sir Neville Henderson, British ambassador to Germany, with Hermann Goering, head of the Luftwaffe, *in 1938.*

clear that the air-raid alert had been sparked by a single light aircraft. This was carrying French liaison officers to a meeting with their British counterparts – but they had neglected to inform anyone that they were on their way, and the air defences had assumed the worst. German aircraft were too busy in Poland for the *Luftwaffe* to launch bombing raids on London or Paris. Indeed, postwar research has demonstrated that the *Luftwaffe* was nowhere near strong enough to conduct the 'knockout blow' that had so concerned the British Government in the latter half of the 1930s.

The Poles Withdraw; The French Advance

The declaration of war meant little to those fighting in Poland. As more units reached the front, the Poles were able to increase the level of resistance, and the German advance gradually slowed. Nonetheless, the Germans continued to enjoy success. The Poles looked to establish a line along the River Warta, but the German Tenth Army seized the town of Tschenstochau early on the morning of 3 September, and quickly established bridgeheads across the river. The Fourteenth Army now began its offensive

1939

DECEMBER

14 December The USSR is expelled from the League of Nations.

15 December The German pocket battleship *Graf Spee* is trapped in Montevideo harbour following the Battle of the River Plate.

16 December The Soviet advance into Finland stalls.

Polish troops move towards the front during the first days of the war. The Polish army was caught before it had fully mobilized.

towards Cracow, and the Poles realized that their two main fronts were on the verge of collapse. On 5 September, a general withdrawal to the River Vistula was ordered, in the hope that a new defensive line could be established in sufficient strength to beat back the Germans.

Meanwhile, the French put the final touches to a plan that would demonstrate support for Poland. On 7 September, French troops moved into the Saar region of Germany. It was little more than a gesture: the invasion force moved extremely slowly, seeming to take inordinate care to avoid inflicting casualties on the enemy. German troops withdrew in good order and waited to see what would happen next. The French penetrated to a depth of 8km (5 miles) in the course of the next five days, before their advance was halted, and then dug in. It was a half-hearted

attack, but it did have an indirect benefit. The German high command could not be absolutely certain that the Allies would not launch a further, larger attack in the West, which forced it to make sure that there were sufficient troops ready to defend Germany. This in turn meant that it was not possible to provide enough troops in Poland to guarantee a rapid encirclement of Warsaw.

The solution was to reinforce General Heinz Guderian's XIX Corps, and then use it to attack Polish forces behind the Narew while the remainder of the Fourth Army drove the Poles back towards the capital. Guderian's highly mechanized forces were able to operate semi-autonomously, not hindered by the slower pace of resupply that usually affected infantry formations. With potent air support from both dive- and medium-bombers operating under the protection of the *Luftwaffe*'s fighter units, XIX Corps represented a potent, highly manoeuvrable threat to the Poles.

The pace of the German armoured forces was such that they frequently overtook the retreating Polish units, making it extremely difficult for the Poles to muster an effective defence against the

17 December The *Graf Spee* is scuttled on departure from Montevideo.

18 December Half of a force of RAF bombers attacking shipping in the Schilling Roads is lost.

21 December The Finnish Army launches a counterattack against Soviet forces.

next assault. The Germans crossed the River Pilica on 5 September and manoeuvred northeast towards Warsaw and the Vistula. Intelligence reports indicated that the Poles were trying to organize a new army formation at Radom, so the commander of the Tenth Army, General Reichenau, was ordered to envelope the Polish positions around Radom and thus prevent the new Polish army from entering the conflict. Three army corps were tasked with the destruction of the Radom Army, and the battle began on 8 September; three days later, Radom was captured, along with the majority of the Polish troops.

Meanwhile, armoured formations from the Tenth Army seized the Vistula crossing at Pulawy. The Panzers were forced to halt temporarily while they waited for more fuel to arrive, which gave the German infantry formations an opportunity to catch up with them, preparatory to more operations east of the river.

On 8 September, the 4th Panzer Division reached the outskirts of Warsaw. Early on 9 September, the Germans launched an attack on the city itself. This became bogged down

German soldiers pick their way though the ruins of a building on the outskirts of the Polish capital during the Battle of Warsaw. Despite the odds, the defenders managed to hold out for just under three weeks.

after a few hours, and the Germans prudently chose to pull back. This gave them the opportunity to work out how best to coordinate armour and infantry, since unsupported tanks proved particularly vulnerable when fighting in built-up areas.

The Last Throw of the Dice

Cracow fell on 6 September, and the Fourteenth Army advanced towards the Polish defences on the River San. The plan was to overwhelm the defences and then drive towards Chelm, enabling a link-up with Guderian's forces and

1939

DECEMBER

29 December Finnish counter-attack north of Lake Lagoda.

31 December The Finns claim to have driven the Red Army back across the Soviet–Finnish border on the Sumomussalmi–Kemijarvi front.

1940

JANUARY

7 January Stalin places General Semyon Timoshenko in command of Soviet forces in Finland.

German troops pause on a Warsaw street, shortly after the capital had fallen into their hands on 30 September 1939, after the besieged city had been forced to surrender due to lack of food and water.

thus encircling Polish forces to the east of Warsaw. Meanwhile, the Eighth Army was closing on Lodz. This meant that its left flank was dangerously exposed, so units based on the German frontier were moved forward to provide protection.

The strength of the Poznan Army had, however, been underestimated by German commanders. It had not yet been fully engaged in the fighting, since it had been bypassed by the German drive into the centre of Poland. On 8 September, General Kurtzeba, the commander of the Poznan Army, was given permission to mount a counterattack against the Eight Army, using both his forces and the remaining units in the Pomorze Army. This gave him a strength of 12 divisions, with which he launched a counterattack on 9 September, across the River Bzura. The Battle of the Bzura surprised the Germans, and was fought with great intensity over the course of the next two days. The Germans were driven backwards, a success that proved only temporary.

General Gerd von Rundstedt, the commander of Army Group South, and Erich von Manstein, his Chief of Staff, saw an opportunity. If the 170,000 Polish troops now concentrated around Kutno could be encircled, the Poles would lose more than one-third of their combat forces. The Germans manoeuvred their forces so that Kurtzeba was threatened with encirclement, rapidly increasing the number of units under the direct command of the Eighth Army to enable this. The Polish situation worsened when it became clear that the Lodz Army was falling back towards Modlin, making it impossible for this force to link up with Kurtzeba.

8 January The Finns counterattack on the Central Front. There are elebrations in Helsinki following the defeat of Soviet forces at Sumomussalmi.

10 January Hitler sets the date for the invasion of Western Europe as 17 January. Plans fall into Allied hands after a German aircraft comes down in Belgium.

16 January Hitler postpones the invasion of Western Europe and orders planning for an attack on Scandinavia to begin.

27 January Hitler takes personal charge of plans to invade Norway.

On 12 September, Kurtzeba launched an attack, aiming to break out to the southeast, but the attack petered out over the course of the next three days. Another attempt on 16 September ended with similar results, and the failure meant that the Germans were able to squeeze the Kutno pocket even further. The *Luftwaffe* was called upon to attack the Kutno pocket on 17 September, suspending operations against Warsaw to increase the number of aircraft available. The weight of the bombardment against the Polish defences began to tell: 40,000 Poles were captured on 17 September, and a final attempt at breaking out failed. A few small units managed to escape, but it was obvious that the Polish Army was disintegrating and would soon not be large enough to engage the enemy in conventional battle.

The Final Assault on Warsaw

By 15 September, the Germans had successfully encircled the Polish capital, with the Tenth Army holding the area to the south of the city, and the Third Army occupying the northern approaches to Warsaw. The next day, the *Luftwaffe* dropped leaflets demanding that the city surrender. The response was defiant, prompting an intensification of the bombardment against the city.

The Germans now planned to reduce Warsaw. Initial attacks into the suburbs were met with fierce resistance, and made little progress. It was clear that the Poles had a plentiful supply of ammunition, and that large numbers of the civilian population had been organized into local militias to bolster the forces defending their capital. This prompted more detailed planning for a final assault on Warsaw, a process that was complicated by an unexpected development.

The Soviets Arrive

At this point, the Red Army invaded Poland. This was a shock not only to the Poles, but to the German Army as well. The Soviet forces crossed the border in strength on 17 September 1939, bypassing many Polish frontier units. Hopes that they had come to aid the

Poles were dashed, however, when units overrun by Red Army spearheads were disarmed and any resistance crushed. The Soviet intervention convinced the Polish Government that the time had come to

A Soviet soldier meets with his German counterparts at Brest-Litovsk on 22 September 1939.

1940

JANUARY

29 January The Soviets seek to reopen negotiations with the Finns.

FEBRUARY

1 February A Soviet attack across Viipuri Bay is disrupted.

5 February Britain and France agree to send an expeditionary force to aid the Finns.

leave and continue resistance from exile; its members fled to Romania, only to be interned after the Romanians succumbed to pressure from the Germans. This left the Poles temporarily leaderless.

The arrival of the Red Army posed some difficulties for German commanders, who now found it necessary to withdraw to the positions specified by the pact. There were a number of minor skirmishes when German units mistook the lead elements of the Red Army for Poles. None was particularly problematic, and on 22 September a combined German–Soviet parade took place at Brest-Litovsk.

The withdrawal in the south of Poland was complicated by the nature of the fighting. The Germans were in the process of investing Lvov, and a withdrawal to accommodate the arrival of the Red Army would leave a substantial, if hard-pressed, Polish force in existence. However, on 20 September, just as the Germans were preparing to leave Lvov to the Red Army, the Poles surrendered. The Germans now pulled back to the west, bypassing several surviving formations of Polish troops. These remnants of the Polish Army were able to cross the Polish frontiers, some 90,000 men reaching Hungary and Romania, with another 15,000 or so men reaching Lithuania. From here, a large number headed to France, to form a Polish army-in-exile.

The Final Assault

The withdrawal complicated the plan to capture Warsaw. Hitler refused to allow an assault to be launched from the east of the city, since this area fell under Soviet control. The attack therefore

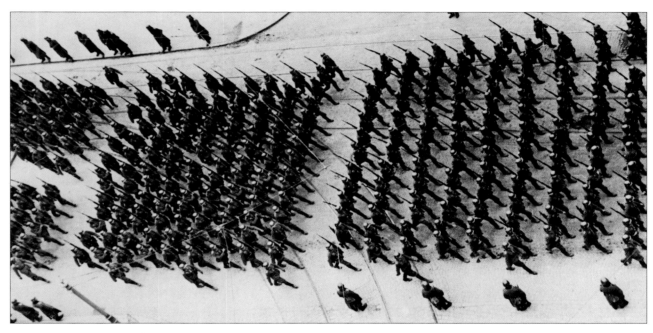

A German victory parade in Warsaw on 5 October 1939, in the presence of Adolf Hitler. The Eighth Army marched through the streets, which had been forcibly cleared of Polish civilians. The state of Poland no longer existed.

9 February The Red Army launches an offensive against the Mannerheim Line.

11 February The Mannerheim Line is breached at Summa. A Russo–German economic agreement is reached.

15 February Summa falls to the Red Army.

had to be launched from the western side. The Eighth Army was given the task, and began by ensuring that the encirclement of the city was such that no civilians could escape. The rationale for this was to place further pressure on the city's food supplies: if civilians escaped, the number of mouths to feed would decrease, enabling the garrison to sustain itself (and its food supply) for longer. The *Luftwaffe* also increased attacks on filtration plants and pumping stations, making it more difficult for the population to obtain water. Many were now forced to drink water from the Vistula, increasing the risk of disease from the untreated liquid. Electrical supplies were also cut off thanks to the extensive bombing, while the flour mills were targeted and destroyed.

On 26 September, the Eighth Army began the assault on Warsaw, and broke through the outer defensive line. The Poles requested a ceasefire at the end of the day, but the Germans countered with a demand for unconditional surrender. Realizing that the final outcome was in no

Polish prisoners of war await transportation to prison camps shortly after the end of the Polish campaign.

doubt, the Poles agreed to the demands. The fighting stopped the following afternoon.

Modlin continued to resist, but once Warsaw had fallen, the Germans were able to bolster the attacking forces. The artillery used at Warsaw was moved to Modlin and employed in a massive bombardment of the Polish defences,

which began to crumble under the weight of fire. The outer defences at Modlin were breached on the same day as Warsaw surrendered, and by 28 September, the position was hopeless. An armistice was agreed later that day, and the Modlin garrison surrendered the following morning.

1940

FEBRUARY

16 February British prisoners of war aboard the German ship *Altmark* are rescued by the Royal Navy in Jossingford, Norway.

17 February The Red Army breaches the Mannerheim Line.

20 February Hitler appoints General von Falkenhorst to command the German attack on Norway.

The Balance Sheet

The fall of Modlin brought an end to almost all fighting in Poland, apart from that around the Baltic. The Helda garrison managed to hold on until 1 October before succumbing – which marked the end of the Polish campaign.

The Polish army had been destroyed as a viable fighting force in a little over five weeks. More than 65,000 Polish soldiers died, 130,000 were wounded, and 250,000 men were taken prisoner. Another 100,000 escaped, and made their way to Britain or France. German losses were considerably less, with about 10,000 fatalities and 30,000 wounded.

The consequences of the Polish defeat were stark. Britain and France had been unable to respond in any meaningful manner, while the Soviet–German agreement to partition Poland meant that the nation once again disappeared off the map. A German–Soviet 'Treaty of Delimitation and Friendship' was signed on 28 September. This gave Stalin the opportunity to exert control over the Baltic states, and Lithuania, Latvia and Estonia disappeared under Soviet control through the mechanism of cooperative treaties between their reluctant governments and Moscow. Stalin was now sufficiently emboldened to press his territorial claims against Finland.

The Winter War

On 12 October 1939, negotiations opened between the Soviet Union and Finland. Stalin demanded that Finland cede land on the shores of Lake Lagoda and the Gulf of Finland while leasing the ports of Viipuri and Petsamo in exchange for parts of Soviet Karelia – terms that were not attractive to the Finns.

The Finnish Government was only too aware that Stalin's treatment of the Baltic states had begun with an apparent willingess to compromise. It also feared that Stalin would consider the acquisition of Finnish territory as merely the start of a process of absorbing Finland back into Russia, from which the country had become independent during the chaos of the 1917 Revolution. The Government therefore continued with negotiations but also refused to acquiesce. By the end of November, Stalin's patience was exhausted, and he ordered Foreign Minister Molotov to break off negotiations. Two days later, on 30 November 1939, Soviet forces crossed the Finnish border.

Finnish troops in position near Illomantsi at the start of the Russo–Finnish (or 'Winter') War.

23 February The Soviet Union issues its peace terms to Finland.

28/29 February Soviet troops overrun Finnish defences on the Karelian Isthmus.

MARCH

1 March The Soviet peace offer to the Finns expires. US Secretary of State Sumner Wells begins a tour of the warring nations in attempt to bring about peace.

Stalin appointed Marshal Semyon Timoshenko to take command of the forces fighting on the Finnish front.

To general admiration, the Finns managed to hold off the numerically superior forces. This gave an early demonstration that Stalin's wholesale purging of the Red Army high command had been unwise. The loss of a number of the most competent Soviet commanders to the firing squad and the gulag meant that the Red Army was much less capable than it might have been. The Finnish Army inflicted heavy losses on the Soviets. Operating on home ground, it exploited the terrain and weather conditions to the full. It withdrew to the Mannerheim defensive line in good order on 3 December, and Soviet attacks on these positions three days later were all rebuffed.

The Finns gathered international support. While Denmark, Norway and Sweden declared their neutrality on 7 December, Britain and France decided to provide support, the French even going so far as to make plans for sending troops. However, it soon became apparent that sending aid would be difficult, for it would be impossible to transport men or war materiel through the neutral Scandinavian nations.

By the end of December, the Red Army had proved unable to defeat the Finns, and a Finnish counterattack on 29 December north of Lake Lagoda only added to Stalin's embarrassment. The next day, the Russian 163rd Division was destroyed at Suomussalami, a disaster followed the next week when, between 5 January and 8 January 1940, the Finns attacked and destroyed the Soviet 44th Motorized Division. By this time, Stalin's patience with his commanders had evaporated, and he appointed General Semyon Timoshenko as commander-in-chief of Soviet forces in Finland.

New Offensive

Timoshenko immediately began plans for a new offensive, but was aware that it would take time to bring better trained and better equipped troops into the line. The Soviets were therefore forced to limit their activity to artillery bombardment against the Mannerheim Line. In the interim, Stalin sought to reopen negotiations, asking the Swedish Government to act as an intermediary. Negotiations had not progressed far by 1 February, when Timoshenko launched a major offensive across Viipuri Bay.

Fortune now changed for the Soviets. On 5 February, the French and British confirmed

1940

MARCH

3 March The Red Army launches an offensive along whole front.

6 March Finnish representatives arrive in Moscow to discuss peace. Hitler adopts a new plan for invasion of the West.

8 March Viipuri falls to the Red Army. Stalin refuses an armistice. A Finnish delegation in Moscow is instructed to sue for peace.

their intention to send an expeditionary force to aid the Finns – a move that would involve ignoring Norwegian neutrality, landing the force in the north of the country to avoid disruption from attacks. It was too little, too late.

The Soviets breached the Mannerheim Line on 11 February, forcing the Finns to pull back to their second line of defence. From this point onwards, the Soviets began to gain the upper hand. On 23 February, Stalin announced his conditions for peace. These were similar to his original demands, requiring control over the shores of Lake Lagoda and the Karelian Isthmus, the signing of a mutual assistance treaty, and a lease on the Hango peninsula for 30 years. The only concession to the Finns was a guarantee to evacuate Petsamo. Stalin gave the Finns until 1 March to respond

When the Soviets broke through the second Finnish defensive line on 28/29 February, it seemed that the Finns had little option other than to accept these terms. Nonetheless, they continued the fight. The ultimatum expired, and the Soviets launched an offensive along the full length of the front on 3 March. The Finns realized that they could not resist for much longer, and

sent a delegation to Moscow to negotiate.

When Viipuri fell on 8 March, the delegates attempted to secure an armistice, but their request was refused: the Soviets would cease fire only if the Finns agreed to a peace settlement. The Finnish Government had no choice. The peace treaty was signed on 12 March 1940, and the Finns were forced to cede the Karelian

Isthmus, including Viipuri, Lake Lagoda and the Petsamo area. Hostilities ended the next day.

For the people of Britain and France, the fighting seemed very far away. Although there had been contact between Allied and German air and naval forces, activity had been sufficiently limited for people to talk of a 'Phoney War'. It was not long before it became all too active.

Men of the Finnish 24th Infantry Regiment leaving Kiviniemi for Ilmee at the end of the Winter War. The Finns made good use of their ski-troops, outmanoeuvring the Red Army until the numbers arrayed against them proved too much.

12 March A peace agreement between the USSR and Finland is signed in Moscow.

15 March The Finnish parliament ratifies the peace terms offered by the USSR.

The End of the Phoney War

Once Poland had fallen, the warring parties prepared for the worst. What they got were some bombing raids, a certain amount of air-to-air combat and some desultory exchanges of fire, leading one American journalist to refer to the conflict as the 'Phoney War'. It was the lull before the storm.

U nable to send forces to assist the Poles, the British undertook a series of naval operations and bomber raids against Germany. These were limited to naval targets, and the first of these, on 4 September 1939, proved to be a disaster. A force of 30 aircraft sent to bomb the Schilling Roads lost seven of its number and inflicted minimal damage. Further daylight attacks – including another on the Schilling Roads on 18 December – suffered serious losses

Left: Dornier bombers of the Luftwaffe head for their targets in southern England on Eagle Day.
Right: Winston Churchill and Brendan Bracken head for the debate that led to the resignation of Chamberlain.

and proved that unescorted bombers could not hope to survive. This swiftly led to a switch to night attacks – with a concomitant loss of accuracy.

The British Expeditionary Force (BEF) crossed to France on 9 September. It would be another eight months before it saw any action. On 6 October, Hitler proposed a peace settlement, but this was rejected by the Allies. Three days later, Hitler gave orders that Western Europe was to be attacked in the near future. Faced with the prospect of poor weather, however, as well as a General Staff that insisted on more time, Hitler was forced to postpone his plan several times.

As a result, the first months of the war did indeed support the perception that somehow this was not a 'proper' war.

The Storm Breaks

Nonetheless, both sides planned for operations. The Allies concluded that a German attack should be met by moving forward into Belgium. The Belgians, though, were anxious to maintain their neutrality, lest they provoke Hitler, and this prevented the Allies from reconnoitring for suitable positions.

Meanwhile, Hitler continued his plans for the attack in the West. On 10 January 1940, he informed his generals that the attack would begin on 17 January. At this point, fate intervened: a German light aircraft carrying two officers with detailed plans for the invasion of the Low Countries strayed off course and force-landed in Belgium. The plans were not destroyed, and Hitler had to assume that they had been compromised. He postponed the attack, unaware that the Allies considered the plans to be an elaborate deception.

In early March, the details of the invasion changed again. Generals Gerhardt von Rundstedt and Erich von Manstein suggested a thrust through the Ardennes. This was heavily wooded territory and widely considered to be unsuited for armour. Indeed, the Allies

German troops march through a burning town in Norway. Despite the best efforts of the Norwegians and an Anglo-French expeditionary force, the German invasion could not be turned back.

1940

MARCH

16 March First British civilian fatality from German bombing.

18 March Summit meeting between Hitler and Mussolini; Mussolini agrees to enter the war on the side of Germany.

20 March Edouard Daladier resigns as French prime minister and is replaced by Paul Reynaud.

28 March Anglo-French agreement to start mining Norwegian waters from 8 April.

APRIL

2 April Hitler issues orders for an attack on Norway the following week.

5 April Prime Minister Neville Chamberlain makes his infamous 'Hitler has missed the bus' speech. The Allies inform Norway and Sweden that they will begin mining Norwegian waters.

7 April RAF reconnaissance aircraft discover German shipping heading towards Narvik and Trondheim.

9 April German troops invade Norway and Denmark. Royal Navy ships are involved in fighting around Bergen.

considered it quite implausible that the main thrust of an enemy attack could come from this direction.

As 1940 continued without any major action on land, some observers suggested that Hitler had prevaricated for too long, allowing the British and French to build up their strength along the likely line of a German attack. On 5 April, Neville Chamberlain claimed that Hitler had 'missed the bus'. Three days later, the Germans invaded Norway.

Norway

Despite declaring its neutrality, Norway was of clear strategic importance. Germany's supply of Swedish iron ore went through the Norwegian port of Narvik, while bases in the country would allow Germany to launch air attacks against northern Britain and to provide an anchorage for maritime operations.

On 27 January, Hitler had drawn up the first plans for the invasion of Norway, even as the Allies were endeavouring to find a way of

British prisoners of war are marched away into captivity at Trondheim, May 1940.

interdicting the iron ore supply. Then, on 16 February, the British destroyer HMS *Cossack* pursued the German transport ship *Altmark* into a Norwegian fjord, boarded it and released the prisoners of war it was carrying (captured from ships sunk by the *Graf Spee*). The Norwegians protested at this

violation of territorial waters, but their complaints were rebuffed. The British Government pointed out that the German

10 April Denmark surrenders. Major naval engagements take place between British and German ships. The German cruiser *Konigsberg* is sunk by a British dive-bombing attack.

11 April The first British troops are despatched to Norway.

13 April Oslo is occupied by German forces.

15 April Allied landings at Harstad.

16 April Allied landings at Namsos.

18 April British troops land at Aandalesnes and move towards Lillehammer.

21 April British and Norwegian troops are driven from Lillehammer.

24 April French reinforcements arrive at Aandalesnes. The Norwegian attack at Narvik is driven back.

Dutch volunteers march off to join the attempts to resist the German invasion. The Dutch were unprepared for the German assault and surrendered after four days, when it became clear that to fight on was pointless.

ship had entered Norwegian waters first, and made it clear that the Royal Navy would certainly act if the Norwegian authorities were not prepared to do so. Hitler was now convinced that the Norwegians could not be relied upon to stand up to the British.

On 28 March 1940, the British and French agreed to mine Norwegian waters, to prevent German shipping from passing through them. The decision was announced on 5 April, the same day that Chamberlain was suggesting that Hitler had missed his chance. In fact, the orders for the invasion of Norway had been issued on 2 April, and the German invasion force was spotted on the 7th. Two days later, German troops landed in Denmark and Norway. Copenhagen fell within 12 hours, and the Danes had little option other than to surrender on 10 April.

The Germans had a less easy time in Norway: fierce fighting between their ships and those of the Royal Navy broke out on Norwegian waters, and the Germans lost several ships between 10 and 12 April. British troops landed at Harstad in the Lofoten Islands opposite Narvik on 15 April; the next day, French and British units landed at Namsos;

1940

APRIL

26 April The British decide to abandon southern Norway. Allied troops in northern and central Norway begin to withdraw to concentrate forces around Narvik.

27 April Germany officially declares war on Norway.

29 April King Haakon and the Norwegian Government are evacuated from Molde to Tromsø.

30 April The British withdraw from Aandalesnes.

MAY

2 May Namsos force is evacuated.

3 May Hitler postpones the date of the attack on Western Europe to 6 May.

6 May Hitler again postpones the date of attack on Western Europe.

8 May Neville Chamberlain resigns as British prime minister. Hitler decides that the attack on the West will begin on 10 May.

10 May Hitler launches the invasion of the Low Countries. Winston Churchill becomes British prime minister at the head of a coalition government.

on 18 April, British troops landed at Aandalesnes. The plan was for the forces at Namsos and Aandalesnes to link up and retake Trondheim. However, the Aandalesnes force commander was persuaded to assist the Norwegians at Lillehammer. They were driven back by heavy German fire. Meanwhile, the Namsos force, weaker than had been intended, was unable to progress into Trondheim. Over the course of the next week, the Germans counter-attacked in central Norway, and drove the Allies back towards Aandalesnes. On 26 April, the Inter-Allied Supreme War Council concluded that all forces should be evacuated from central Norway to be concentrated against Narvik.

The evacuation was completed by 3 May, and the Allies advanced towards Narvik. By the third week in May, the road to Narvik was open. By the end of the month, the German troops based there were short of supplies and on the verge of collapse. On 28 May, the Allies launched a final assault on Narvik and took it. However, during the advance on the town, the strategic situation had altered: the Germans had invaded Belgium and Holland on 10 May, and Norway seemed to be of far less importance.

The Allies decided to evacuate, and did so between 3 June and 8 June. The final tragedy of the campaign came on the last day, when the British carrier HMS *Glorious* was sunk with almost all hands.

France and the Low Countries

The Germans invaded Belgium and Holland early on 10 May, beginning with attacks on airfields and airborne landings to seize key bridges. The BEF and three French armies responded by moving north into Belgium along the River Dyle and the Meuse. Nor was the drama of the day yet complete: Neville Chamberlain resigned as British prime minster that same evening and was replaced by Winston Churchill.

On 12 May, the Germans secured the north bank of the Meuse. The next day, the Germans crossed the river on either side of Sedan, and it was clear that the Allies were in serious difficulty. The RAF launched a series of attacks on the 14th to cut the Meuse crossings, but suffered grievous losses in the process – and to no effect. The same fate befell the efforts of the French Air Force.

General Maxime Weygand was recalled to France in May 1940 to replace General Gamelin as supreme commander.

12 May British bombing attacks on Albert Canal bridges are repulsed with heavy casualties.

13 May The Germans cross the River Meuse at Sedan.

14 May German armoured forces break through Allied lines at Sedan. The Germans bomb Rotterdam.

15 May The Dutch Government surrenders. Local Defence Volunteers are established in Britain.

16 May Allied armies begin the withdrawal from Belgium.

17 May Brussels falls.

18 May Antwerp falls to German forces. The Germans capture St Quentin and Cambrai.

19 May General Weygand is appointed as commander of the French forces in place of General Gamelin. World War I hero Marshal Pétain is appointed deputy prime minister.

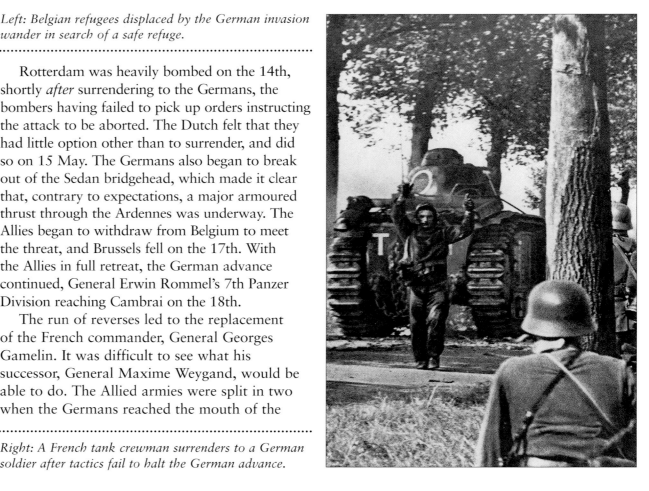

Left: Belgian refugees displaced by the German invasion wander in search of a safe refuge.

Rotterdam was heavily bombed on the 14th, shortly *after* surrendering to the Germans, the bombers having failed to pick up orders instructing the attack to be aborted. The Dutch felt that they had little option other than to surrender, and did so on 15 May. The Germans also began to break out of the Sedan bridgehead, which made it clear that, contrary to expectations, a major armoured thrust through the Ardennes was underway. The Allies began to withdraw from Belgium to meet the threat, and Brussels fell on the 17th. With the Allies in full retreat, the German advance continued, General Erwin Rommel's 7th Panzer Division reaching Cambrai on the 18th.

The run of reverses led to the replacement of the French commander, General Georges Gamelin. It was difficult to see what his successor, General Maxime Weygand, would be able to do. The Allied armies were split in two when the Germans reached the mouth of the

Right: A French tank crewman surrenders to a German soldier after tactics fail to halt the German advance.

1940

MAY

20 May Amiens falls. Rommel surrounds Arras and German forces reach the Belgian coast at Noyelles, splitting the Allied armies in two.

21 May The BEF launches a counterattack at Arras.

22 May German Panzer forces turn to attack Channel ports.

23 May The evacuation of Boulogne begins. General von Rundstedt orders Panzer divisions to halt to resupply and re-equip.

25 May Boulogne falls and the BEF begins to retreat to Dunkirk.

26 May Operation Dynamo begins as an armada of ships leaves British ports to evacuate the BEF from France.

27 May Evacuation of the BEF from Dunkirk begins.

27/28 May Allied forces recapture Narvik from the Germans.

A column of wounded British soldiers at Dunkirk.

River Somme on 20 May, prompting the British to counterattack at Arras in a bid to relieve the pressure. This attack against the 7th Panzer Division was supported by a French thrust to the south, but a shortage of tanks and a lack of coordination between the two forces meant that Rommel was no more than temporarily discomfited and was able to push off the assault.

The German advance continued, and Boulogne and Calais fell on 25 and 27 May respectively. The rest of the Panzer forces halted, Von Rundstedt believing that a pause was necessary to effect repairs and resupply. With the BEF, Belgians and First French Army isolated, this seemed a reasonable enough decision, particularly when Hermann Goering, head of the *Luftwaffe*, informed Hitler that the trapped armies could be destroyed from the air. However, the pause gave the commander of the BEF, General Lord Gort, time to assess the situation. He concluded that a large counter-attack proposed by Weygand would not work, and that it was his duty to save as much of the BEF as possible. He therefore issued orders that the BEF was to fall back on Dunkirk, and prepare to be evacuated.

Operation Dynamo

The Royal Navy now set in train its plan for the evacuation of Dunkirk, Operation Dynamo. This had been prepared over the course of the previous six days as it became clear that elements of the BEF might have to be rescued, but the scale of the operation was far greater than anticipated.

The evacuation began on 27 May, as King Leopold of Belgium announced his intention to surrender, the formalities of which were completed the next day. The evacuation continued, although being harassed from the air, and over the course of the next eight days, more than 330,000 British and French troops were evacuated to Britain. The success of the operation provoked considerable pride in Britain, not least because many of the ships involved were civilian craft, several of which were not well suited for crossing the Channel and were manned by their civilian crews. Churchill deflated the mood by noting that wars were not won by evacuations, but he also roused the nation with a speech promising that 'we shall fight on the beaches', and pledging that Britain would never surrender.

28 May King Leopold of Belgium orders his army to surrender.

29 May Hitler orders the main offensive to be switched towards southern France.

31 May Churchill flies to Paris.

JUNE

4 June The last evacuation ship leaves Dunkirk in the early hours. German troops enter Dunkirk. Churchill makes his 'We shall fight on the beaches' speech.

4/8 June Allied forces withdraw from Narvik. King Haakon and his government are evacuated to form a government-in-exile in London.

5 June The Germans start to attack French armies in the south. General Charles de Gaulle is appointed Under-Secretary of State for War.

6 June The German breakthrough reaches the River Aisne.

9 June French forces on the Somme are defeated.

One aspect of the evacuation went unnoticed by the public. The RAF flew constant fighter patrols over France and Belgium in a bid to prevent German bombers from reaching the evacuation beach. They were unable to stop all the bombers and suffered heavy losses, but they did take control of the air from the *Luftwaffe,* for perhaps the first time. It would not be the last.

The Drive South

The Germans now switched the thrust of their main attack towards the south of France. On 9 June, the French were routed on the Somme, and the success of the Germans prompted Mussolini to declare war on Britain and France on the 10th. President Roosevelt responded by offering material aid to the Allies.

Paris was declared an open city the next day, and the Germans entered the capital on the 14th. On the same day, the Maginot defensive line, which was supposed to prevent a German invasion, was penetrated near Saarbrücken. The

Hitler took particular delight in the French surrender, and undertook a victory tour of Paris to celebrate.

1940

JUNE

10 June Norway surrenders. Italy declares war on Britain and France. The French Government leaves Paris for Tours. President Roosevelt promises to provide material assistance to France and Britain.

11 June Paris is declared an open city. Italian aircraft bomb Malta, Aden and Port Sudan. The British bomb Turin and Genoa, and targets in Libya and Eritrea. British armoured cars cross the border into Libya and attack an Italian supply convoy.

12 June Five Allied Divisions (four French, one British) surrender at St Valéry.

14 June The Germans enter Paris. The Maginot Line is breached near Saarbrücken. British troops capture Fort Capuzzo and Fort Maddelena.

16 June The French Government decides to seek armistice. Reyanud resigns and is replaced as prime minister by Pétain.

18 June The last British troops leave France. General de Gaulle broadcasts from London to the French population, calling for volunteers to join Free French forces.

French Government decided that it had no option other than to seek an armistice. Prime Minister Reynaud resigned, and was replaced by the hero of World War I, Marshal Henri Pétain. The last British troops left France on 18 June. Later that day, General Charles de Gaulle, who had escaped to Britain, broadcast to the French nation from London. He called for defiance, and for volunteers to join the Free French forces, which would ultimately help drive the Germans out.

On 22 June, the French signed an armistice. Hitler's sense of grievance over World War I was demonstrated by his insistence that the surrender should take place in the same railway carriage used for signing the armistice of November 1918. (Once the

....

Charles de Gaulle escaped to London after the French surrender.

ceremony was over, Hitler ordered the carriage to be transported to Berlin for public display.) Hostilities in France ended on 25 June, with the armistice leaving the southern part of the country under Pétain's government, based in the town of Vichy.

Britain now stood alone. Churchill had already warned the nation, on 18 June: 'What General Weygand called the Battle of France is now over. I expect the Battle of Britain is about to begin.'

The Battle of Britain

Losses sustained during the Battle of France and the evacuation of Dunkirk left the RAF with barely enough aircraft to defend Britain from air attack. It was

clear, though, that the Germans would be unable to invade unless they defeated RAF Fighter Command. As long as the British had the means of defending the Royal Navy from the depredations of German bombers, the Navy would be able to decimate any invasion fleet.

Fighter Command was divided into a number of Groups, the most important being 11 Group, which covered the south coast and London. The British also had the advantage of a radar network that gave early warning of the arrival of an attack. Despite the odds stacked against it, Fighter Command was able to inflict serious damage upon incoming *Luftwaffe* attacks.

The initial stage of the air battle took place above Channel convoys. The German bombers were provided with considerable cover by escort fighters, and these were able to inflict such damage on the convoys that the Admiralty temporarily suspended them. A lull occurred at the end of July, marking the end of the first phase of the battle.

On 6 August, Goering set the 10th as the opening day of the main offensive against Britain. Bad weather put it back until the 13th. In the interim, the *Luftwaffe* attacked coastal

20 June Italian troops invade the south of France.

22 June An armistice is signed between France and Germany.

24 June An armistice is signed between France and Italy.

25 June Hostilities end in France. The Germans control northern France, leaving the south to be governed from Vichy by Marshal Pétain.

26 June Turkey declares its neutrality.

28 June Italian Governor-General of Libya, Marshal Balbo, is killed in an air crash and is replaced by General Rodolfo Graziani.

30 June German forces occupy the Channel Islands.

airfields and radar stations. The latter were critical targets, but fortunately for the British, Goering seems not to have appreciated their importance, and did not give priority to heavy, repeat attacks.

When the main offensive began, the results were disappointing for the Germans. They failed to destroy their targets and suffered heavy losses amongst their Stuka dive bombers. Indeed,

these had to be withdrawn from the battle, as they were too vulnerable to fighter attack – a fact that had not been realized given the lack of enemy fighters in Poland and Western Europe. As a result, a further heavy attack was planned for the 15th, codenamed 'Adler Tag' (Eagle Day). Nearly 1800 sorties were flown by the Germans, including attacks from Norway against northeast England. The Norwegian-based force suffered heavy losses, but the weight of German attacks against airfields began to tell, and the RAF was now under considerable pressure. On 18 August, the Germans inflicted serious damage on a number of fighter airfields, causing major disruption to command and

A convoy in the Channel comes under air attack. Such convoys were temporarily halted to prevent further losses.

control. Moreover, the weight of attacks in recent days had led to heavy RAF pilot casualties, and the survivors were extremely tired. Fortunately for the RAF crews, the weather intervened, and they gained some time to recover.

Pilots of 85 Squadron, RAF, in front of a Hawker Hurricane.

1940

JULY

2 July A German military directive ordering preparations for an invasion of Britain is laid down.

3 July The Royal Navy bombards the French fleet at Oran and Mers-el-Kebir to prevent ships from falling into German hands.

4 July Italian troops attack British positions at Kassala and Gallabat.

5 July Vichy France breaks off diplomatic relations with Britain.

6 July The first U-boat base in France opens at Lorient.

9 July The first battle takes place between British and Italian naval forces in the Mediterranean. The Italians break off and head to port.

10 July German air attacks on docks in South Wales mark the opening of the Battle of Britain.

11 July Pétain is declared French head of state.

16 July Hitler issues a directive for the invasion of Britain.

The Third Phase

The third phase of the Battle of Britain began on 24 August 1940, and continued to concentrate on airfields. Goering, however, made a considerable error of judgement, calling off attacks on the radar system because the results appeared to have been negligible. Furthermore, German intelligence was of poor quality, and suggested that the RAF had almost been destroyed by this point. This was far from correct, despite the fact that the pressure on Fighter Command was beginning to tell.

Respite came from an unpredictable event. On the night of 24/25 August, a German bomber, returning to base with its bomb load on board, followed normal procedure and jettisoned its bombs. As the result of a navigational error by the crew, however, the bombs fell not on open countryside but on London. The British were unaware that this was in contravention of standing orders that the city was not to be bombed under any circumstances, and they retaliated against Berlin the following night. This prompted a shift in tactics: outraged by the attack, Hitler considered bombing London.

This decision was based on wildly optimistic assessments of the RAF's strength – or rather, weakness. The German High Command was convinced that a single decisive battle would destroy the few remaining British fighters and bring victory. Hitler ordered the attacks on London to begin, and this gave the fighter airfields the respite they so desperately required.

On 7 September, the Germans switched their attack to London, and over the next few days,

Tower Bridge against a background of smoke and flame caused by the first major German air raid on London.

AUGUST

19 July Hitler makes a plea to Britain to make peace; his offer is rejected immediately. General Sir Alan Brooke is appointed Commander-in-Chief of British Home Forces.

21 July The Baltic states are subsumed into the USSR.

22 July Churchill orders the formation of Special Operations Executive (SOE) to aid resistance movements throughout Europe.

30 July The first phase of the Battle of Britain ends.

31 July Hitler informs the German High Command that he intends to invade the Soviet Union in spring 1941.

1 August Hitler directs that the *Luftwaffe* should begin operations to gain air superiority over Britain from 6 August.

4 August The Italians invade British Somaliland.

6 August Hermann Goering sets 10 August as the start date for a main air offensive.

St Paul's Cathedral during the great fire raid of Sunday 29 December 1940.

the city was subjected to attacks both day and night. However, the move to London took the bombers out of the range of escorting fighters, providing an opportunity the RAF was able to exploit. Casualties amongst the German bomber force increased considerably, both in terms of aircraft and men. On 10 September, Hitler postponed the invasion of Britain, Operation Sealion, until at least the 24th. Five days later, the *Luftwaffe*

attempted to draw the RAF into another decisive battle and suffered a serious reverse. British claims to have shot down 185 German aircraft were exaggerated, but the Germans had to accept that they had not managed to gain air superiority. This prompted a reassessment of operations, and the attrition suffered led to a decision to conduct the bombing campaign at night only. Then, on 17 September, Hitler postponed Sealion indefinitely. Finally, on 24 October, he abandoned it completely. The Battle of Britain was at an end.

Mussolini's Frustration

Mussolini faced an embarrassing problem. He regarded himself as the 'senior partner' amongst the Axis nations, but his position was increasingly undermined by the fact that his forces had failed, while the German armed services had been spectacularly successful. Hitler's willingness to undertake military action without consultation was a further source of irritation to the Italian dictator, who felt marginalized. To an extent, Mussolini had only himself to blame. His decision to enter the war only when it appeared that Britain

1940

AUGUST

8 August The *Luftwaffe* renews attacks against shipping in the English Channel.

10 August Poor weather forces the postponement of the start of German air offensive against Britain.

12 August German attacks begin on British radar sites and airfields.

13 August Churchill and Roosevelt sign the Lend-Lease agreement. The largest air attacks on Britain to date are generally ineffective.

15 August Adler Tag (Eagle Day) – maximum effort by the *Luftwaffe* against Britain.

17 August The Italians complete the occupation of British Somaliland. The British garrison is evacuated by sea. Hitler announces a total maritime blockade against Britain.

18 August 'The Hardest Day' – the Germans inflict heavy damage on Fighter Command airfields. Bad weather forces them to reduce attacks over the next few days.

was on the verge of defeat had not earned Hitler's respect.

Mussolini's frustration was heightened by his suspicions over Hitler's intentions in the Balkans. The collapse of the Austro-Hungarian empire led to the creation of Hungary, Romania and Yugoslavia, yet none of the three nations was satisfied by the territory awarded by the terms of the peace settlement. The Hungarians were irritated that Transylvania had been handed to Romania, particularly the area occupied by ethnic Magyars. Despite discussions between the two nations, no agreement over the future of Transylvania could be reached.

Both nations were prepared to fight, and were prevented only because Hitler made it clear that Germany would intervene to prevent conflict. Germany relied heavily on Romanian oil, and Hitler could not afford to allow a Balkan conflict to threaten supplies required by the army. Mussolini also had an interest, tending to favour Hungarian claims to Transylvania. The interest of the two Axis powers persuaded both the Romanians and Hungarians to seek arbitration. The powers gave their judgement on 30 August 1940, and the decision satisfied neither the Hungarians nor the Romanians. Transylvania was divided between the two countries, infuriating the Romanians, who had already been forced to hand territory over to the USSR. On 4 September, General Ion Antonescu forced King Carol of Romania to abdicate in favour of his son, Prince Michael, and Antonescu imposed a dictatorship.

Since the Italians favoured the Hungarians, Antonescu continued Carol's policy of seeking German patronage. A Romanian military delegation visited Berlin two days before Antonescu's coup, and invited Hitler to provide military assistance. A division of German troops was despatched to Bucharest, the first elements arriving on 7 October 1940. Mussolini informed his foreign minister on 12 October that he was tired of Hitler's failure to consult him, and that unfavourable public opinion in Italy meant that 'equilibrium' must now be restored in the Balkans. This he proposed to do by invading Greece.

Hitler meets the Romanian leader Ion Antonescu at the Reich Chancellery, Berlin.

19 August Mussolini issues a directive that Graziani is to invade Egypt on the same day that the German invasion of Britain takes place.

20 August Churchill makes his speech praising 'the Few'.

22 August A British reinforcement convoy for Egypt sets sail.

24 August The third phase of the Battle of Britain begins. German bombs fall on London.

25/26 August The RAF bombs Berlin.

26 August Two Panzer divisions are sent to Poland to begin preparations for an invasion of the USSR.

30 August The British Mediterranean Fleet is reinforced.

SEPTEMBER

4 September Hitler makes a speech declaring that British cities will be razed to the ground in retaliation for attacks on Germany.

The Greek Campaign

Italian forces were ordered to invade Greece a mere 12 days after Mussolini's decision. The Italian Army was aghast, having recently demobilized more than 500,000 men. Requests for a delay went unheeded – until the eleventh hour. So it was not until 28 October that Italian troops crossed the border between Albania and Greece. Just the day before, Hitler, on a visit to Vichy France, had been warned by the German ambassador in Rome that the Italians were on the verge of invading Greece. Hurrying to meet Mussolini at the Brenner Pass, he arrived at 10 a.m. on the 28th, to be told by the proud dictator 'We are on the march!'

Mussolini had anticipated an easy victory; his confidence was misplaced. Underestimating the Greeks, he demanded their surrender in the aftermath of relatively light air attacks on a variety of targets throughout Greece. The monarch, King George II, and his prime minister, General Joannis Metaxas, rejected the demand and instituted a general mobilization.

Mussolini allegedly had little admiration for Hitler, despite the German military successes.

Bad weather now interfered with Italian operations, most notably those by the air force, meaning that the Greek mobilization proceeded with little hindrance. Within a week, the Greek forces were able to counterattack, and did so on 4 November. They were outnumbered, but the Italians were unfamiliar with the demands of fighting in the mountainous terrain, and began to fall back. Indeed, Greek troops crossed the Albanian frontier on 21 November 1940, and took a number of towns. However, winter was beginning to close in, and by 5 December, they had lost momentum. Both sides now settled in for the winter.

Hitler's Balkan Ambitions

Hitler was distinctly unimpressed, but appreciated that it was necessary to assist the Italians. The invasion had made enemies of the Greeks, who might now be prepared to allow the British to base aircraft on their territory. From there, they would be able to target the oil infrastructure in Romania. Assisting Mussolini was the only way to remove the threat. On 13 December 1940, he issued instructions to secure the southern flank of his proposed invasion of

1940

SEPTEMBER

5/6 September London is bombed as the *Luftwaffe* begins the move to night operations.

7 September London is subjected to massive air attacks. The Night Blitz begins.

10 September Hitler postpones Operation Sealion until 24 September, and four days later until 27 September.

13 September The Italian invasion of Egypt begins.

15 September 'Battle of Britain Day' – the culmination of the daylight fighter battles.

16 September The Italian advance reaches Sidi Barani, then halts to allow construction of defensive positions.

17 September Hitler postpones Operation Sealion indefinitely.

21 September General Sir Archibald Wavell, the British commander in Egypt, begins planning for a counterattack.

After the Greeks drove the Italian invasion force back into Albania, Hitler sent troops to ensure that Greece could not become a base from which the Allies could threaten the southern flank of his attack on the Soviet Union.

Russia. Troops were to be sent through Hungary to Romania, from where they could invade Greece if British forces began to arrive there.

Romania and Hungary had already joined the Tripartite Pact, in November 1940, and Hitler now hoped to force the Bulgarians to join, to allow access to Russia through their territory. Negotiations over the passage of troops began on 1 January 1941, but the Bulgarians hesitated. On 13 January, Hitler demanded that the Bulgarians join the Tripartite Pact, but the Sofia government was reluctant.

On 24 January, the Italians launched a counterattack against the Greek forces in Albania. At this point, the British intervened, attempting to establish a counter-Axis grouping in the Balkans. The Yugoslav Government refused to negotiate with the British, but the Greeks were enthusiastic. On 14 February, Hitler, suspicious of the Yugoslav Government, decided that he must force Yugoslavia to join the Tripartite Pact. Rebuffed, he invited Prince Paul to discuss the matter, and demanded that German troops be allowed to pass through his territory. On 25 March, the Yugoslav Government signed the Tripartite Pact.

OCTOBER

NOVEMBER

24 September A British reinforcement convoy arrives in Egypt, docking at Port Said.

30 September The final major daytime air attack on Britain.

29 September A convoy to Malta from Alexandria fails to provoke an Italian naval response.

8 October The second Malta supply convoy. The Italian attempt to interfere with the return voyage ends with the sinking of several Italian ships.

17–20 October U-boats sink 32 ships from convoys SC7 and HX79.

28 October Italian troops invade Greece.

4 November The Greeks mount a counterattack that drives the Italians back into Albania.

11/12 November Battle of Taranto – Italian naval strength is severely reduced by an attack by Royal Navy aircraft.

By this time, British troops had begun to arrive in Greece, the first of them landing on 7 March 1941. The risk to the security of the Romanian oil fields weighed heavy on Hitler's mind. Any doubts about the need for action were overcome by the remarkable set of events in Yugoslavia at the end of March. On the 27th, a coup was launched by a group of Yugoslav air-force officers opposed to the Tripartite Pact. Paul was deposed as Prince Regent, and the 17-year-old Prince Peter installed as monarch. He was a mere figurehead, power lying with General Dusan Simovic, who led the new government. Simovic announced his objections to the Tripartite Pact, and made it clear that he was prepared to negotiate with the British about forming an anti-Fascist coalition and to seek an accommodation with the USSR.

This was too much for Hitler, and he ordered the invasion of both Greece and Yugoslavia.

Invasion and Collapse

Axis forces invaded Yugoslavia and Greece on 6 April 1941. An air attack on Belgrade inflicted many casualties, and much of the Yugoslav air force's aircraft was destroyed on the ground in

Italian troops visit the Acropolis on a sightseeing tour, once the Greeks had surrendered.

1940

NOVEMBER

14/15 November An air raid on Coventry causes severe damage and marks the commencement of heavy attacks on British industrial cities.

26 November British Training Exercise Number 1 for General O'Connor's Western Desert Force in preparation for a counterattack against Italian forces in Egypt.

27 November The naval engagement off Sardinia ends inconclusively when the Italians withdraw and are not pursued.

DECEMBER

5 December The first iteration of a plan for invasion of the USSR is completed by German General Staff and presented to Hitler.

6 December British Training Exercise Number 2 takes the Western Desert Force to holding point some 32km (20 miles) away from Italian defensive positions.

9 December Italian camps at Nibeiwa, Tummar East and Tummar West are captured by the 4th Indian Division. British warships bombard Maktila and Sidi Barrani.

10 December Sidi Barrani and Maktila are surrounded by the British.

11 December Sidi Barrani fall to the British.

German bombing raids. Despite their best efforts, the Yugoslavs found it difficult to defend their territory. Within two days, their forces had begun to collapse under the weight of the German advance. Meanwhile, the Germans were making progress towards the Greeks' Metaxas and Aliakmon defensive lines. The British contribution to the defence of the country,

W Force, could not withstand the assault, and on 10 April, the troops were forced to withdraw from the Aliakmon Line, to take up a new position around Mount Olympus.

In Yugoslavia, the Italians advanced along the Yugoslav coast, and on 13 April, the Germans entered Belgrade. Three days later, Sarajevo fell, and it was clear that resistance

German soldiers on the way to Yugoslavia, checking buildings for signs of the enemy in April 1941.

could not continue. On 17 April, the Yugoslav government surrendered.

The situation in Greece was no better for the Allies. On 18 April, the Germans broke through the British positions on the Aliakmon Line, creating a gap between British and Greek forces. To make matters worse, the Greek commander, General Papagos, refused to allow a withdrawal from Albania. This meant that the eastern part of the country was held by the four

Italian troops attack a Yugoslav position during the early days of the invasion of the country in April 1941.

1941

JANUARY

13 December Hitler directs that the Balkan states are to be invaded to protect the southern flank of the assault on the USSR.

18 December Directive Number 18 is issued by Hitler, confirming his plan for invasion of the Soviet Union, Operation Barbarossa.

20 December All Italian troops are driven from Egyptian soil.

1 January The Western Desert Force is renamed XIII Corps.

5 January Bardia falls to Australian troops.

6 January Churchill makes reinforcement of Greece a priority.

7 January British forces besiege Tobruk.

8 January Hitler announces his intention to provide military support to Italy.

divisions of the BEF's W Force – and little else. The German assault came as the British were waiting for much of their equipment to arrive, making their task even more difficult. By 19 April, the position had become so perilous that the Greeks agreed that W Force should be evacuated. The British commander, General Henry Maitland Wilson, ordered a withdrawal towards the Peloponnesian ports, while a protective rearguard was maintained at Thermopylae. Evacuation began on 22 April, by which point the Greek First Army had surrendered – twice. The first surrender was taken on 20 April by Sepp Dietrich, the commander of the SS Liebstandarte Adolf Hitler. He granted terms of surrender that were relatively light, allowing the Greek soldiers to return home. Mussolini was outraged, and on 21 April 1941, a much harsher set of surrender terms was imposed upon the unfortunate Greeks.

King George and his government were flown to Crete by the RAF on 23 April, and it was clear that the end of the campaign in the Balkans was approaching. The British rearguard at Thermopylae was forced to withdraw towards the evacuation ports on 24 April, and the last Greek resistance outside Athens collapsed on the 27th, allowing German troops to enter the capital. The British evacuation was completed the next day, the troops being taken to Crete. The evacuation itself was a success, but W Force had left almost all of its equipment behind.

The Greeks and Yugoslavs were left to fight a resistance campaign against the occupying troops.

The Yugoslav Partisans

On 4 July 1941, Jospi Broz, a leading member of the prewar Yugoslav Communist Party and the man better known as 'Comrade Tito', called for a national revolt against the 'Fascist hordes'. The Partisan war began almost immediately, with acts of sabotage across the country; in Montenegro, the Italian occupying forces were badly defeated.

Tito assumed that the conflict to liberate Yugoslavia would be long and difficult, and he

A crowd of Yugoslav soldiers, milling around in the aftermath of the announcement that the Government had surrendered.

1941

JANUARY

10 January Roosevelt introduces the Lend-Lease bill to Congress. The *Luftwaffe* attacks British shipping in the Mediterranean, badly damaging aircraft carrier HMS *Illustrious*.

11 January German aircraft sink the cruiser HMS *Southampton*.

17 January The Italians evacuate Kassala and Gallalabat.

19 January British troops occupy Kassala and drive into Eritrea.

22 January Tobruk falls into British hands.

23 January The British 4th Armoured Brigade reaches the Egyptian town of Mechili.

24 January British forces under General Andrew Cunningham invade Italian Somaliland.

Tito (centre) pauses for a photograph during a break in the fighting in the fourth Axis offensive against the Partisans. The Axis powers did not have the manpower to overcome the resistance movement in Yugoslavia.

it possible for the Partisans to control large swathes of territory, running them as liberated areas. Over the next three years, the Germans launched a series of anti-Partisan offensives, but never managed to crush the movement. The scale of these operations was considerable. For example, in January 1943 the Partisans faced more than 150,000 German troops, three divisions of Italian troops, and 18,000 Chetniks and troops from the Croatian puppet government. Nonetheless, they inflicted severe damage on the Italians and routed the Chetniks – who were unable to reconstitute themselves as a major force for the remainder of the war. Tito's forces headed into Montenegro, pursuing what was left of the Chetnik forces as they went.

A further offensive – the fifth – did damage the Partisans, but they remained a potent force: by the end of 1943, Tito had 300,000 men and women in his organization and controlled two-thirds of Yugoslavia. It came close to defeat only in a seventh German offensive, launched in 1944. Tito was almost captured, but he escaped, and the final chance for the Germans to defeat the Partisans had passed.

was proved correct. The task was complicated by another resistance group, the Chetniks, headed by Draza Mihajlovic. Mihajlovic was an ardent royalist, while Tito wished to establish a communist state. The Chetniks therefore regarded Tito's Partisans as a more dangerous threat than the Germans, and in fact chose to collaborate with the Germans and Italians, with the aim of destroying them.

German Offensives

Yugoslavia's terrain hindered German attempts to control the country. And the fact that so many troops were required in the USSR made

FEBRUARY

27 January The British occupy Mechili.

29 January Anglo-American staff talks begin.

3 February The Battle of Keren (Somaliland) begins.

4 February Aerial reconnaissance reveals Italian forces withdrawing from Benghazi.

6 February Australian troops enter Benghazi. Hitler appoints General Erwin Rommel to command German forces in Libya.

6/7 February The Battle of Beda Fomm. The Italian break-out fails and troops are forced to surrender. Italians are now cleared from Cyrenaica.

8 February The Royal Navy's Force H bombards Genoa.

The Balkans Liberated

On 20 August 1944, the Red Army invaded Romania, and the Romanian front collapsed. King Carol II took the opportunity to sack his government, and made clear his intention to seek an armistice with the Allies. Some 6000 SS troops were despatched to Bucharest to prevent this, but the Romanian garrison fought them off. The Germans now concluded that the only way to sustain their position in the country was to kill the king. An assassination attempt was made on 24 August, when the *Luftwaffe* dive-bombed his palace. The king survived, but many civilians were killed, and the only consequence was to turn the Romanians against their erstwhile allies. Instead of simply seeking an armistice, Romania declared war, on the same day that Soviet troops entered the country.

The Germans promptly began withdrawing into Bulgaria, causing great concern in Sofia. Bulgaria was a member of the Axis, but was not at war with the USSR. Allowing German troops to make use of their territory would probably lead

German prisoners are escorted through Bucharest by Romanian soldiers after the Romanians changed sides.

to war with the Soviets, so Bulgarian troops disarmed the Germans and sent them to internment camps. However, given that the Soviets controlled Romania, it was impossible to keep Bulgaria out of their sights.

Bulgaria Turns

Attempts to negotiate failed. The Government proclaimed that it was no longer at war with the Western allies, but the Soviets were not convinced.

1941

FEBRUARY

12 February The Battle for Keren ends inconclusively. Rommel arrives in Libya.

14 February German forces begin to arrive in Libya.

23 February The Greek Government accepts a British offer of troops.

24 February British and German forces skirmish in Libya for the first time.

25 February The 11th African Division takes Mogadishu from the Italians.

MARCH

1 March The 11th African Division embarks on the pursuit of Italian forces towards the Ogaden Plateau.

4 March A British contingent leaves Egypt for Greece.

7 March British and Commonwealth troops land in Greece.

On 5 September 1944, they declared war, prompting the Bulgarians to declare war against Germany, fighting alongside the Soviets. This gave the Soviets control of a front more than 676km (420 miles) long.

The Germans were forced to reorganize to meet this threat, and withdrew from Greece. As they retreated, the country collapsed, Greek royalists and communists turning on one another. On 12 October 1944, British troops landed in Greece, intending to help the exiled government regain power. What they found instead was a country torn by civil war. The country would be free of German troops by 4 November 1944, but the civil war would continue until 1948.

Hungary Falls

The Hungarian Government feared that it would be next to fall to the Soviets – a fear that proved correct. The Hungarians attacked into Romania on 5 September 1944, causing the Soviets to redirect some of their units towards the Hungarian border. This led to panic in Budapest, and the Government now told the Germans that unless more troops were provided, it would act in the country's interests – implying that it might act as the Romanian Government had done.

The Hungarian leader, Admiral Horthy, opened secret negotiations with the Soviets. This did not prevent a Soviet offensive on 6 October 1944, against Debrecen, which ran into trouble within three days. Even so, Soviet forces were less than 113km (70 miles) from Budapest, worrying the Government further. To bolster Horthy's resolve against the Soviets, Hitler ordered the kidnapping of his son. The plan backfired, simply persuading Horthy to step down in favour of Ferenc Szálasi.

Szálasi took over on 16 October, but there was little he could do. The Soviets surrounded the twin cities of Buda and Pest by Christmas, and then attacked. Pest's layout made the going difficult, and the fighting was heavy. The Soviets literally had to blast the

Wehrmacht horse-drawn artillery troops enter Bulgaria during the German *withdrawal from Romania, initiating concern in the Bulgarian Government.*

8 March Lend-Lease becomes law in the United States.

11 March Build-up of the first wave of German forces for the Afrika Korps in Tripolitania.

15 March The second battle for Keren begins.

16 March British troops land at Berbera in British Somaliland.

19 March Churchill forms the Battle of the Atlantic Committee to coordinate British efforts against German U-boats.

20 March The 11th African Division and the Berbera Force link up, having driven the Italians from both British and Italian Somaliland.

24 March Rommel drives the British from El Agheila.

27 March High ground above Keren is occupied, forcing the Italians to withdraw from the town below.

defenders out, building by building and street by street, until the surviving Germans and Hungarians surrendered, on 18 January 1945.

Buda was equally difficult to take, and the Soviets reduced the city by taking the same methodical approach. On 13 February 1945, aware that resistance was hopeless, the remaining defenders surrendered at 10 a.m.

The Last Act

The Soviets now advanced into Austria, reaching Vienna on 7 April. After six days, the city fell.

The last major activity in the Balkans came in Yugoslavia. The Soviets entered the country on 11 October 1944, prompting the collapse of German resistance in Belgrade. On 7 March 1945, Tito formed a provisional government, and with his Soviet allies set about removing the last German troops. On 8 May 1945, Zagreb was liberated. A few pockets of German resistance held out for another week, but the war in the Balkans was over.

Soviet troops advance along a street during the fighting that punctuated the battle for control of Budapest.

1941

MARCH

28 March The Battle of Cape Matapan between British and Italian naval units. Five Italian ships are sunk and the battleship *Vittorio Veneto* is damaged.

31 March An American team arrives in Greenland to consider using it as a base for maritime patrol aircraft.

APRIL

1 April The Eritrean capital Asmara falls to the British. Raschid Ali seizes power in Iraq.

2 April Naval attacks by the Italian Red Sea Squadron end in disaster with five ships sunk and two captured by the British.

4 April Germans enter Benghazi unopposed.

6 April Axis forces invade Yugoslavia and Germany.

8 April Skopje and Nis fall to Axis troops.

9 April The Germans capture Salonika.

Troops with a 76.2mm (3in) Infantry Gun Model 1927 (76-27) of the South-Western Front commanded by D. Solodnov waiting in ambush during Operation Barbarossa.

Operation Barbarossa

Hitler finally attacked the Soviet Union on 22 June 1941. The forthcoming conflict would be a huge affair, since the two opposing armies were each some three million strong.

The Germans began with the advantage. Firstly, Stalin ignored the intelligence that pointed to a German attack, refusing to believe that the Germans would violate the non-aggression pact, so he did not place his forces on alert. Secondly, the Red Army had been weakened: the brutal purges ordered by Stalin in the mid-1930s meant that many of the country's best military leaders had been executed, imprisoned or exiled. A number of leading aircraft designers had also been purged, meaning that modern aircraft had gone undeveloped, leaving the Soviet Air Force desperately exposed. The consequences were many and serious: senior commanders were less than adept, appointed for reasons of loyalty rather than talent; troops were under-trained; and the Soviet equipment programme was short of talented designers. Finally, the Germans had more experience than their Soviet counterparts, which would provide an initial advantage.

10 April British forces start to withdraw from the Aliakmon Line. Zagreb falls to the Germans and Croatia announces independence from Yugoslavia.

11 April The Pan-American security zone is extended, increasing the limit within which the US Navy will protect merchant vessels. Rommel begins an attack on Tobruk.

12 April American troops land in Greenland.

13 April Germans occupy Belgrade. Japan–Soviet Neutrality Pact is signed.

17 April Yugoslavia surrenders.

18 April A brigade of Indian troops lands at Basra.

20 April The Greek First Army surrenders to the Germans.

The German High Command (Oberkommando der Wermacht; OKW) knew that the Soviets could simply withdraw into the vast Russian interior, and wait for the arrival of winter to aid them. Moreover, the Soviets had learned much about fighting in winter conditions during the war in Finland. It was clear that only a rapid advance would bring victory, but Hitler and the OKW now had a sharp difference of opinion. The OKW advocated a drive on Moscow to capture the capital, Hitler wanted to seize Leningrad, the birthplace of the Bolshevik revolution. He was certain that the Soviets would soon collapse, and his view prevailed.

The opening weeks of Barbarossa seemed to prove him right. The Soviets suffered great losses, and the Germans advanced rapidly. By mid-July 1941, however, the Germans began to have difficulties supplying their forward troops, while there were many pockets of Soviet forces as yet undefeated all along the line of advance. The scale of resistance proved demoralizing: by

German armour passes through a burning village during the early part of Operation Barbarossa.

1941

APRIL	MAY

22 April British troops begin to evacuate Greece.

23 April King George of Greece and the Greek Government are evacuated to Crete.

25 April The Afrika Korps drives the British from Halfaya Pass. Hitler issues instructions for the capture of Crete.

27 April The Germans occupy Athens.

28 April The last British troops are evacuated from Greece.

29 April Raschid Ali's forces besiege the British base at Habbaniyah. The Second brigade of Indian troops lands at Basra.

5 May Haile Selassie returns to Addis Ababa. Major-General Bernard Freyberg is appointed as commander of British forces in Crete.

6 May The third brigade of Indian troops lands at Basra.

A German anti-tank gun unit seen on the outskirts of a Russian village during Operation Barbarossa. These were extremely useful in urban fighting, capable of taking out many types of armoured vehicles in use at the time.

the end of August 1941, 10 per cent of the Field Army had been killed or wounded or had gone missing. Replacements arrived slowly, meaning that the German Army was 200,000 men below strength. By September, it had become obvious that the USSR would not be defeated easily.

Operation Typhoon

On 6 September, Hitler issued a directive that made Moscow the next objective. Operation Typhoon would be a familiar *blitzkrieg*-style attack, the armour penetrating deep into the Soviet lines and encircling enemy positions,

thus enabling the infantry to destroy them. It was a simple plan, but it ignored the fact that Typhoon would take place when the autumn rains were likely to make the few Russian roads impassable, dramatically hampering movement. A further problem came from the assumption that the Soviets would have just 60 divisions left at this point in the campaign. In fact, the true number was 212.

While preparing his strategy, Stalin did have to consider the possibility of an attack from the east. Eventually, he decided this was unlikely, on the grounds that the Japan's attention was focused on preparations for war with the United States. This gave him the confidence to move some of his combat-experienced divisions from the Far East. And it meant that Marshal Georgy Zhukov, effectively exiled when posted to High Command in the east, returned to Moscow to take charge of the resistance.

The German attack began on 30 September, three days after the start of the autumn rains. Soviet resistance was determined, and was punctuated by a series of sharp counterattacks that took the Germans by surprise. Combined with the weather, it brought the operation to a

8 May U-110 is captured by HMS *Bulldog*. A German Enigma encryption machine is captured.

9 May The British brigade 'Habforce' enters Iraq from Palestine.

10 May Rudolf Hess, Hitler's deputy, flies to Scotland.

10/11 May The last night of Blitz on Britain sees the heaviest attack on the war on London.

12 May A convoy arrives at Alexandria with more tanks and aircraft to enable the British offensive against the Afrika Korps.

15 May The British launch Operation Brevity, regaining the Halfaya Pass and taking Sollum and Capuzzo.

16 May Rommel counterattacks and drives the British back to their start line.

18 May Habforce arrives at Habbaniyah. The German battleship *Bismarck* leaves port in Gydnia for operations in the Atlantic, accompanied by the cruiser *Prinz Eugen*.

near-halt on 30 October. The OKW was forced to admit that the army would be unable to take Moscow before 1942. The arrival of winter frosts, however, solidified the ground, meaning that the advance resumed on 7 November. By 23 November, the Germans were within 48km (30 miles) of Moscow. It was the nearest they came.

The Soviets launched a counterattack on 29 November. German forces were over-extended, but Hitler forbade any withdrawal. Instead, he sacked all three Army Group commanders, and removed a number of others. This was pointless; a change in personnel could not alter the fact that winter would fall before the Germans were in Moscow. On the night of 4 December, temperatures fell to -35°C (-31°F), and Hitler was forced to end the attack.

The Siege of Leningrad

Had Hitler not been so eager to capture Leningrad, this situation might have been averted. Taking it proved much less easy than anticipated, the Soviets in the path of Army Group North putting up severe resistance. The first German artillery shells landed in the city on 1 September 1941, and a week later land communications between Leningrad and the rest of the Soviet Union were cut off. The city was encircled by 15 September and a siege began.

The decision to switch the main attack towards Moscow meant that the German forces outside Leningrad were not strong enough to assault the city. The Soviets now strived to keep

A convoy of supply trucks approaches Leningrad prior to the city being cut off by the Germans.

1941

MAY

19 May The British seize Fallujah from the Iraqis.

20 May The German attack on Crete begins. Malme is in German hands by nightfall.

21 May *Bismarck* is sighted by RAF reconnaissance aircraft. The Home Fleet is alerted and sent out in pursuit.

22 May Soddu falls to the 11th and 12th African Divisions, ending the campaign in southern East Africa. General Freyberg decides to concentrate the forces on Crete around port of Suda.

23 May *Bismarck* and *Prinz Eugen* are sighted by HMS *Suffolk* in the Denmark Strait.

24 May The British fleet intercepts *Bismarck*. HMS *Hood* is sunk and HMS *Prince of Wales* damaged and forced to break off action. Contact with *Bismarck* is lost.

25 May German reinforcements arrive at Maleme, beginning the second stage of the German offensive on Crete.

26 May *Bismarck* is located by an RAF flying boat. Swordfish torpedo bombers from HMS *Ark Royal* attack *Bismarck* and damage its steering gear.

the city supplied. Provisions were ferried across Lake Lagoda by barge, but the rate of supply was inadequate, pointing up the foolishness of the decision not to build up food stocks prior to the attack.

Rations had to be dramatically reduced as food ran out. The Leningrad Scientific Institute looked into alternative food sources, and developed artificial flour from shell packaging. A variety of substances, such as sawdust, were added to the 'bread' made from the artificial flour. The population received only one-tenth of their daily calorific requirements, and deaths from cold, malnutrition and medical conditions ran into the thousands.

On 9 November, the Germans took Tikhvin, from where the supply convoys to Lake Lagoda originated. Fortunately for the Leningraders, Tikhvin was recaptured a month later, by which point Lake Lagoda had frozen to a thickness that allowed lorries to be driven straight across it into the city. Even then, the amount of supplies that could be carried into Leningrad was inadequate. It would be a long, hard struggle until the siege could be lifted – a struggle that took 900 days.

The Battle for Moscow

On 6 December, Soviet forces counterattacked on the Kalinin front, achieving almost complete surprise. Chaos reigned in the German lines, and the salients north and south of Moscow collapsed. On 6 December, the other fronts attacked as well, and the Germans were unable to hold off the assault. The Red Army was not yet capable enough to exploit their advantage, and as the Germans settled into strongly constructed defensive positions known as 'hedgehogs', the counterattack slowed.

German infantry and accompanying armour move into Kiev during operations in the Ukraine. Initially, the Germans were welcomed as liberators from Stalin by many Ukrainians, but their brutality turned possible allies into opponents.

27 May *Bismarck* is intercepted and sunk by the battleships *King George V* and *Rodney*. The first convoy to enjoy the protection of continuous escort sails from Canada. Freyberg concludes that he cannot win the Battle for Crete and organizes an evacuation. In Iraq, British forces begin to advance towards Baghdad. Rommel recaptures the Halfaya Pass.

30 May Raschid Ali leaves Iraq.

31 May British forces enter Baghdad and agree an armistice with the Iraqis.

JUNE

8 June British and Free French forces invade Lebanon and Syria.

14 June All German and Italian assets in the United States are frozen.

15 June Hitler confirms the date of the invasion of the USSR. The British begin Operation Battleaxe in the Western Desert.

The Germans had made gains elsewhere, however. Odessa fell on 16 October, followed a day later by Taganrog. Kharkov fell on the 24th, and all of Crimea, bar Sevastopol and Kerch, was in German hands by the 27th.

By spring 1942, though, both sides were at a standstill. Hitler now turned his attention to the Caucasus and southern Russia, a useful source of oil supplies. To deny these same supplies to the Soviets would, of course, provide a second, not inconsiderable benefit.

The Caucasus

During the first phase of the operations, the River Volga was to be cut above Stalingrad, preventing oil supplies from reaching the Soviets. This was to be followed by an attack against the Caucasian oilfields. The Kerch Peninsula was attacked on 8 May 1942, and seized by 16 May. A Soviet offensive south of Kharkov on 12 May drove the Germans back, but German Sixth Army attacked into the Isyum salient on the 18th. Izyum and Barvenkova were captured the next day, trapping the Soviet forces.

German attention turned towards Sevastopol. An initial attack in 1941 had been beaten off,

A German soldier takes cover while fighting rages nearby during the early phases of the German assault on Kharkov.

1941

JUNE

17 June Operation Battleaxe ends in failure as the Afrika Korps drives the British back to their start line. The Finns begin mobilization of forces.

21 June Free French forces occupy the Syrian capital, Damascus.

22 June Hitler launches Operation Barbarossa.

23 June An invasion force penetrates 80km (50 miles) into the USSR.

25 June Dubno is captured.

26 June Finland declares war on the USSR. German Army Group North enters Lithuania; Army Group Centre traps Soviet forces in the Bialystok pocket.

27 June Hungary declares war on the USSR.

but the fighting dragged on. By early June, the Germans were ready for their final assault against the besieged city. Beginning on 6/7 June 1942, the attack took 27 days to complete. The garrison fought desperately, until it became clear that the only option was to evacuate. The evacuation began on 30 June, and by 4 July, the Germans had secured the city.

Elsewhere, Army Group B reached the Don at Voronezh and took the town, at the same time that Army Group A attacked into the Donets Basin. On 25 July, Army Group A broke out of its bridgeheads on the lower Don, and linked up with Army Group B. The German advance was thus progressing steadily into the Caucasus, and on 9 August, the Germans took

the Maykop oilfields. Running out of fuel, they now discovered that the Soviets had destroyed the facilities, thus denying them the resources they required. This meant that the German main objective could not be achieved, and attention turned to Stalingrad.

Stalingrad and Kharkov

As with Leningrad, Stalingrad had a symbolic significance. Hitler believed that its capture would be a massive blow to Soviet morale and a huge propaganda benefit for the Nazis. The plan initially called for Stalingrad to be neutralized or captured during the course of the Caucasus offensive, but when the Red Army staged its counteroffensive at Voronezh, Hitler changed the emphasis: Stalingrad was to be assaulted, taking equal priority with the oil fields. This represented a diversion of effort, but Hitler overruled the objections and General Friederich von Paulus's Sixth Army was detailed to seize the city. Paulus did not have enough troops to encircle Soviet positions, and was instead forced to conduct a frontal assault into urban terrain, an operation fraught with danger.

German pioneers advance in company with tanks across a possible mined area during the drive on Moscow.

28 June Albania declares war on the USSR.

29 June The Finns attack the Karelian Peninsula.

JULY

1 July Riga falls.

2 July The Germans break through the Stalin Line on the Latvian border.

3 July Red Army units in the Bialystok pocket surrender.

5 July General Wavell is relieved of his command of British forces in North Africa and is replaced by General Sir Claude Auchinleck.

7 July US Marines relieve the British garrison in Iceland.

12 July The Mutual Assistance Pact between Britain and the USSR is signed.

Stalingrad was defended by Lieutenant-General Vasily Chuikov's Sixty-Second Army. Chuikov had assumed command just three days before the German assault started, and immediately sought to exploit the nature of urban warfare to dislocate the attack. The battle started on 14 September 1942, beginning weeks of fighting. The Germans could not dislodge the defending forces.

A German motorcycle combination approaches the scene of recent fighting during battles in the Caucasus.

Meanwhile, the Soviet High Command prepared a counteroffensive.

Operation Uranus would use over one million Soviet troops, encircling Stalingrad from the north and south. On 11 November 1942, the Germans began another series of attacks, and Chuikov's forces had some difficulty in containing them, prompting the decision to begin Uranus on the 19th. The offensive began in the northern sector. General Nikolai Vatutin's South-West Front and General Konstantin Rokossovsky's Don Front attacked the Romanian forces in front of them. The Soviets found the going slow, but momentum increased as General Andrei Yeremenko's Stalingrad Front attacked on 20 November. By the end of the day, penetrations up to 40km (25 miles) deep had been made in

the German lines. Vatutin captured the only intact bridge over the Don at Kalach on 22 November, cutting off the Sixth Army's line of communications, and the next day, the South-West and Stalingrad fronts linked up. This left the Sixth Army and elements of the 4th Panzer Division trapped in Stalingrad. The Romanian Third Army had been all but destroyed in the attacks, and the Romanian Fourth Army had suffered severe attrition.

Paulus might have considered breaking out from Stalingrad, but on 26 November Hitler ordered him to stand fast. It was not the first, nor would it be the last, occasion when Hitler issued an order that took no account of the reality of the military situation. This time, he was influenced by Hermann Goering, who claimed that the Sixth Army could be kept supplied from the air. It was a foolish claim, for Paulus's daily requirement could not be met by the number of transport aircraft available, and only one of the seven available airfields around Stalingrad was able to accept traffic, at night.

Operation Winter Storm
On 27 November, Hitler created Army Group

1941

JULY				AUGUST		
15 July Soviet forces around Smolensk are encircled. Fighting in Syria ends with the Convention of Acre.	**16 July** German Army Group South creates a pocket at Uman between Kiev and Odessa.	**19 July** Hitler directs that Moscow is not to be the main objective of the offensive, which is now to be directed against Leningrad.	**27 July** Tallinin falls.	**2 August** The United States begins to send Lend-Lease aid to the USSR.	**5 August** Soviet forces in the Smolensk pocket surrender.	**9–12 August** Churchill and Roosevelt meet in Newfoundland and produce the Atlantic Charter.
					8 August Soviet forces in the Uman pocket surrender.	

German anti-tank gunners in action in 1942. The Germans inflicted large losses on Soviet tanks but Russian industrial output was such that the losses were absorbed.

Don under Field Marshal Erich von Manstein, giving him the task of lifting the encirclement of Stalingrad. Von Manstein drew up plans for Operation Winter Storm, which would advance along the axis of the Kotelnikovo–Stalingrad railway and relieve the siege. The date he chose was 3 December, but the plain was short-circuited on 30 November, when the Soviets launched a series of attacks to clear the Germans from the lower Chir. The attacks failed to break through, but the Don and Stalingrad fronts then launched an offensive to split the German pocket in Stalingrad. After five days of heavy fighting, the assault was called off.

Operation Ring

The Soviets now prepared a new plan, Operation Ring, to be conducted in two phases. The first would destroy the southern and western parts of the Stalingrad pocket, the second would annihilate the remaining German forces. Scheduled to begin on 16 December, it was in danger of being delayed when Manstein launched Winter Storm on the 12th. However, the Soviets blocked this attack long enough for more troops to be brought up, and General Hermann Hoth's Group of forces found the going slow. The operation went ahead as planned.

During the first phase, the Soviets also launched Operation Little Saturn. The Italian Eighth Army was completely destroyed, and the airfield at Tatsinskaya, essential for the resupply of forces at Stalingrad, was overrun. Hoth's forces reached within 26km (16 miles) of Stalingrad by 19 December, but could not break through. Manstein proposed that Paulus should break out to link with Hoth, but Paulus was still under instructions to hold until relieved, so he could not release sufficient forces.

On 24 December, the Soviet counteroffensive broadened, and the already battered Fourth Romanian Army was mauled as the Soviets broke through its lines. Manstein was forced to withdraw Group Hoth, and the situation deteriorated to the point that Hitler permitted a withdrawal of Army Group A and Army Group Don to a position 200km (125 miles) from Stalingrad. Hitler claimed that he would still relieve the Sixth Army, but in truth Paulus was on his own.

17 August Odessa is besieged.

26 August British troops occupy the Abadan oil fields.

25 August British and Russian troops invade Iran to secure oil supplies.

27 August The Iranian Government is deposed and the new administration requests an armistice.

SEPTEMBER

4 September Leningrad is under siege. A German U-boat is engaged by American destroyer USS *Greer*.

16 September Roosevelt announces that ships carrying Lend-Lease aid will be escorted by the US Navy out to 26° West.

17 September Anglo-Soviet forces occupy Tehran.

19 September Kiev falls.

24 September Fifteen nations sign the Atlantic Charter.

A German gun team in action during the fighting in Stalingrad.

The End in Stalingrad

On 1 January, Yeremenko's Stalingrad Front was renamed the South Front, and he was given the task of continuing to attack Manstein's forces. The final attack on Stalingrad was scheduled for 6 January 1943, but was postponed for four days to allow for the huge deployment of troops required. Rokossovosky offered Paulus surrender terms on the 8th, but these were rejected. The Soviet attack began as planned on the 10th, and made a steady advance. On 12 January, the western end of the German pocket was overrun, and the airfield at Karpova fell the next day. The night-flying airfield at Pitomnik was captured on the 16th, and four other airstrips fell the next day. The Germans were in danger of losing their ability to resupply the Sixth Army.

On 22 January, the final phase of the Soviet offensive began. Paulus signalled Hitler with a stark appreciation of the situation, implying that the Sixth Army should surrender. This was ignored. The same day, Soviet forces split the remainder of the German pocket into two smaller pockets in the north and south of the city. The final German aircraft left the city on the 23rd, and it was now a matter of time before the end came. Paulus sought permission to attempt a breakout, but was again refused. The Sixth Army held on, although the food shortage was such that the wounded and sick could not be fed, the supplies going to those still capable of fighting.

On 30 January 1943, Hitler promoted Paulus to field marshal. It was a none-too-subtle message: no German field marshal had ever surrendered, so Paulus could now be counted on, couldn't he, to 'do the decent thing' and commit suicide as the battle drew to its inevitable end.

The next day, 31 January, the Sixty-Second Army surrounded Paulus' headquarters, prompting his surrender. The northern pocket fought on for two more days, but surrendered after a massive artillery bombardment. The Battle for Stalingrad was over, and the war had reached a turning point.

The Role of Industry

The German failure to overcome the USSR by the end of 1942 meant that factors other than martial skill and good fortune came into play on the Eastern Front. In a state of total war, the

1941

SEPTEMBER

25 September Army Group South launches an offensive into the Crimea.

26 September The first Arctic convoy carrying war materiel to the USSR leaves Britain. The formation of the British Eighth Army in the Western Desert.

27 September The campaign in East Africa resumes after a halt imposed by poor weather, with the capture of the Wolchefit Pass.

29 September Tripartite conference in Moscow between US, USSR and Britain to discuss aid to Russia.

30 September The attack towards Moscow, Operation Typhoon, is launched. Pockets are created at Vyazma and Bryansk.

OCTOBER

6 October Churchill promises Stalin that a supply convoy from Britain will be sent to the USSR every 10 days.

10 October General Zhukov assumes command of the West Front to defend Moscow.

14 October The Bryansk pocket surrenders.

16 October The evacuation of government and industry from Moscow begins; Stalin declares he will remain in the capital. Odessa falls.

ability of one side to out-produce the other may take on huge significance, particularly if this is coupled with a vast source of manpower for the front line. The Soviet Union had both the capacity to out-produce the Germans, and the men and women to make full use of the equipment sent from the factory to the front line.

To understand just how impressive was the manufacturing achievement of the USSR, consider this simple fact: Soviet factories produced around twice as much war materiel as German industry in 1942, despite the fact that Soviet industry had access to only about one-third of the steel and coal supplies available to Hitler. The reason for this lay in the careful development of industrial capacity. Before the war, Soviet factories that produced tractors as the main business also turned out some tanks; when war came, the ratio of tank-to-tractor production was reversed, guaranteeing a rapid build-up in Red Army armoured strength. Production for agriculture inevitably fell, but did not disappear entirely, enabling a balance to be struck between feeding the front line with armaments and feeding the nation as a whole.

Soviet industry was able to produce nearly 240 million tons of munitions in 1942, a dramatic increase on the 1940 figures – and a figure that is even more impressive when the disruption caused by evacuating industry is taken into account. The overall output from Soviet industry was prodigious. Between 1943 and 1945, more than 80,000 aircraft, 73,000 armoured vehicles and 324,000 artillery pieces were made. To provide just one example, a total of 36,000 Ilyushin Il-2 'Sturmovik' attack aircraft were built, making it the most heavily produced aircraft in history (a figure that is almost certainly never to be beaten).

Industrial output alone did not defeat Hitler on the Eastern Front, but any assessment of the fighting that took place from 1943 onwards must take it into account. The sheer scale of the troops, machines and other equipment involved is difficult to grasp, but without this industrial capacity, a Soviet victory on the Eastern Front would have been impossible to achieve.

A German machine-gun position on the outskirts of Stalingrad.

---

17 October American destroyer USS *Kearney* is torpedoed by a U-boat and badly damaged.

19 October The Vyazma pocket surrenders.

24 October Army Group South captures Kharkov.

27 October The Crimea falls.

30 October The German advance halts as bad weather makes ground impassable.

31 October A torpedo attack by a U-boat sinks the American destroyer USS *Reuben James*.

NOVEMBER

3 November Kursk is captured by the Germans.

7 November The advance on Moscow resumes.

13 November America repeals its Neutrality Act.

16 November Kerch falls to German forces.

18 November The British launch Operation Crusader in the Western Desert.

The Atlantic War

The war at sea was of critical importance to Britain, given the country's reliance upon imported foodstuffs and war materiel. The German surface fleet was small in comparison to the Royal Navy, and the major threat to British shipping came from the U-boat.

Unfortunately, the Admiralty had decided that the submarine threat had been made irrelevant by the development of the ASDIC detection system (better known today as sonar). This overlooked the fact that ASDIC worked only when submarines were submerged, and that the submarines of the period operated on the surface for as long as possible to extend their endurance. Submerging offered protection when attacking a ship, but was not always necessary: U-boat commanders developed the technique of attacking on the surface at night, when it was almost impossible for lookouts to spot them.

The Admiralty's decison meant that the British were more interested in the threat from the German

Left: A convoy of merchant ships is escorted across the Atlantic by the Royal Navy.
Right: Graf Spee burns after being scuttled in the entrance to Montevideo harbour, December 1939.

surface fleet, rather than the U-boats. The Germans had only 57 U-boats at the start of the war, and limited their use in accordance with an edict from Hitler that the submarines were not to embark on a major offensive. He still believed he could reach an accommodation with the Allies, and was also concerned that an unrestricted submarine offensive might alienate neutral nations who lost vessels. He permitted only limited operations, against military vessels or clearly identified merchant ships.

The first major naval activity occurred on the day the war began, when a U-boat sank the liner HMS *Athenia*. This convinced the British that the Germans had embarked on unrestricted submarine warfare, and they introduced convoying for their shipping as a result. Worse was to follow. The aircraft carrier *Courageous* was sunk on 17 September 1939 by U-29, a result of the misguided decision to use aircraft carrier groups to hunt U-boats. The *Ark Royal* had nearly been hit by the U-39 just a few days earlier, surviving only because the torpedoes had exploded short of the target. In fact, during the first year of the war, faulty German torpedoes would save a number of ships.

A close up of the stricken Graf Spee *as she burns in Montevideo harbour, December 1939.*

The River Plate

The first major surface action of the war occurred 12,875km (8000 miles) from Europe. The German pocket battleships *Deutschland* and *Graf Spee* were ordered to attack British shipping in the Atlantic on 27 September, and set about their task with alacrity. *Graf Spee* sank five ships in three weeks, before heading for the Indian Ocean. The Admiralty organized a number of task groups to find the pocket battleships, but these failed to locate them for some time.

Worse was to come for the Royal Navy on 14 October, when U-47 managed to slip into the anchorage at Scapa Flow and sink the battleship *Royal Oak*. This was a blow to British morale, and a propaganda coup for the Germans, who had more to crow about as the *Graf Spee* continued its successful campaign against British shipping. The captain of the *Graf Spee*, Hans Langsdorff, moved back into the South Atlantic, and sank two more merchant ships, one on 3 December and another four days later.

By this point, there were six British task groups hunting for the ship. The *Graf Spee* was finally located off the River Plate by Force G,

1941

NOVEMBER

20 November Tobruk garrison is given the order to break out. The Germans capture Rostov-on-Don.

22 November Gondar falls to the British, ending the campaign in East Africa.

23 November German troops come within 48km (30 miles) of Moscow.

24 November Rommel's 'dash for the wire' to Egyptian-Libyan border in an attempt to cut Eighth Army supply routes.

26 November Rommel begins the withdrawal from the border as fuel supplies run out.

29 November Soviet counterattack on Rostov.

under Commodore Henry Harwood. Spotting their smoke, Langsdorff mistook Force G for destroyers escorting a convoy, rather than three cruisers. He attacked, and after two hours of fighting HMS *Exeter* and *Ajax* had been badly damaged. This left only HMS *Achilles* to follow the *Graf Spee*, which had been so badly damaged that it required repairs. Langsdorff had no choice but to put into Montevideo harbour.

The Uruguayan authorities reminded the German captain that this was a neutral port, which meant that

the time allowed for repairs was limited. The British realized that the best chance they had of dealing with the *Graf Spee* was to intercept it as it left harbour, but the forces capable of dealing with a pocket battleship were not in place. They therefore devised a bold plan to trick Langsdorff into believing that a far superior force would be waiting for him. Their signalling was deliberately careless so that it could be intercepted, while agents in Montevideo spread rumours that a battleship squadron had arrived. On 17 December, the *Graf Spee* left harbour, and Langsdorff scuttled the ship before reaching the open sea.

For Britain, this was to be one of the few high points in the sea war for some time to come.

The U-boats Arrive

On 17 August 1940, the Germans began a total maritime blockade of Britain. The capture of French bases meant that the U-boats had a far shorter transit time to their operational areas in the Atlantic, thereby increasing the submarines' endurance. During July and August, some 700,000 tons of shipping were sunk by the U-boat fleets, a source of considerable concern to the British. This was partially alleviated when the Lend-Lease Act came into force on 2 September, and the Americans supplied 50 ageing destroyers to Britain, the first eight of which were handed over four days later.

However, the British were still at a disadvantage, since there were not enough escorts to cover all the convoys. Moreover, air

The battlecruiser Gneisenau *and her sister-ship* Scharnhorst *were amongst the most powerful ships in German service.*

DECEMBER

5 December The German drive on Moscow halts. Britain declares war on Finland, Hungary and Romania. General Konev's Kalinin Front counterattacks across the upper Volga.

6 December Zhukov's West Front begins a counterattack.

7 December Zhukov begins a further attack to south of Moscow. The Afrika Korps withdraws to Gazala, and the siege of Tobruk is lifted.

9 December The ban on U-boats operating in American waters is lifted by Hitler.

11 December Germany declares war on the United States.

12 December All Vichy French ships in US ports are requisitioned.

13 December Timoshenko's South-West Front counterattacks between Yelets and Livny. Field Marshal von Brauchitsch orders a German withdrawal.

cover was virtually nonexistent, since the RAF did not have enough aircraft, while many of the craft that were available lacked the range to provide cover into the Atlantic.

The U-boats were thus able to inflict serious damage on a number of convoys in September and October, aided by the fact that they were able to read the signals from Allied merchant shipping. The only saving grace for the British was the bad weather in November and December, which reduced the rate of sinkings. Even so, the amount of tonnage lost (more than 600,000 tons) was alarming. To make matters worse, the Germans resumed surface action. The pocket battleship *Admiral Scheer* and the battlecruisers *Scharnhorst* and *Gniesenau* caused considerable damage to convoys between November 1940 and March 1941, sinking 115,000 tons of shipping before returning to port.

There was, however, some hope. In March 1941, the Royal Navy sank U-47, U-99 and U-100 in the space of 10 days. A combination of more ships, better training and the introduction of radar able to detect surfaced U-boats made the task easier, while the use of signals intelligence to work out the location of U-boats allowed safer routing of convoys. Nevertheless, the battle hung in the balance, and on 19 March 1941 Churchill created the Battle of the Atlantic Committee to coordinate activities. Shipping losses for March, despite the Navy's success, were 517,000 tons, an unsustainable rate.

The situation did not improve until 8 May 1941, when U-110 was forced to the surface after attacking convoy OB318. As the U-boat

The Enigma code-breaking machine provided important information on enemy positions.

surfaced, her captain saw not one but two British destroyers bearing down on his vessel, apparently preparing to ram it. He ordered his crew to abandon ship, and in their haste, the charges for scuttling the submarine were not set. The captain of one of the two British ships, Commander A.J. Baker-Cresswell, noticed that the U-boat was not sinking, and thought that there might be a chance of capturing it. He ordered full astern, and his ship, HMS *Bulldog*, pulled up just feet away from U-110. The accompanying HMS *Broadway* also stopped. A boarding party searched U-110 and discovered that the radio operator had failed to destroy his Enigma signals encryption machine and the accompanying code books. These soon played a major part in reducing the capability of the U-boats.

The End of the 'Happy Time'
With the Enigma machine and code books in British hands, the situation changed. Able to interpret German signals, the codebreakers at Bletchley Park were able to provide information that allowed convoys to be routed away from the positions of enemy submarines. The rate of

1941

DECEMBER

14 December Hitler sacks von Brauchitsch and overturns his order to withdraw.

15 December Stalin instructs government ministries to return to Moscow. The Eighth Army attacks Gazala.

18/19 December Italian naval special forces cripple battleships HMS *Valiant* and *Queen Elizabeth* in Alexandria harbour.

19 December Hitler announces that he is taking command of the German Army.

21 December Large-scale air attacks on Malta begin.

22 December Churchill and Roosevelt meet in Washington.

1942

JANUARY

6 January The US Congress approves additional spending on war production.

12 January U-boats launch Operation Drumbeat – attacks on shipping off the American eastern seaboard. The German battleship *Tirpitz* is ordered to Norway.

sinking declined dramatically, while several German supply ships were located and sunk by the Royal Navy.

Britain received a further advantage when the United States offered help, despite technically being neutral. On 11 April, Roosevelt gave instructions that the US Navy's neutrality patrols were to operate further out into the Atlantic. The patrols were to protect American merchant shipping out to 26° West, which meant that the British and Canadians had to cover far fewer convoys. The escorting ships also radioed sightings of U-boats to their charges. The signals were decoded and easily intercepted by the Allies (as Roosevelt probably intended), making it almost impossible for the Germans to achieve surprise. To add to Hitler's suspicions that Roosevelt was in effect embarking upon an undeclared naval war with Germany, American troops occupied Greenland on 12 April, thus providing a useful base for patrol aircraft, and on 7 July American troops relieved the British troops guarding Iceland.

The battleship Bismarck *being launched. It was the most notorious of the German ships during World War II.*

17 January Bardia is recaptured by the Eighth Army.

21 January Rommel launches an offensive into Cyrenaica.

22 January The Afrika Korps captures Agedabia.

23 January *Tirpitz* reaches Trondheim.

26 January American troops arrive in Northern Ireland.

29 January Rommel captures Benghazi.

29/30 January Unsuccessful bomber raid against the *Tirpitz*.

FEBRUARY

1 February The new Engima cipher is adopted by the U-boat fleet, rendering communications traffic unreadable by British codebreakers.

2 February A supply convoy for Malta leaves Alexandria, but all three supply ships are sunk by an air attack.

This gave Roosevelt the opportunity to provide escorts to convoys heading to and from Iceland, again increasing the pressure on the U-boats. By midsummer, the U-boat arm found that it was unable to damage British shipping in the same way, and morale began to dip. The period of success known as the 'Happy Time' was over.

Sink the Bismarck

At this point, the Germans suffered a further blow. The battleship *Bismarck* had left harbour bound for the Atlantic on 18 May, accompanied by the heavy cruiser *Prinz Eugen*. The two ships were sighted by reconnaissance aircraft on the 21st, and the British Home Fleet was sent to intercept them in the Denmark Straight. The two ships were located on the 23rd, and the Home Fleet intercepted them the next day. In the battle that followed, the *Bismarck* hit the battlecruiser HMS *Hood,* which blew up, sinking with all but three of her crew.

This was an enormous blow to British pride, since the *Hood* had been regarded as the pride of the Royal Navy. The *Bismarck* now had to be

Seen at sea, the Bismarck *enjoyed a short but spectacular career. She was sunk on 27 May 1941.*

sunk. As the two German ships separated, the Admiralty ordered Force H from Gibraltar, complete with aircraft carriers and battleships, to intercept.

Contact with *Bismarck* was lost, until sighted by an RAF Catalina flying boat on 26 May. A strike by Swordfish torpedo bombers from HMS *Ark Royal* nearly ended in disaster when they attacked HMS *Sheffield* by mistake. However,

---

1942

FEBRUARY

4 February The German offensive comes to a halt in front of the Gazala–Bir Hachim line.

7 February A supply convoy sails from Malta, carrying Spitfire fighters aboard aircraft carriers HMS *Argus* and *Eagle*; aircraft are flown off once in range of the island.

8 February The Red Army cuts off 90,000 German troops at Demyansk.

11 February The 'Channel Dash' begins as German ships *Scharnhorst*, *Gneisenau* and *Prinz Eugen* leave port in Brest for Germany.

13 February The 'Channel Dash' ends with German ships reaching the safety of German ports.

16 February U-boats launch a major anti-shipping offensive off the US eastern seaboard, sinking 71 ships during the remainder of the month.

23 February Air Chief Marshal Sir Arthur Harris takes over as head of RAF Bomber Command.

MARCH

19 March The Soviet Second Shock Army is surrounded between Novgorod and Gruzino.

this proved a blessing in disguise, since the few torpedoes that were dropped exploded on impact. The chastened aircrews flew back to *Ark Royal* and had their aircraft loaded with differently fused weapons. They launched a further strike, and early on the evening of the 26th, managed to hit *Bismarck*, wrecking the battleship's steering gear. This slowed her

considerably, and meant that it was only a matter of time before Force H was able to intercept. The battleships *King George V* and *Rodney* found *Bismarck* on the 27th, and pounded the enemy ship into oblivion. The *Bismarck's* crew put up a gallant fight, but the ship was left blazing from end to end. The cruiser HMS *Dorsetshire* administered

the *coup de grâce* with torpedoes, and the *Bismarck* slipped beneath the waves, taking more than 2000 men with her.

On the same day as the *Bismarck* was sunk, the first convoy with continuous escort across the Atlantic set sail.

The Americans Enter the Fray

American participation in the Battle of the Atlantic increased in intensity following the extension of the Pan-American security zone. On 4 September, the USS *Greer* exchanged fire with a U-boat, prompting Roosevelt to warn that Axis warships entering the zone did so at their own risk. This was followed 12 days later by the announcement that it was not only US-registered ships that would receive escorts but all ships carrying Lend-Lease materiel.

A clash between the Americans and the Germans was now almost inevitable. On 17 October, the USS *Kearney* was torpedoed and badly damaged, and exactly two weeks later, the USS *Reuben James*, escorting convoy HX156,

The American destroyer Reuben James *was the first American warship to fall victim to German U-boats.*

20 March Air attacks on Malta intensify.

22 March Battle of Sirte Gulf.

29 March Third supply convoy of Spitfires to Malta.

21 March Second supply convoy of Spitfires to Malta.

28/29 March The RAF bombs Lübeck, inflicting heavy damage. Hitler orders retaliatory attacks on historic British towns.

30/31 March Second unsuccessful bombing raid against the *Tirpitz*.

APRIL

1 April American authorities begin to introduce a convoy system along the US eastern seaboard to reduce losses to enemy submarines.

5 April Hitler issues orders for a summer offensive in Russia.

was sunk with the loss of most of her crew. On 6 November 1941, the blockade runner *Odenwald* was captured by the US ships *Somers* and *Omaha*. The fact that the German ship was disguised as a American vessel made Germany even more unpopular in the United States, allowing Roosevelt to repeal the Neutrality Acts on 13 November. This gave him the power to bring the United States into the war, though public opinion remained divided. Fate intervened: on 7 December 1941, the Japanese attacked Pearl Harbor, and on the 11th, Hitler declared war.

The Second 'Happy Time'

The United States could now bring its vast industrial power to bear. But its entry into the war also meant that the U-boats could attack US shipping without worrying about the political consequences. Initially, the Americans were unprepared to deal with the arrival of U-boats off the eastern seaboard, lacking the ships, aircraft and experience to address the threat. During January 1942, the majority of ships sunk went down off the eastern seaboard. Silhouetted against the lights of coastal towns and cities,

they made easy targets for the U-boats, and it took some time for the merits of a blackout to be appreciated.

To make matters worse, the Germans adopted a new cipher for their Enigma machines on 1 February. The analysts at Bletchley Park now had to start all over again in their attempts to decode signals. This meant that the U-boats were able to enjoy even greater success. Yet by April, the Americans had started to fight back in a meaningful manner. Convoying was introduced along the eastern seaboard, thus helping to reduce sinkings, and on 18 April a blackout was instituted after local authorities understood that denying U-boats the ability to see their targets against the coastline was more important than any potential damage to the tourist trade. On 1 August, the Americans introduced an interlocking convoy system that linked all shipping from the Caribbean to the eastern seaboard. Admiral Karl Dönitz, commander of the U-boat arm, had always known that such a step would reduce sinkings, and he now moved his forces to the North Atlantic. The second 'Happy Time' was over.

Admiral Karl Dönitz, the head of the German U-boat arm, and later head of the German Navy.

1942

APRIL

8 April Anglo-American talks on the opening of a second front against Hitler begin in London.

10 April The Soviet ambassador in Washington demands the opening of the second front.

20 April American carrier USS *Wasp* flies in 46 Spitfires to Malta.

24 April German air raid against Exeter, the first in retaliation for Lübeck.

26 April The intensity of air attacks forces the withdrawal of a British submarine squadron from Malta.

27/28 April Third unsuccessful bombing raid against the *Tirpitz*.

30 April Hitler and Mussolini set the date for the invasion of Malta: 10 July.

MAY

8 May Manstein launches an attack in the Crimea to clear the Kerch Peninsula.

Final Crisis

By now, however, the Allies had taken steps that would dramatically improve their effectiveness against the U-boat threat. The use of radar on escort vessels had increased, while direction-finding equipment allowed escort ships to locate U-boats from their radio transmissions.

RAF Coastal Command, originally ill-equipped, now had stronger forces and more modern aircraft. It is true that some types were either no longer wanted by Bomber Command or were considered second-rate, but also available were more of the long-range Catalina flying boats and the Consolidated B-24 Liberator. Designed as a bomber, the Liberator had the range to cover the 'Atlantic Gap' in which the U-boats could operate without fear of air attack other than from the small air groups carried on escort carriers. That said, the Gap could not be closed completely until 1943, since the Liberators were initially available in small numbers only. However, escorts were also better armed, the Hedgehog bomb-throwing system enabling them to blanket an area with bombs, each of which was capable of destroying a submarine.

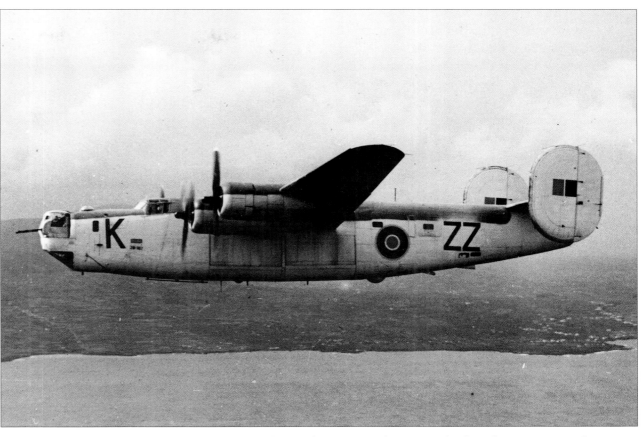

A Consolidated B-24 Liberator bomber in the colours of RAF Coastal Command. The Liberator was used as a very long range patrol aircraft, and was vital for the provision of air cover for convoys in the middle of the Atlantic.

9 May A further 60 Spitfires are flown to Malta.

10 May General Albert Kesselring, German Commander-in-Chief South, erroneously reports that Malta's defences have been neutralized; Axis aircraft over Malta find themselves outnumbered by defending fighters for the first time.

12 May Soviet offensive south of Kharkov.

13 May British Chiefs of Staff approve an amphibious raid against Dieppe.

16 May Manstein clears the Kerch Peninsula.

18 May German counterattack against Soviet forces around Kharkov.

23 May Air Chief Marshal Harris issues orders for a raid against Hamburg by 1000 bombers.

26 May Rommel launches a new offensive in the Western Desert.

Nonetheless, the last months of 1942 were a period of considerable concern for the Allies, as the rate of sinkings in the North Atlantic remained at worrying levels. In November, some 126 ships were sunk, and the Admiralty observed that the situation with escorts had 'never been tighter'. The U-boats seemed to have gained the upper hand once more.

Brighter news came in December, when Bletchley Park broke the Enigma cipher again, revealing the movement of U-boats. However, the codebreakers now had to wade through a mountain of previously unreadable material, which meant that they were unable to provide up-to-date information, and the sinkings continued. Convoys ONS154 and TM1 were severely mauled by the U-boats between 26 December 1942 and 8 January 1943. Further losses increased the sense of gloom, and when convoys HX229 and SC122 suffered heavy losses between 15 and 19 March 1943, it appeared that the Germans might be on course for victory.

The Final Victory
Between 4 and 7 April, convoy HX231 was attacked by a pack of U-boats – but this time,

An atmospheric photograph of an Allied convoy, taken from an accompanying aircraft during 1942. The provision of escort and air cover made the work of the U-boat arm more difficult as the war went on.

1942

MAY				JUNE

26 May The Anglo-Soviet Treaty is signed. Both nations pledge not to make separate peace with Germany.

27 May The Afrika Korps pushes northeast of the Gazala Line.

29 May Soviet forces south of Kharkov are cut off and forced to surrender.

30/31 May The first 1000-Bomber Raid occurs, but against Cologne rather than Hamburg, which is saved by bad weather preventing an attack against it.

31 May The 'Battle of the Cauldron' begins with a combined Italian/Afrika Korps attack on the British 150 Brigade.

1/2 June The second 1000-bomber raid against Essen.

2 June Manstein launches an attack on Sevastopol. Axis troops overrun 'the Cauldron'.

the U-boats were vigorously hunted. Commander Peter Gretton's HMS *Tay* sank the U-635, while a Liberator despatched U-632. Four more U-boats sustained such heavy damage that they limped home. The three merchant ships sunk represented a poor return for these casualties.

In the early hours of 4 May 1943, convoy ONS5 was set upon by 40 U-boats, and six ships were sunk. During the day, U-630 was sunk by a Royal Canadian Air Force Canso flying boat, but the U-boats returned to sink seven more ships. Still, the cost for the Germans was high: the same number of U-boats had been damaged. Then, on the morning of the 5th, U-192 was sunk by HMS *Pink*, and the U-boats failed to find another victim until nightfall. They sank another four ships, but the escorts now gained the upper hand. U-638 was depth-charged, and sank; HMS *Vidette* blew U-125 to pieces with its hedgehog bomb system; U-531 was rammed by the escort HMS *Oribi*, and sank; U-438 was located by the radar of HMS *Pelican*, and it too sank. U-boat headquarters called off the attack the next morning. Eight U-boats had been lost and five more badly damaged.

Next it was the turn of convoy HX237 to come under attack. It completed its Atlantic

A U-boat is depth-charged from an anti-submarine aircraft. These could even locate U-boats at night.

crossing on 16 May 1943, having lost three ships, but the escorts had sunk three U-boats and damaged two more. Finally, on the evening of 18 May, convoy SC130 was approached by 33 U-boats. The convoy was warned of the presence of submarines, and the escorts came close to sinking a U-boat the following night. At first light, a Liberator appeared over the convoy and reported that U-boats had surrounded it. Over the course of the next 12 hours, the submarines tried to attack, but to no avail. U-381 was sunk by a bombardment of hedgehog bombs from two escorts; U-954 was sunk by the Liberator; U-273 was sunk by a Lockheed Hudson that arrived to provide additional air cover; and U-258 was located on the surface by another Liberator that arrived over the convoy, and it too sank. On the morning of 21 May, the U-boats were called off, having lost five of their number. They had not fired a single torpedo.

Some 31 U-boats had been lost by 22 May. Dönitz knew that he was beaten. He ordered his submarines out of the North Atlantic to the waters south of the Azores. The struggle would continue until 1945, but the Battle of the Atlantic was over.

11 June Supply convoys from Gibraltar and Alexandria head for Malta. Bir Hakim falls to Rommel and the Battle of Knightsbridge begins.

13 June The Battle of Knightsbridge ends with a British withdrawal.

14 June Malta supply convoys come under heavy air attack.

15 June Malta supply convoys are attacked again, and the weight of attack prevents them from completing their mission.

18 June Tobruk is surrounded by the Afrika Korps. Churchill starts talks with Roosevelt about plans for launching offensive operations against Germany.

21 June Tobruk falls to Rommel.

23 June Rommel resumes his advance.

The War in the Desert

In the run-up to World War II, Britain realized that the outcome of the war might be decided in the Mediterranean and the Middle East, a vital source of oil supplies and the main line of communication with India and the Far East.

The Italian declaration of war on 10 June 1940 was, therefore, a serious threat to Britain's position in the Mediterranean. Hostilities opened on 11 June, when the Italian Air Force raided Malta nine times, and bombed Port Sudan and Aden. Meanwhile, RAF Bomber Command raided Turin and Genoa, and British armour crossed into Libya to ambush Italian trucks by Fort Capuzzo. The fort, and its near-neighbour at Maddalena, were captured on 14 June, but the small British force only destroyed the guns of each position before withdrawing. Meanwhile, the British prepared a defensive line at Mersa Matruh.

The First Attack
The Italians opened the first major operations with an attack in the Sudan on 4 July. They took the British positions at Kassala and Gallabat on the borders of Abyssinia and Eritrea, but made no further advance. Then, on 4 August, a 25,000-strong force invaded British Somaliland. The small British

Left: General Bernard Montgomery, seen in the desert around the time of the second Battle of El Alamein. Right: A wrecked Italian CR42 fighter aircraft lies alongside the highway from Sollum to Sidi Barrani.

British troops are seen on exercise in Egypt, late 1940.

garrison had little option other than to withdraw, and was evacuated on 17 August by the Royal Navy. The Italians were now in a position to threaten the entrance to the Red Sea, but had to face the problem of a British-inspired revolt in Abyssinia. Sporadic fighting continued in the region while the British built up their strength in the Middle East.

On 13 September, the Italians invaded Egypt, crossing the frontier and occupying Sollum. The British Western Desert Force (WDF) conducted a pre-planned fighting withdrawal to Mera Matruh, aiming to delay the Italian advance. Sidi Barrani fell on 16 September, at which point the Italians halted. General Sir Archibald Wavell, the Commander-in-Chief Middle East, began planning for a counterattack on 21 September, by which time the arrival of reinforcements would give him a much greater armoured strength than the Italians. Realizing this, the Italian commander, General Rodolf Graziani, refused to make any further advance, despite pressure. Frustrated by the failure to

push on towards Egypt, Mussolini turned his attention to Greece.

On 28 October, Italian troops crossed the border between Albania and Greece. The Greeks mounted a vigorous counterattack and also accepted support from Britain. Although declining direct assistance, they welcomed an offer to send a brigade from the Middle East to garrison Crete on their behalf.

Wavell's Counterattack

Wavell, aware of the situation in East Africa and the possibility that he would have to send troops to Greece, was able to plan for an offensive in North Africa. On 26 November 1940, the WDF began Training Exercise Number 1, a dress rehearsal for the offensive itself. On 6 December Training Exercise Number 2 took place, involving a march to

1942

JUNE

25/26 June The third 1000-bomber raid against Bremen is the last raid on this scale until 1944.

26 June The Afrika Korps attacks at Mersa Matruh.

27 June British positions at Mersa Matruh are outflanked, forcing them to withdraw.

27 June–5 July Convoy PQ17 for Russia is decimated by German air and submarine attacks, losing 23 out of 33 ships.

28 June The Germans capture Fuqa.

29 June Mersa Matruh is captured by the Afrika Korps.

30 June The Sevastopol garrison begins evacuation by sea. The German Sixth Army attacks the Soviet South-West Front. The British Eighth Army is back on the El Alamein defensive line.

point 'Piccadilly', 96km (60 miles) south of Maktila. The WDF concentrated here, and on 9 December launched Operation Compass. The Italian camps at Nibeiwas and Tummar were captured, and the next day Sidi Barrani was surrounded. By 20 December, the Italians had been driven from Egypt, and the British pursued them into Libya. Bardia was taken on 5 January 1941 and Tobruk was besieged on the 7th. After two weeks' fighting, Tobruk fell, and Wavell was ordered to push on to Benghazi. The Australians captured it on 6 February, and Italian attempts to break through the British positions at Beda Fomm were defeated. This was the first major British land victory of the war – but the success was not to last. On the day that Benghazi fell, he appointed General Erwin Rommel to command the German Afrika Korps, to give aid to the Italians.

The Afrika Korps Arrives

Rommel landed at Tripoli on 12 February. Twelve days later, the first clash took place at Nofilia, when British and German troops met while carrying out reconnaissance along the coastal road from Sirte. Even as the German

Italian troops surrendering at Bardia, Libya, during Wavell's advance into Cyrenaica. When the Bardia fortress fell, the British took more than 32,000 prisoners and captured valuable weapons and armour.

JULY

1 July Rommel makes an unsuccessful attack on the El Alamein line.

2 July Further indecisive attacks are made by the Afrika Korps around El Alamein and the Ruweisat Ridge.

3 July The Afrika Korps advances 14km (9 miles) along the Ruweisat Ridge before being halted. Rommel orders his troops on to the defensive. Manstein takes Sevastopol.

4 July The first air attack in the European Theatre of Operations by US Army Air Force aircraft against airfields in the Netherlands. Auchinleck makes an unsuccessful armoured counterattack on German positions.

5 July The British make unsuccessful attempts to outflank Afrika Korps' positions. German Army Group B reaches the River Don.

build-up of forces continued, the British were forced to send four divisions to Greece to assist in the defence of that nation. This seriously weakened the British force, and on 24 March, the Afrika Korps captured El Agheila. A week later, a further attack at Mersa Brega presaged a German advance to Agedabi, from which the British withdrew. Benghazi fell into Rommel's hands on 4 April, and by the 25th, the British had been forced back to their start line of five months before, the besieged Tobruk being all that remained of their gains.

A convoy carrying tanks and aircraft arrived in Egypt on 12 May, allowing Wavell to launch a new offensive. Operation Brevity was intended to drive Rommel back into Libya, and began on 15 May. The Halfaya Pass, Sollum and Capuzzo were recaptured, but the Germans counterattacked the next day and retook the two latter positions. Rommel awaited the arrival of 15th Panzer Division, and then retook the Halfaya Pass on 27 May. The failure of Brevity increased the

General Erwin Rommel, commander of the Afrika Korps, November 1941.

pressure on Wavell from Churchill, who wanted Tobruk to be relieved. This led to Operation Battleaxe, which began on 15 June. It was a dispiriting failure, and by the evening of 17 June, the offensive had been driven back to its start line, having suffered heavy tank losses. As a result, Wavell was replaced by General Sir Claude Auchinleck on 5 July 1941.

A New Offensive
Auchinleck issued orders for a new offensive, Operation Crusader, to relieve Tobruk and reconquer Cyrenaica. This was to be undertaken by Lieutenant-General Sir Alan Cunningham's XIII Corps (the renamed Western Desert Force). By 26 September, 30 Corps had arrived in the Middle East, and the Eighth Army was formed to control both of them, under Cunningham. Crusader began

1942

JULY

7 July Army Group B attacks into Donets Basin.

8 July The first Panzer Army crosses the Donets.

9 July Rommel attacks New Zealanders holding Deir el Munassib, only to discover they had withdrawn to new positions shortly before the assault.

10 July Australians and South Africans attack from the El Alamein Box, making small gains.

12/13 July The Afrika Korps makes a further unsuccessful attack against El Alamein Box positions.

15 July New Zealanders attack at Ruweisat, but make little progress.

18 July Army Group B resumes its advance on Stalingrad.

22 July The British offensive sees XII Corps break through at Ruweisat, but it makes little further progress.

An Afrika Korps Panzer tank moves along a desert road in the early days of the German campaign. The Panzers were superior to Allied armour in North Africa.

British prisoners of war in Libya head towards captivity. Despite strong counterattacks in the region, Rommel outmanouevred Wavell.

on 18 November 1941, and made good progress. The Tobruk garrison was now ordered to break out, but was blocked by the Afrika Korps.

Reorganizing his forces, Rommel counter-attacked on 24 November; by the end of the day, he had reached the Egyptian frontier. At

this point, Wavell visited Cunningham and discovered him on the verge of collapse from nervous exhaustion; he replaced him with Lieutenant-General Neil Ritchie. Rommel's offensive now slowed, thanks to attacks by the Desert Air Force and a lack of fuel supplies. On 26 November, he was forced to turn about to

deal with the link-up of the Tobruk garrison and troops from the New Zealand Division at El Duda. Attempts to put Tobruk under siege again failed, and Rommel withdrew to Gazala on 7 December. The Eighth Army attacked eight days later, and Rommel withdrew again, reaching the Tripolitanian frontier on 6 January 1942. Bardia

AUGUST

23 July General von Bock is dismissed as head of Army Group B.

25 July Roosevelt decides that Operation Torch – the invasion of French North Africa – must take place by the end of October.

27 July Australians attack at the Miteriya Ridge, but come to a halt quickly. Auchinleck calls off the offensive, bringing the first Battle of El Alamein to an end.

30 July Auchinleck informs the British Government that he will be unable to make another attack until September.

1 August The Allies introduce an inter-locking convoy system, reducing U-boat successes in American waters.

3 August Churchill flies to the Middle East to evaluate the situation. He decides to split the Middle East Command into two, and to give Lieutenant-General William Gott command of the Eighth Army.

7 August Gott is killed in an air crash. Lieutenant-General Bernard Montgomery is posted to command the Eighth Army. The idea of splitting Middle East Command is abandoned. Auchinleck is moved to India and General Sir Harold Alexander is given command in the Middle East.

9 August General Dwight D. Eisenhower is appointed to command Operation Torch.

fell into British hands on 17 January. Crusader had been a hard struggle, but was a British success. It was to be short-lived.

The Threat of Malta

The setback caused by Crusader did not deter Rommel. On 21 January 1942, after receiving more tanks, he launched an attack into Cyrenaica. He took Agedabia the next day, Msus on the 25th and Benghazi on the 29th, before halting in front of the Gazala-Bir Hachim line on 4 February. At this point, he paused, since he did not have sufficient strength or fuel to attack. He was also certain that the British would be unable to carry out offensive action for some time, given their losses. The Afrika Korps was also unable to conduct offensive action, and Rommel pleaded with Berlin for more troops so that he could exploit his success and drive on towards the Suez Canal. He was told to wait, both the Italian and German high commands believing that Malta had to be captured to protect the Axis supply lines. He waited until May, when he was instructed to launch a limited offensive against Tobruk.

A transport convoy negotiates a desert road. Maintaining a robust supply line was vital to success in the North African campaign, and the Axis powers realized that capturing the island of Malta was key to this supply line.

1942

AUGUST

9 August The Germans occupy Maikop oil fields.

10 August Paulus, commander of the German Sixth Army, crosses the River Don and reaches the outskirts of Stalingrad.

12–16 August Churchill visits Moscow for discussions with Stalin, and persuades the Soviet leader that opening a second front in 1942 will be impossible.

13 August Montgomery assumes command of the Eighth Army.

15 August German troops reach the Caucasus mountains.

19 August Operation Jubilee is launched against Dieppe. The raid is a failure.

21 August Eisenhower draws up a revised outline plan for Operation Torch.

30 August Rommel launches an offensive towards Alam Halfa Ridge.

Malta under heavy aerial bombardment. The citizens of Malta were awarded the George Cross in 1942 in recognition of their bravery during the Axis campaign.

By this point, the Italians and Germans were attempting to reduce the British garrison on the island of Malta. From 20 December 1941, the island had come under heavy air attack, in preparation for an invasion. Malta's fighter defences were limited at first, and although the British assigned more Hurricanes to defend the island, the latest models of the Bf109 were superior to the British fighter. Inevitably, the decision was taken to supply Malta with Spitfires – a difficult proposition, which required the Spitfires to fly from Royal Navy aircraft carriers. Forty-seven were flown off on three days in March (the 7th, 21st and 29th), but the rate of attrition to the island's defending aircraft was such that even more were required. Moreover, the air attacks intensified from 20 March, meaning that even more Spitfires were needed. The American carrier USS *Wasp* (larger than the British carriers) flew off 46 Spitfires on 20 April. The intensity of the fighting was such that almost all were destroyed or unserviceable within 72 hours. The weight of air attack forced the withdrawal of the 10th Submarine flotilla from the island, a blow to the Royal Navy, which had been conducting effective attacks on Axis supply convoys with the flotilla; the RAF had also enjoyed success with anti-shipping strikes launched from the island.

By 30 April, both the Germans and Italians believed that Malta was now all but defenceless, and it was agreed that the invasion of the island should take place after Rommel had captured Tobruk. On 10 May, Albert Kesselring, the Commander-in-Chief South, announced that Malta had been neutralized. However, the determination of the island's defenders had been underestimated. Just the day before Kesselring's

SEPTEMBER

31 August The German attack at Alam Halfa is repulsed.

1 September The second German attack at Alam Halfa is repulsed.

2 September The Afrika Korps withdraws to the start line, marking the end of Rommel's attempts to reach the Suez Canal. Convoy PQ18 leaves Britain for Russia. Thirteen ships are sunk on the voyage.

5 September Churchill and Roosevelt agree on their preferred planning concept for Operation Torch.

13/14 September British raid on Tobruk to destroy harbour installations is unsuccessful.

14 September Paulus resumes the attack on Stalingrad, without result. Montgomery issues a plan for Operation Lightfoot, an offensive against the Germans opposite El Alamein.

announcement, another 60 Spitfires had been flown in from the carriers HMS *Eagle* and USS *Wasp*. The Italian and German aircrew sent to raid the islands therefore got an unpleasant surprise, being outnumbered for the first time.

The struggle continued, however. Two Allied convoys from Gibraltar and Alexandria were sent on 11 June, but were forced to turn back, leaving Malta critically short of supplies.

The Third Offensive

Rommel began his third offensive on 26 May 1942, and swiftly pushed towards the Gazala Line. He attacked the feature known as the 'Cauldron' on 31 May, breaking through on 2 June. A British counterattack failed, and worse was to come: the Battle of Knightsbridge on 11 June turned into a disaster for the Eighth Army. The British withdrawal left Tobruk exposed, and on the 18th, the Afrika Korps isolated the fortress. It fell on 21 June, representing a major defeat for the British. Ritchie was relieved of the

German Panzergrenadiers advancing in North Africa.

command of the Eighth Army four days later, and Auchinleck took command. This was not enough to prevent Rommel from taking the Mersa Matruh position, leaving the Eighth Army back on the El Alamein line on 30 June.

Rommel launched another attack the next day, which petered out on 3 July. Auchinleck counterattacked, and a series of attacks and counterattacks punctuated the next three weeks until the First Battle of Alamein ended in stalemate. The reverses in the desert led Churchill to divide the existing commands in Africa, with Auchinleck commanding the Middle East, and General Sir Harold Alexander the Near East Command. Lieutenant-General William Gott was to take command of the Eighth Army, but he was killed in an air crash on 7 August, and Lieutenant-General Bernard Montgomery was appointed in his place. The decision to split Middle East Command was also abandoned, and Alexander took command while Auchinleck went to India.

Montgomery's first challenge was an attack launched by Rommel on 30 August. This was the same day that Operation Pedestal succeeded in getting a supply convoy through to Malta,

1942

SEPTEMBER

17 September Churchill demands that 'Lightfoot' begin before the end of the month.

20 September The date for Operation Torch is set as 8 November.

23 September Alexander persuades Churchill that 'Lightfoot' cannot take place before October. Rommel flies to Germany to recuperate from illness.

30 September Attack by the British 44th Division at Munassib Depression to test the strength of German defences.

OCTOBER

22 October General Mark Clark holds a secret meeting with the commander of the French Algerian Division, securing his agreement to cooperate with the Torch landings.

23 October The lead elements of the American Western Task Force, which is to land at Casablanca, sets sail from the United States.

23/24 October The second Battle of El Alamein begins.

25 October The British attack slows; Rommel returns to North Africa.

relieving the pressure on the island. For Rommel, the situation was less fortunate. Four of his six supply ships had been sunk, which meant that to capture the Alam Halfa Ridge and break through to Cairo, he would have to rely on capturing British fuel stocks. Nevertheless, the Afrika Korps attacked, to be repulsed by the Eighth Army on both 31 August and 1 September. Rommel was forced back, and the failure at Alam Halfa marked his final attempt at reaching Cairo.

Montgomery now prepared to go on the offensive. However, to the frustration of Churchill, who wanted an early victory, he spent several months ensuring that his forces were trained properly. Not until the night of 23/24 October did Montgomery attack at El Alamein.

El Alamein

The battle opened with a massive bombardment from British guns, and the initial attacks met with success. However, by 26 October, the advance slowed, and Montgomery ordered a temporary halt to proceedings. While he altered his plans, Rommel counterattacked but was beaten off. Then, on 29 October, Montgomery

Australian troops storm a German strongpoint under the cover of smoke during the second Battle of El Alamein. Allied success here marked the end of Germany's expansionist plans in the war.

issued plans for Operation Supercharge, altering the direction of advance from the coastal sector to further inland. It began in the early hours of 2 November 1942, and soon put the Afrika Korps under pressure. Rommel decided that he

had to withdraw before his fuel ran out, making it impossible for him to extricate his forces. The Eighth Army pursued the retreating Germans as they headed towards western Libya. Tobruk was regained on 13 November, and by

NOVEMBER

26 October Montgomery halts his attacks to allow forces to regroup. The first wave of troops leaves harbour in Scotland, destined for landings at Oran and Algiers.

27 October Italian and German counterattacks are beaten back.

29 October Montgomery modifies his plan, with the main weight of the next attack to be inland rather than along the coast.

2 November Army Group A is halted by the Red Army just outside Ordhonikidze, marking the limit of the German advance in the Caucasus.

3 November British forces break in to Axis positions.

4 November Break-out begins as British armour commences pursuit of the Afrika Korps.

5 November Torch convoys begin to enter the Mediterranean.

6/7 November Heavy rain impedes the British pursuit of Rommel.

Trucks carrying infantry through an enemy minefield in North Africa come under heavy shell fire.

20 November, Benghazi was in British hands once more. Rommel halted at El Agheila, and despite orders to remain there, pulled out on 13 December, with the aim of joining with Axis forces in Tunisia.

This was not the only tale of woe for the Axis, since the defeat at El Alamein coincided with the Allied invasion of North Africa.

Operation Torch

The Allies drew up various plans to invade North Africa during the course of 1942, finally deciding on the overall plan in September. The purpose of the Operation, codenamed 'Torch', was twofold. Firstly, to satisfy Stalin's demands for a second front, and secondly, to attack the Axis forces in Tunisia. The first Allied soldier to land in North Africa was General Mark Clark, who was landed in Algeria by a British submarine to meet General Charles Mast, commander of French forces in Algeria. Mast agreed to facilitate the landings, due on 8 November. The two invasion fleets came from the United States and Scotland, and set sail on 23 and 26 October respectively, reaching the Mediterranean on 5 November. The landings took place at Casablanca, Oran and Algiers on 8 November, meeting some resistance. The Vichy French protested, but Marshal Pétain secretly told the High Commissioner in Algiers, Admiral François Darlan, to negotiate with the Allies. On 10 November, Darlan ordered Vichy French troops to end resistance, and an armistice was signed. The Allies now began to move towards Tunisia, aiming to trap the Axis forces between the Torch invasion and the units of Middle East Command following up the victory at El Alamein.

The Final Round

The Axis position in North Africa was perilous. Resistance to the Torch landings was fierce and imposed considerable delay upon the Allies, but it was not enough to hold the numerically superior opposition at bay for any length of time. And as the Allied troops gained more experience, they became more formidable opponents for the Afrika Korps. The only saving grace for the Germans retreating from El Alamein was the fact that Montgomery pursued in a methodical fashion that let them avoid a rout. He reached Sirte on

1942

NOVEMBER

8 November Operation Torch begins. Marshal Pétain declares the French will resist but secretly instructs Admiral Darlan, High Commissioner in Algiers, to open negotiations with the Allies.

10 November Darlan orders Vichy French forces to cease resistance.

11 November The French in Morocco and Algeria sign an armistice with the Allies. The Germans occupy Vichy France in retaliation. Elements of General Anderson's First Army land at Bougie. The Sixth Army renews its attack on Stalingrad.

12 November British troops make amphibious and airborne landings at Bône.

13 November The British retake Tobruk.

15 November The Eighth Army captures Derna.

16 November The British capture Souk el Arba with an airborne assault.

25 December 1942, and then paused to secure his supply lines.

On 12 January 1943, aircraft from the Desert Air Force launched raids in support of an offensive south of Buerat by 30 Corps. Progress was slow, as the advancing troops had to deal with minefields and difficult terrain. Montgomery instructed the 51st Highland Division to press on. The Division entered Homs on 19 January, convincing Rommel to abandon his defensive line. Contrary to his expectations, though, Montgomery made his main thrust along the coast road, aiming for Tripoli. On the night of 22/23 January, Rommel abandoned the city, and British forces entered Tripoli on 23 January without opposition.

Rommel's army had now been driven out of Egypt, Cyrenaica, and nearly all of Libya and Tripolitania. The Axis position in North Africa was critical.

Tunisia

Rommel fell back on the Mareth Line defensive position, reaching Tunisia on 13 February. He had not given up, however, and on the next day, launched an assault against the inexperienced American 2nd Corps. Concluding that the Allies might strike against the coast from Gafsa, he decided that the best defence was to attack the Americans before they were ready.

There were a number of difficulties, however. Both Rommel and Colonel-General Jürgen von Arnim tried – and failed – to obtain the other's mobile forces for the attacks being planned. Arnim planned to attack through Faid to Sidi Bou Zid, and simply could not hand over troops to Rommel.

Arnim's attack began first, on 14 February, and went well. By 0600 on the first day, German troops were 8km (5 miles) west of the Faid Pass. The inexperienced American troops could not stop German forces from linking north of Sidi Bou Zid. A newly confident Rommel now ordered that the attack on Gafsa

Unloading of personnel and equipment from the combined British–American convoy at St Leu.

17 November Montgomery reaches Msus.

19 November The Soviet South-Western and Don Fronts launch an offensive against German and Romanian forces to the north of Stalingrad.

20 November The Stalingrad Front attacks. The South-West Front penetrates German lines to a depth of 40km (25 miles). Benghazi is retaken by the Eighth Army.

22 November Vatutin's South-West Front captures the bridge over the Don at Kalach.

23 November Link-up of the South-West and Stalingrad Fronts encircles the German Sixth Army and part of the 4th Panzer Division.

24 November Rommel halts the withdrawal at El Agheila as the British make an operational pause to prevent overextension of supply lines. The Allies resume the advance into Tunisia from French North Africa. Goering announces that he can keep the Sixth Army supplied from the air.

should begin on 15 February. An American counterattack ran into difficulties and only just managed to withdraw.

On 17 February, the Americans order Feriana and Sbeitla to be abandoned, and Gafsa and Tozeur; Sbeitla and Sidi Bou Zid fell shortly afterwards. Rommel ordered the Afrika Korps to take the Kasserine Pass.

The Kasserine Pass

The Germans faced a combination of American units known as Stark Force after the commanding officer of the US 26th Infantry Regiment, Colonel Alexander N. Stark. They attacked on 19 February, and the inexperienced American forces were forced to withdraw to Djebel el Hamra.

Disembarkation of US troops during Operation Torch.

On 21 February, the Germans advanced towards Thala and Djebel el Hamra, but were blocked by the Americans at el Hamra. The British 26th Armoured Brigade was pushed back south of Thala, but put up fierce resistance and Rommel realized he would be unable to break through. On the afternoon of 22 February, he ended the offensive and turned his attention to southern Tunisia for a blow against the Eighth Army.

The Battle of Medenine

Rommel's next planned attack was against Montgomery's position at Medenine. Signals interception revealed this, and by early March the British had quadrupled their strength. When the Germans attacked on 6 March, they ran into serious difficulties.

German tanks suffered heavy losses, and heavy defensive artillery fire made it almost impossible for the German infantry to advance. Rommel called off the attack.

The Mareth Line

The failure at Medenine convinced Rommel that the German and Italian forces had to abandon North Africa, but he was unable to make Hitler

1942

NOVEMBER

26 November Hitler orders the Sixth Army to remain in Stalingrad rather than attempt a break-out.

27 November Hitler creates Army Group Don, under Manstein, to relieve the Sixth Army. The French fleet at Toulon is scuttled to prevent the Germans from seizing it.

28 November 36 Brigade of the First Army is stopped at Bald and Green Hills by the Germans.

DECEMBER

2 December The Soviets began an attempt to drive a gap between German forces around Stalingrad.

12 December Manstein launches Operation Winter Storm in an attempt to relieve the Sixth Army.

13 December Rommel begins to withdraw towards Tunisia.

16 December Operation Little Saturn is begun by Soviet forces in an attempt to cut across Manstein's lines of communication. The main German transport airfield at Tatsinskaya is overrun.

attack on 26 March, supported by heavy air cover and artillery.

The British reached El Hamma by dawn on 27 March, the advance only slowing in the face of a German counterattack that allowed the majority of Axis forces to retreat to Wadi Akarit. However, without reinforcement, holding Wadi Akarit was impossible, so the Axis troops withdrew to Enfidaville. As they joined to defend their last remaining foothold in North Africa, the Allies drew up plans to ensure victory.

For the Allies, the best approach to Tunis was through the Medjerda valley, by clearing the hills on either side of Medjez el Bab, thus opening a gap for armour to exploit. Alexander hoped to take the Tunisian ports, so he ordered the First Army to attack on 22 April against the Axis forces between Medjez al Bab and Bou Arada. Montgomery, however, proposed to carry out an attack by four divisions (three infantry and one armoured), aiming to punch at least 32km (20 miles) into enemy lines. Alexander decided that he could afford to allow Montgomery to carry out the attack, which meant that resources were not concentrated within the First Army area to the extent originally planned.

Sherman tanks move up during the advance on Kasserine, Tunisia, February. 1943. The combined American and British defence of the Kasserine Pass resulted in yet another defeat for Rommel's forces.

or Mussolini appreciate the extent of the danger.

Meanwhile, Montgomery made plans to break through the German defensive positions on the Mareth Line. Beginning on 20 March, a frontal assault was launched against the enemy defensive positions. It made only a small dent in the Axis lines and was driven back by the end of

22 March. The secondary attack, a flanking move on El Hamma, enjoyed more initial success, but was held up. Montgomery now modified his plan and concentrated his forces on the inland flank, a step detected by Axis reconnaissance aircraft. This prompted Arnim to withdraw his forces just before the new

19 December German troops reach the Myshkova, but are unable to penetrate any further towards Stalingrad.

21 December Churchill and Roosevelt agree to a summit meeting at Casablanca.

22–25 December Battles for Longstop Hill.

24 December The Stalingrad Front breaks through the Fourth Romanian Army positions and attacks towards German positions on the lower Don. Manstein is forced to withdraw.

26 December Rommel reaches Buerat.

28 December Further German withdrawals put army groups over 160km (100 miles) away from Stalingrad.

29 December The Soviet High Command directs that German Army Group A in the Caucasus is to be attacked, with the aim of taking Rostov and cutting off the German escape route from Crimea.

30 December The Soviet High Command directs that the offensive to destroy German forces should begin on 6 January 1943, later postponed to 10 January.

Bouncing the Enemy

Montgomery's plan was to 'bounce' the Germans out of Enfidaville. When he realized the strength of enemy defences, though, he became less confident.

On the night of 19/20 April, the 4th Indian Division launched the attack. Enemy resistance was fierce, and little of the ground needed for the next phase of the operation had been taken by daybreak. This presented the commander of 10 Corps, Sir Brian Horrocks, with an uncomfortable choice: he could press on, with the likelihood of significant casualties, or he could remain in place, with a similar probability of casualties but with a greater opportunity of damaging the enemy as they counterattacked. Either decision implied a slow battle of attrition.

During the course of the day, 50th Division took Enfidaville, but the rest of the Corps could not make any decisive showing on the battlefield. It was obvious that the main effort must pass to the First Army and US 2nd Corps.

The most important area for the new assault

German tanks at the Battle of Kasserine. Rommel captured Kasserine on 19 February 1943.

was covered by British 5 Corps. Taking the features known as 'Longstop Hill' and 'Peter's Corner' would enable a direct approach on Tunis. The Germans appreciated this, and attacked to disrupt the offensive on 20/21 April, on both

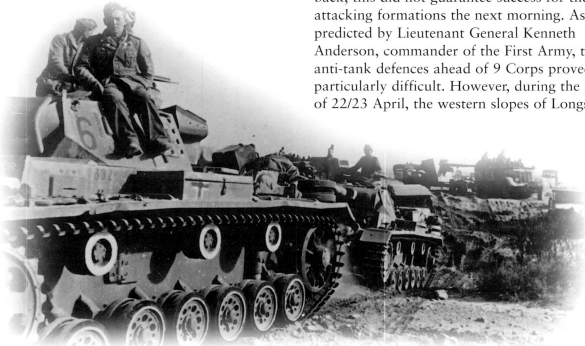

5 and 9 Corps' fronts. They did manage to delay a brigade of 46th Division, but all of 5 Corps was able to advance to its start line on time.

The British Advance

Although the German attacks had been pushed back, this did not guarantee success for the attacking formations the next morning. As predicted by Lieutenant General Kenneth Anderson, commander of the First Army, the anti-tank defences ahead of 9 Corps proved particularly difficult. However, during the night of 22/23 April, the western slopes of Longstop

1943

JANUARY

3 January Army Group A begins to withdraw from the Caucasus. French forces take the Kairouan and Karachoum Passes from the Italians, but lose the Fondouk Pass.

8 January Surrender terms are offered to Paulus, but rejected.

10 January Soviet forces open an offensive against the Stalingrad pocket.

12 January The western side of the Stalingrad pocket is overrun. Operation Iskra is launched in attempt to lift the siege of Leningrad.

13 January The Voronezh Front attacks across the Don. Rommel begins the withdrawal from Buerat.

16 January The Soviets overrun the Pitomnik airfield.

Hill were taken, and after three more days of fighting the Germans were removed.

Von Arnim realized that his position was untenable, and sought to counterattack, but was thrown back by 30 April. By this point, the Allied offensive was becoming disjointed, so Montgomery offered the 7th Armoured and 4th Indian Divisions and 201st Guards Brigade to Alexander, allowing the First Army to be reinforced.

This did not escape the attention of the Germans. Arnim understood that an assault in the Medjerda valley would follow, and there was little he could do to stop it. The final push began at 0300 on 6 May, and by 0930 a large hole had been created in the enemy defences, allowing armour to drive through. The next day, British troops captured Tunis, while the US 2nd Corps reached Bizerta. On 12 May, Arnim surrendered to the 4th Indian Division, and the Italian commander, Field Marshal Messe, followed suit next day.

At 1316 local time on 13 May, Alexander signalled London, his simple message ending: 'We are masters of the North African shores.' Attention now turned to Italy.

A victory parade in Tunis following the Allied victory in North Africa in 1943. French troops march past the saluting base before Generals Eisenhower, Alexander, Anderson and Giraud.

18 January General von Arnim begins an offensive to retake the Kariouan and Karachoum Passes. Hungarian and Italian troops on the River Don are encircled.

22 January The final phase of the Soviet offensive around Stalingrad begins. The German Sixth Army is cut in two by attacks, leaving small pockets north and south of city.

23 January The Eighth Army enters Tripoli.

24 January Hitler orders that there should be no attempt at a break-out from Stalingrad. The Soviet Bryansk and Voronezh fronts begin the encirclement of the German Second Army.

25 January Voronezh falls to the Red Army.

27 January German Army Group Don withdraws behind the lower Don.

30 January Hitler promotes Paulus to field marshal. The French are driven from Faid by the Germans.

31 January Paulus surrenders the remnants of the Sixth Army in the south of Stalingrad; the northern pocket fights on.

Defeat in the East and Italy

After crushing the German Sixth Army, the Soviets continued offensive operations into the New Year. On 29 January 1943, Operation Gallop was launched, attacks along the entire German front enjoying considerable success.

The front collapsed and the Soviets pushed deep into the German rear areas. Despite offering stiff resistance, the Germans were unable to stop the onward march of the Soviet forces. By 14 February, they were in danger of being surrounded in front of Kharkov itself. Their commanders now hesitated, and the resistance became fragmented. Following heavy street fighting on 15/16 February, Kharkov was retaken.

Left: Soviet T-34 tanks roll through Kharkov. The city changed hands several times during the course of the war.
Right: General Erich von Manstein examines a map.

The Fourth Battle of Kharkov

The successes of the Soviet offensive worried Field Marshal Erich von Manstein, commander of Army Group Don. The length of frontage under his control was too great for the forces available to him, and the need to shorten the line was pressing. He persuaded Hitler to let him withdraw from the salient around Rostov and the Donbas area to a better position on the River Mius. In the face of the Soviet advance, though, this position also looked untenable, and Manstein faced the prospect of Army Group Don being cut off. He launched a counterattack. The tempo

of recent operations, he judged, would have worn down his opponents, making them vulnerable. The offensive began on 20 February and made rapid progress against the Soviets, who were poorly positioned to meet the unexpected counterattack. By 25 February,

the Soviets were exhausted, and went over to the defensive, enabling Manstein to launch the second phase of his campaign.

The Germans closed in on Kharkov once more, and by 10/11 March the city was on the point of falling into their hands. After a few more

days' fighting, it did. Despite this success, the Germans were not in an enviable position by April 1943. They had suffered huge losses, three German armies having been destroyed between November 1942 and the halt in late March 1943.

Operation Citadel

The end of Manstein's counteroffensive against Kharkov left the Soviets holding a significant salient, centred on the town of Kursk. Hitler decided that this offered the ideal opportunity to destroy the two Soviet army fronts holding the area – Central and Voronezh.

However, he now made a crucial mistake, choosing to postpone the offensive until enough Panther and Tiger tanks and self-propelled guns were available. The Soviets were therefore able to increase their strength, thereby making it more difficult to make a breakthrough. To make matters worse, Soviet intelligence-gathering capabilities had improved dramatically since the invasion of June 1941. Indeed, it is possible that Zhukov knew that Kursk would be the target for the next German offensive even before Hitler had told some of his generals who would conduct the attack.

SS troops at Kharkov in the immediate aftermath of the fighting that led to the Germans recapturing the city for the final time. Kharkov was finally liberated in August 1943.

1943

FEBRUARY

2 February The northern Stalingrad pocket surrenders.

4 February The Red Army conducts an amphibious landing near Novorossisk on the Black Sea coast, to cut off the German Seventeenth Army.

7 February Montgomery begins an advance into Tunisia, hampered by heavy rain.

8 February The Soviets recapture Kursk.

14 February The Soviets retake Rostov and Voroshilovgrad. Arnim cuts off US forces around Sidi Bou Zid.

15 February Rommel takes Gasfa. The Eighth Army reaches the Mareth Line. The Soviet offensive against the Demyansk salient begins.

Zhukov brought in troops from other fronts to defend the salient, and plans were made to follow up a German attack with a huge counteroffensive along the entire southern part of the front. By July, the Germans had concentrated nearly 3000 tanks, but the Soviets had quietly prepared a series of strong defensive positions. Between April and July, they built seven defence lines, and a final line of defence behind the salient, to deal with the possibility of a breakthrough.

As a result, an immense force opposed the Germans. There were nearly one million men and 3300 tanks directly opposite them, and another 380,000 men and 600 tanks held in reserve. And these figures, although impressive enough, represent only the tactical-level defences against an assault. The operational line behind the salient had a further 500,000 men and another 1500 tanks available, ready for deployment where required. Furthermore, large numbers of Soviet aircraft were in the area, to provide direct air support against the attack.

The offensive thus began with the attacking forces heavily outnumbered by opponents who had the protection of strong defensive positions and massive reserves.

Following preparatory operations the day before, the Germans opened Operation Citadel at 0430 on 5 July 1943. Shortly after 0500, the first reports of tank and infantry attacks came from Soviet frontline positions. The Germans gained ground to a depth of 7–10km (4–6 miles), and General Rokossovsky secured agreement from Stalin that the Twenty-Seventh Army should be sent forwards to assist.

When it became clear that the situation on the Voronezh Front was even more serious than that facing Central Front, Stalin sent the forces there instead. By 1800 on 6 July, both sides were pouring men and materiel into the battle, the armour of both sides moving on a scale never seen before or since, in formations up to 200 strong. Some 4000 Soviet and 3000 German tanks and assault guns were on the verge of entering the battle, which continued with ever greater ferocity; the Soviet High Command estimated that nearly 600 German tanks were knocked out on the first day of the fighting.

....

General Konstantin Rokossovsky, commander of the Soviet Central Front, and victor of the Battle of Kursk.

By the morning of 7 July, the Germans were threatening the high ground near Olkhovatka, which gave command of the battlefield. Rokossovsky promptly reinforced the approaches to Olkhovatka, both sides suffering huge losses. By 10 July, the Germans were regrouping, and it was clear that the climax of the battle was approaching.

---

16 February The Germans evacuate Kharkov.

17 February German forces in the Demyansk salient withdraw in good order. Rommel takes Feriana and makes for the Kasserine Pass.

19 February Rommel takes the Kasserine Pass.

20 February Rommel is stopped at Sbiba. Pavlograd and Krasnograd are recaptured by General Vatutin's South-West Front. Manstein launches a counteroffensive.

24 February The Allies retake Sbiba.

25 February The Allies retake the Kasserine Pass, Sbeitla and Sidi Bou Zid. Vatutin orders his Sixth Army to go on the defensive.

LT-34s charge towards the enemy at Prokhorovka Station, the scene of the largest tank battle in history – during Battle of Kursk.

an attack towards Prokhorovka would force them to move units from their flanks in support. The vulnerable flanks might then be attacked, and the Germans encircled.

At dawn on 11 July, the Germans attacked Prokhorovka and Oboyan. A massive battle took place between three SS divisions and the 5th Guards Tank Army. The battle for Prokhorovka was in the balance by nightfall, and the 5th Guards Tank Army was sent in to the fray once more, counterattacking vigorously. Both sides took huge casualties. The Germans lost more than 300 tanks (including 70 Tigers), while about 50 per cent of the 5th Guards Tank Army was destroyed. Even so, the Soviets had achieved their aim. The German attacks had been halted, while the Soviets still had their reserves.

The Germans continued probing attacks for three more days, but it was clear that they would not be able to break through at Prokhorovka or even bypass it. Effectively, the battle was over, particularly because the

The Clash of Battle

The Germans had penetrated nearly 32km (20 miles) towards Oboyan, but this breakthrough was not sufficiently deep. The axis of their attack now shifted towards the railway junction at Prokhorovka – soon to become the site of the largest tank battle the world has ever seen.

In response to the threat to Prokhorovka, armour and troops were moved to strengthen the Voronezh Front. If the Germans could break through here, they would be in a position to unhinge the Soviet defences. General Vatutin regarded the threat as an opportunity, however. The Germans had suffered massive losses, and

1943

MARCH

3 March The German offensive drives Vatutin's forces back to the northern Donets.

4 March The second phase of Manstein's offensive begins, with the aim of recapturing Kharkov.

6 March The Battle of Medenine sees a German attack repulsed.

9 March Illness forces Rommel to leave North Africa. He is replaced by Arnim as Commander-in-Chief Army Group Africa.

15 March The Germans succeed in regaining Kharkov.

17 March General George S. Patton's forces capture Gafsa and advance to secure Montgomery's left flank.

18 March Belgorod is recaptured by the Germans.

invasion of Sicily prompted the transfer of forces to the Western Front, at the expense of 'Citadel'. This meant that the Germans had no option but to head back to their start points of 5 July. The operation to take Kursk was over.

The Soviets now attacked, with General Knoen's Steppe Front and General Vatutin's Voronezh Front launching their own offensive – Operation Polkovodets Rumyantsev. When Rumyantsev began on 3 August, the Germans were taken by surprise and by nightfall on the second day, Belograd was back in Soviet hands. This allowed an advance towards Bogodukhov and Kharkov. On 21 August, Kharkov changed hands for the fourth – and final – time.

The offensive continued, and by 25 October, the Soviets had cut off German forces in the Crimea. Another German counterattack battered some of the Soviet advanced forces around Krivoi Rog, but could not prevent the Soviets advancing on Kiev. The offensive began on 3 November, and the city was back in Soviet hands within 48 hours. As Christmas approached, the Germans held just a few small sections of the western bank of the Dnepr, hoping to hold on until the Soviet offensive had exhausted itself.

Ukraine and Crimea

The Soviets now looked to begin the re-conquest of western Ukraine. On 24 December, the 1st Ukrainian Front launched a massive preparatory bombardment against Army Group South's positions to the west of Kiev. As the day drew to a close, the Soviets had advanced to a depth of 32km (20 miles), and the Germans were in disarray.

Despite poor weather, the advance continued. The rail link between Army Group Centre and Army Group South was cut on 5 January 1944,

German armour heads towards the battlefield at Kursk, July 1943. The Germans suffered enormous tanks losses.

APRIL

20 March Montgomery begins his attack on the Mareth Line.

6 April The Eighth Army breaks through at Wadi Akarit.

12 April Stalin takes the decision that Soviet forces in the Kursk salient will remain on the defensive to meet the expected German attack.

22 April The Allied First Army a launches series of attacks.

MAY

4 May Hitler postpones the Kursk offensive (Operation Citadel) until more Tiger and Panther tanks are available.

6 May Final Allied assault against the remaining Axis positions.

7 May Bizerte and Tunis fall to the Allies.

8 May The Allies begin an aerial bombardment of the Italian island of Pantelleria.

and a hole 240km (150 miles) wide and 80km (50 miles) deep was made in the German front before the attack began to lose momentum. Even then, this gave the Germans only a temporary respite. The 2nd Ukrainian Front launched an offensive of its own, which reached the outskirts of Kirovgrad. Then a combined attack by both the 1st and 2nd Ukrainian Fronts trapped 50,000 Germans in the Korsun–Shevchenkovsky salient.

They retreated, a move that went well at the beginning, but as the Soviets appreciated what was happening, the remaining soldiers were shelled. The withdrawal broke down into a rout, command and control disappearing as officers were killed, wounded or otherwise separated from their men. Thousands of soldiers were killed trying to cross the Gniloi Tikitsch river, which was in full spate as a result of the thaw.

The Soviet momentum did not slacken, and on 4 March a new attack forced the Germans back across the Dniestr. By 12 April, the Germans had to withdraw from the Crimean peninsula, and four days later, they were driven back into Sevastopol. The Soviets attacked on 6 May, and it became clear that the Germans

would be unable to hold out. The Germans had taken no less than 250 days to take the city from the Soviets; the Soviets now recaptured it in three. They then set about destroying the remaining German forces in the Crimea. A huge Soviet attack followed swiftly, and by midday on 12 May, the remnants of the Seventeenth Army surrendered, some 25,000 men from an army that had once been 110,000 strong.

Liberating Leningrad

Meanwhile, the Soviets sought to lift the siege of Leningrad. The city had been besieged for nearly three years, and although a corridor had been opened into the city in 1943, it was well within the range of German artillery and therefore did not alleviate the city's suffering. In addition, Stalin was anxious to deal with the problem posed by the Finns, fighting as co-belligerents

Soviet armour waits outside Kiev during the heavy fighting that led to the liberation of the city and much of the Ukraine during the winter of 1943. During their occupation, the Germans massacred thousands of civilians.

1943

MAY	JUNE	JULY		
11 May Axis forces in the Cape Bon peninsula surrender, ending the war in North Africa.		**4 July** The Battle of Kursk begins.		
	11 June British troops land on Pantelleria to take the surrender of the Italian garrison.		**10 July** The launch of Operation Husky, the Allied landings in Sicily.	**12 July** Patton begins to advance inland from the Sicilian landing beaches. The Soviet counterattack begins at Kursk.
16/17 May 617 Squadron of the RAF carries out an attack against German Ruhr dams.				**13 July** Hitler calls off Operation Citadel.

with the Germans to overturn the peace treaty that had been signed after the Winter War.

General Govorov's Leningrad Front and General Meretsov's Volkhov Front were told to combine for offensive operations in the Novgorod–Luga sector, beginning on 14 January 1944. The attack was preceded by an overnight raid by heavy bombers on German artillery at Bezzabotny. Then, at 0935, an artillery bombardment against the German positions began, and in a barrage lasting for 65 minutes, 100,000 shells were fired. The Second Shock Army moved forward as soon as the bombardment ended, gaining 2740m (3000yd) along an 8km (5 mile) frontage, with some units reaching the German second line of defence.

By 19 January, the 2nd Shock and 42nd Armies had linked up near Ropsha, and the next day the Soviet breakthrough was complete. The Soviets moved into a pursuit phase, chasing the Germans as they pulled back. Leningrad's encirclement ended on 26 January, when the Moscow–Leningrad railway line was cleared of all German troops.

All that remained was to remove Finnish forces from the territory they had occupied since 1941. The Finns could see that the Soviet success against Army Group North rendered their position difficult, and they attempted to open negotiations with Stalin through diplomatic contacts. In the meantime, General Meretskov was given command of the Karelian Front, and launched the Svir–Petrozavodsk offensive on 10 June, and the Leningrad Front attacked the Karelian Isthmus near Vyborg. Operations lasted until 9 August, when the Finns were driven back to the line of the 1939 Finnish–Soviet border. Aware that there was nothing more that they could do, the Finns sought peace, and an armistice was signed on 4 September.

Operation Bagration

Even as the spring 1944 offensives drew to a close, the Soviet High Command had begun planning for the next offensive – to attack Army Group Centre's positions in Belorussia, with the initial aim of recapturing Minsk. The offensive, named Operation Bagration after a famed Russian commander of the nineteenth century, would encircle the German army groups in the Minsk–Vitebsk–Rogachev triangle, and destroy them.

Bagration began on 23 June 1944, and within three days the 1st Byelorussian Front had broken in to the German positions around Bobruisk.

....

German prisoners of war are marched through Leningrad.

15 July The Soviet Central Front begins to attack the German Ninth Army.

16 July Patton begins the attack towards Palermo.

17 July The Soviet South-West Front attacks towards Kharkov.

23 July American troops enter Palermo.

24/25 July Operation Gomorrah, combined Anglo-American bomber raids against Hamburg, inflicts massive damage on the city.

25 July Mussolini is arrested and deposed as Italian leader.

26 July The German withdrawal from Orel begins.

31 July The Americans capture San Stefano.

The Soviets drove forward, encircling first German LIII Corps, then the German Fourth Army. In each case, a timely withdrawal would have saved the German formations, but Hitler refused permission. IX Corps was destroyed at Vitebsk, after permission to abandon it came too late, then 70,000 men of Ninth Army were trapped in the Bobruisk pocket. On 29 June, the city was stormed and the remainder of the German forces was wiped out.

The Fourth Army escaped thanks to the subterfuge of its commander, General Tippelskirch. He fabricated his situation reports to Hitler, sending him sets of orders that indicated he was standing fast, while issuing his troops with orders for withdrawal. Despite this, on 30 June, the bulk of his forces were trapped to the east of the River Berezina, where they were killed or captured *en masse*.

Army Group North suffered at the hands of the Soviet advance as well. German forces around Minsk were trapped by 3 July. The city itself fell on 4 July, and in the desperate fighting that followed over the next week more than 43,000 Germans were killed.

The Soviets then pushed into Lithuania, heading for Vilnius. Arriving on 8 July, they encircled the city and captured it five days later. The 2nd Byelorussian Front came to within 80km (50 miles) of East Prussia, while the 1st Byelorussian drove into Poland and crossed the Vistula. Finally, on 29 August, Operation Bagration came to an end. Soviet forces had advanced between 547km (340 miles) and 604km (375 miles) along an 1125km (700 mile) frontage. Army Group Centre had been rendered ineffective, and other German formations mauled. The Soviets were now in an ideal position for an advance towards Germany itself.

....

Troops from the 3rd Ukrainian Front advance during Operation Bagration.

1943

AUGUST

3 August Axis forces begin to evacuate Sicily, beginning with Italian units.

5 August Montgomery captures Catania. The Soviets liberate Orel and Belgorod as the Germans fall back to the Hagen Line.

6 August The Americans take Troina.

11 August German counterattacks against the Voronezh Front begin, forcing Soviets on the defensive over the course of the following week.

12 August Stalin issues orders for three separate offensives to begin once Kharkov is recaptured. The Germans begin to leave Sicily.

13 August The Anglo-American 'Quadrant' Conference begins in Quebec. Soviet troops reach Kharkov.

Members of the 1st Ukranian Front advance past destroyed enemy vehicles. The joint offensive by the 1st and 2nd Ukrainian fronts routed the Germans at Kirovgrad.

A German field gun in action, June 1944. Despite failures on the Eastern Front, Hitler refused to issue orders for his troops' withdrawal.

Inexorable Advance

The Soviets began planning for their 1945 offensives in October 1944, at a time when Hitler had assumed they would be on the defensive, recovering from losses sustained during Operation Bagration. They were not.

By early January, some 2.2 million Russian troops were assembled opposite the River Vistula, ready to attack. The offensive began in a blizzard, at 0430 on 12 January 1945, with a massive bombardment against German positions. When the bombardment eased, Soviet troops went forward, breaking through the German lines to a depth of up to 3km (2 miles) before they were halted.

At 1000, a second immense bombardment was laid upon German lines. The Fourth Panzer Army's headquarters was wiped out, and without leadership, the formation collapsed as the Soviet tanks and infantry attacked. Soviet exploitation troops swiftly broke through, and by nightfall on 12 January 1945, had reached a depth of 23km (14 miles) along a 40km (25 mile) front. The next day, more than 2000 Soviet tanks cut the lines of communication between Warsaw and Kraków. The Germans withdrew from Warsaw, leaving Kraków and Silesia as the next targets for the Soviets.

Further north, Marshal Zhukov sent his troops into action on 14 January. After

14 August The new Italian leadership begins secret armistice negotiations with the Allies.

17 August Patton enters Messina. The USAAF raid on Schweinfurt and Regensburg suffers heavy losses.

20 August An Italian delegation is informed that the Allies will accept unconditional surrender of Italy. A 10-day deadline is imposed for the Italians to agree.

23 August The Germans withdraw from Kharkov to avoid encirclement. An RAF raid on Berlin suffers heavy casualties.

26 August The Soviet Central Front begins attacks against Army Group Centre.

30 August Taganrog is liberated by the Soviet South Front.

1 September The Allies are informed that the Italians will agree to an armistice. German forces are placed on alert to disarm Italian units in the event of an armistice.

impressive initial gains, Zhukov sent the First and Second Guards Tank Armies into the fray. The weight of assault was such that German Ninth Army began to collapse, allowing the Second Guards Tank Army to sweep northwest, threatening Warsaw. On the night of 16 January, it became clear to the German High Command that to remain in Warsaw would be suicidal. Orders were given that XLVI Panzer Corps

Infantry 'tank riders' of the Soviet Red Army advance into battle, August 1944.

should retire from the city – without reference to Hitler. Outraged by this 'cowardice', Hitler dismissed some generals and imposed a rigid command structure. All commanders from divisional level upwards were now instructed to obtain approval for every move they made, on pain of death. This undercut their ability to respond to events in a flexible and timely fashion just at the moment when this was of critical importance. Zhukov now sent the First Polish Army to retake Warsaw.

Kraków and Silesia

On 17 January, Marshal Konev's 1st Ukrainian Front was ordered to take Kraków and Silesia, as a precursor for an advance towards the German city of Bresalu. The Fifty-Ninth and Sixtieth Armies were employed for these tasks, and made an advance on Kraków. The Germans withdrew to avoid being encircled, and the Soviets entered the city.

Silesia was a more difficult proposition for the Soviets, since it was heavily industrialized. As had been the case at Stalingrad, the nature of an industrialized area – with its large factories and urban areas – offered good defensive

opportunities, but this time to the Germans. An innovative approach was required. Konev sent the Third Guards Tank Army forward, and it crossed the German border on 20 January. Once it had reached the bank of the River Oder, Konev turned it through 90° and sent it along the bank rather than across. The Germans saw it approaching from the west, and the Fifty-Ninth and Sixtieth Armies coming from the east, and realized that encirclement was imminent. They fell back towards the Carpathian mountains, leaving Silesia to the Soviets.

Reaching the Oder

Zhukov now sent the 1st Byelorussian Front to drive on Poznán, the last major Polish city before the German border and the River Oder. As had been the case in Silesia, the troops avoided urban areas and pursued the Germans across central Poland at speed. They then manoeuvred round the south side of Poznan itself on 26 January, a move that trapped 60,000 Germans. Zhukov next drove forward to the Oder, reaching it on the last day of January. The Fifth Shock Army crossed the river and took the town of Kienitz. This was to be

1943

SEPTEMBER

2 September The Soviet Central Front reaches the Bryansk–Konotop railway.

3 September Allied landings in mainland Italy begin.

4 September Merefa is captured.

6 September Konotop falls to Soviet forces. The Americans resume bombing missions against Germany with an attack on Stuttgart.

8 September The Italian surrender is announced.

9 September Stalin proposes an Anglo-Soviet-American meeting at Tehran, and a foreign ministers' conference in Moscow. The Allies land at Salerno.

9/10 September The Transcaucasas Front begins an offensive against the Taman Peninsula.

the last act of the offensive, which was halted by Stalin on 2 February.

Appreciating that rising temperatures and the inevitable thaw would slow down the offensive, Stalin decided it was better to stop and allow his troops to prepare for the last battle – the drive on the Nazi capital. Meanwhile, preparations

against the Germans in the Baltic states were under way. The troops there could have been ignored, but to do so would have been dangerous, since they might have been able to counterattack into the flanks of the Soviet troops heading for Berlin.

The Baltic

On 13 January 1945, the 3rd Belorussian Front attacked towards Königsberg. The Germans put up stiff resistance, and the attack was in danger of stalling. Marshal Chernyakovsky redeployed his forces and broke through on 20 January, heading for Königsberg. Within a week, Soviet forces had nearly surrounded the city, but German assault guns drove Soviet armour back.

Their chance to take the city in a swift attack now gone, the Soviets completed the encirclement of Königsberg on 29/30 January, and laid siege.

....

Soviet forces move into Königsberg, January 1945.

The siege was lifted on 19 February, when the German 5th Panzer and 1st Infantry Divisions broke through Soviet lines, joining with elements of XXVIII Corps attacking out of Samland. The result of this attack was the creation of a narrow corridor from the city to Pillau, which could be used for the evacuation of civilians.

A lull in the fighting followed, not least because Chernyakovsky was killed on the day that the siege was lifted. His replacement, General Vasilevsky, arrived and reorganized the forces, incorporating 1st Baltic Front into his new command. This done, he was ready to resume the attack.

For once, Hitler permitted a limited evacuation, and the German commander, General Otto Lasch, began a limited withdrawal. However, on 2 April, before this was complete, the Soviets resumed their assault. By 6 April, they had broken through the German lines. Two days later, the Eleventh Guards Army linked up with the Forty-Third Army, cutting the last link between Königsberg and the rest of East Prussia. Lasch knew that the position was untenable, and surrendered on 10 April.

10 September The Germans occupy Rome. Mariupol is captured by an amphibious assault.

11 September – Sardinia is evacuated by German forces.

12 September German special forces rescue Mussolini from captivity.

14 September The Germans begin counterattacks against the Salerno beaches.

16 September Novorossisk falls into Soviet hands. The Germans evacuate Bryansk.

21 September The Soviets retake Chernigov, bringing the Central Front to the Dnieper.

22 September Crossings over the Dnieper are taken by the Voronezh Front.

Georgi Zhukov, the military leader who helped relieve the siege of Leningrad.

Soviet armour, led by an IS-2 heavy tank, moves through a captured German town. This final assault, on Germany itself, began in April 1945.

Russian soldiers move through a captured part of Berlin, the damage to buildings showing the ferocity of the fighting.

West Prussia

The final area of concern for the Soviets lay in West Prussia, which also needed to be cleared to ensure that troops could not be employed in a flank attack on advancing Soviet troops. Progress was made, but the thaw turned the ground into swamp, forcing Marshal Rokossovsky to call off the attack on 19 February 1945. At the start of

March 1945, the 1st and 2nd Byelorussian Fronts attacked again. The attack cut the railway to the east of Koeslin, and then pushed towards Danzig and Gdynia. These were the main supply bases for Königsberg and Courland, making the defence of both areas even more difficult. By the middle of March, the Germans were reduced to holding small enclaves in West Prussia. On 18

March, Kolberg fell; Gdynia, 10 days later; and then, on 30 March, Danzig.

At the end of March 1945, therefore, the Soviets were in position for the final push on Berlin. And it was not only the might of the Red Army the Germans would face, but that of the Anglo-American forces now moving to the west of the capital. Defeat was inevitable.

1943

SEPTEMBER

25 September Smolensk and Roslavl are recaptured by the Bryansk Front, which is then dissolved and redistributed amongst other Fronts. Mussolini announces the formation of the Italian Socialist Republic in northern Italy.

OCTOBER

1 October The Allies enter Naples and Foggia.

6 October The Kalinin and Baltic Fronts begin an offensive to open the path towards the Baltic states.

9 October The German Seventeenth Army completes its withdrawal across the Kerch Straits into Crimea. The US Fifth Army (General Mark Clark) pushes towards the River Volturno.

16 October The Soviets begin an attack on the Dnieper bend with the aim of trapping the First Panzer and Sixth Armies. An attack by the Voronezh Front to enlarge Bukrin bridgehead is repulsed.

20 October Reorganization of the Soviet Fronts. Voronezh, Steppe, South-West and South Fronts are retitled 1st, 2nd, 3rd and 4th Ukrainian Fronts; the Central Front becomes the Byelorussian Front; the Kalinin and Baltic Fronts are renamed as 1st and 2nd Baltic Fronts.

The War in Italy

At the Casablanca conference during January 1943, Roosevelt and Churchill discussed strategy. Initially, they disagreed. Roosevelt advocated an invasion of France, contending that operations elsewhere were a diversion from the principal aim of defeating Hitler. Churchill was less convinced. Describing Italy as the 'soft underbelly' of Europe, he argued that the Allies could drive through it into the heart of the continent. He also pointed out that an invasion of Italy might also persuade Turkey to break its neutrality and join the war on the Allied side.

Despite opposition from the US Army Chief of Staff, General George C. Marshall, Roosevelt understood this logic and agreed to a compromise. He was also influenced by the fact that it was obvious the Allies did not yet have the necessary forces to invade France. A lull in fighting, though, would lose the momentum built during the latter stages of the North African campaign, and would also prompt complaints from Stalin about the lack of a second front.

....

Roosevelt, Churchill and their senior military advisers at Casablanca

It was agreed that the Allies should occupy Sicily and then consider an invasion of the mainland. Eisenhower was appointed supreme commander, with three British deputies – General Harold Alexander, Air Chief Marshal Sir Arthur Tedder and Admiral of the Fleet Sir Andrew Cunningham. The plan called for an attack on or around 10 July 1943. Montgomery's Eighth Army would land on the southeast corner of Sicily, and Patton's Seventh Army would land to the left of the British, to protect the flank. Montgomery would then drive up the east coast of the island to Messina. The plan was unpopular with American commanders, who believed (correctly) that Montgomery sought to relegate them to a supporting role, letting him take credit for the victory.

It was not clear whether the defenders of the island would fight. The Axis force was commanded by General Alfredo Guzzoni, who had about 200,000 Italian troops, supported by 30,000 Germans, under his control. Guzzoni was a competent general, but as insurance, the Germans had a separate chain of command headed by Field Marshal Albert Kesselring, the Commander-in-Chief South.

---

23 October
Denpropetrovsk is recaptured by the Soviets.

31 October The foreign ministers' conference in Moscow ends.

NOVEMBER

3 November An offensive is launched across the Dnieper from the Lyutezh bridgehead.

5 November The Battle for Monte Camino begins.

6 November The Soviets liberate Kiev. Field Marshal Albert Kesselring is appointed as supreme German commander in Italy.

8 November British troops reach the River Sangro.

12 November Zhitomir is recaptured by Soviet forces.

Operation Husky

On 9 July 1943, 2500 ships and landing craft, carrying an invasion force of more than 160,000 men, headed for Italian waters. The fleet sailed past Malta – demonstrating just how important it had been to hold the island and prevent it from becoming an Axis base. Poor weather prompted concerns that the invasion force would have to turn back, but Eisenhower decided to continue.

In Tunisia, a fleet of transport aircraft had been awaiting the decision. Once it came, they lifted off, towing the gliders of the British 1st Airlanding Brigade towards Sicily. Unfortunately, their route took them straight into the path of the storm. Aircraft were driven off course and the gliders were tossed about in the gale. This led to tragedy: 69 glider tugs, their pilots and navigators, confused by the storm, released their gliders well short of the correct point, and the fragile transport craft fell into the sea, causing many fatalities among the airborne troops. Meanwhile, the transport aircraft carrying 3000 US paratroops were unable to maintain their course in the teeth of the storm. Very few transports dropped their cargo in the correct place, and only 200 men landed in reasonably close proximity to their objectives. Indeed, the confusion was so great that General James M. Gavin, the American airborne commander, was at first convinced that he had been dropped into mainland Italy. The only positive note about the air landings was that they caused consternation amongst the enemy. There were so many reports of

US paratroops prepare the equipment prior to boarding their transport aircraft for the invasion of Sicily.

1943

NOVEMBER

13 November The Allies recognize Italy as a co-belligerent, formally accepting the Italian wish to change sides.

18 November The Germans launch a counterattack against the Kiev bridgehead. Zhitomir is retaken.

18/19 November RAF Bomber Command raids Berlin and Mannheim, the first occasion when two major raids are launched on a single night. Opening of the 'Battle of Berlin'.

20 November The Eighth Army crosses the Sangro.

23 November Cairo strategy conference between British and American chiefs of staff.

26 November Heavy rain brings the German offensive to a halt. The Byelorussian Front liberates Gomel. The Cairo conference is suspended to allow the Tehran summit to take place.

28 November The Tehran summit of the 'Big Three' begins. Montgomery begins attacks on the Gustav Line.

paratroops and glider landings that the Germans and Italians thought Sicily had been invaded by at least 20,000 and possibly even 30,000 airborne soldiers. In fact, there were just over 4500.

As the invasion fleet approached the beaches, the weather improved, although the US Seventh Army, due to land on the west of Sicily, was some way behind schedule. The Eighth Army was on time, and encountered only light opposition as it went ashore. The Italians defenders had concluded that an amphibious

Landing ships unloading their cargo at Gela, Sicily, 10 July 1943. Codenamed Operation Husky, the Allied invasion of Sicily was the largest amphibious assault of the war thus far.

landing would not be attempted in bad weather, and therefore relaxed after the Allied transport aircraft left. The first assaulting troops met no opposition, and stormed up the beaches to seize the coastal defences. As they realized what

was happening, the Italians opened fire, but their artillery was suppressed by naval gunfire from six British battleships sitting offshore.

It was not long before the advanced elements of the forces ashore in eastern Sicily were moving inland: by 0800, the town of Cassibile

DECEMBER

1 December The Tehran summit ends.

2 December Clark resumes attacks. The British secure Monte Camino.

4 December The Cairo conference resumes.

6 December Eisenhower is appointed as Supreme Commander for the invasion of Europe. The Cairo conference ends.

7 December The Battle of San Pietro begins.

16/17 December Bomber attacks against German V-weapon sites in France.

24 December The railway running west from Vitebsk is cut by Soviet forces. Montgomery is appointed to the command of the 21st Army Group for the invasion of France.

27 December The Eighth Army captures Ortona, bringing the British offensive to an end.

A posed photograph showing Italian prisoners surrendering to British troops during the Sicily campaign.

was in the hands of the British 5th Division. The Americans enjoyed similar fortune. The defences in western Sicily had been alerted to the attack by the British landings, and opened fire on the invasion craft as soon as they were within range of the coastal gun batteries. However, these were engaged and neutralized by naval gunfire, and the Americans went ashore with few problems.

At Licata, American soldiers found an abandoned command post, and as they entered it, heard the telephone ringing. By chance, the war correspondent Michael Chinigo was accompanying these troops, and he answered it. The caller was an Italian officer, anxious to know whether the rumours that the Americans had landed were true. Chinigo was a fluent Italian speaker, and told the caller that the rumours were nonsense. The Italian officer cheered up at this news and rang off, none the wiser.

By the middle of the morning, the invading forces were pushing inland, aided by the fact that the American airborne troops had overcome the problem of not landing in the right place: a number of paratroops met up as they tried to reach their intended drop zones, and decided instead to form themselves into

small units. They then caused havoc behind the Italian lines, hindering the flow of reserves to the invasion area.

The British airborne formations also tried to make the best of a poor situation. Only about 100 of the 1500 men who were supposed to have landed made it on to the island, but they were still able to seize and hold the Ponte Grande bridge over the River Cavadonna. The Italians finally dislodged them late in the afternoon of 10 July. By this point, only 15 British troops were left, and seven were killed in the Italian assault. Undaunted, the eight survivors split into two groups – two men took up positions on a nearby hill and prevented the Italians from moving by sniping at them at every opportunity, while the remaining six made their way back to the invasion area, to find Allied troops. Once they did this, they led a mobile column from the 5th Division to the bridge. The column carved its way through the Italian defences, opening the way for an advance into Syracuse.

The second day of the Sicilian campaign, however, demonstrated that the battle to take the island would not be easy. The Germans and Italians had reorganized overnight, and their

1944

JANUARY

1 January General Carl Spaatz is appointed as commander of American strategic air forces in Europe. General James Doolittle is appointed to command the USAAF Eighth Air Force.

3 January Montgomery holds the first planning conference for Operation Overlord.

8 January Eisenhower and Montgomery leave Italy to prepare for the invasion of Europe, being replaced by Field Marshal Henry Maitland Wilson and General Sir Oliver Leese respectively.

17 January Clark attacks across the Garigliano.

20 January The Allies are halted below Monte Cassino.

22 January Allied landings at Anzio.

FEBRUARY

3 February The Germans counterattack at Anzio.

15 February Allied bombing of the monastery at Monte Cassino precedes a fresh assault on German positions.

response became more coordinated. An attack by 60 German tanks came within 3km (2 miles) of the beaches, and it took time to force them back, aided by naval gunfire.

The following day, the Germans made an airdrop of their own, landing reinforcements at Catania. This marked the start of a major German reinforcement of the island; while the troops were arriving, the Allies continued their advance.

The Drive to Palermo

For the rest of July, the two Allied armies pushed their way forwards, the rivalry between Patton and Montgomery increasing as they moved further north. When the British XXX Corps was held up near Lentini, Montgomery ordered a change of direction around the base of Mount Etna, to enable an assault on Messina from the west. To achieve this manoeuvre, the XXX Corps's commander, General Sir Oliver Leese, had to use Route 124, a road running from Vizzini to Caltagirone. The road was in the American sector, but Montgomery sent Leese up the route without telling the Americans that his troops would be joining them. American and

A German PAK 41 88mm gun in action, Sicily, July 1943. Although the first day of the Sicilian campaign went well for the Allies, the Germans and Italians soon regrouped and launched a counterattack.

16 February Further German counterattacks at Anzio enjoy considerable success.

17 February Allied attacks on Monte Cassino are suspended.

19 February The Allies manage to prevent the beachhead at Anzio from being split in two by the Germans.

21 February The opening of the 'Big Week' air offensive against Germany.

29 February General Vatutin is mortally wounded in an ambush by pro-German partisans. He is replaced by General Zhukov. The Germans begin another round of counterattacks at Anzio.

MARCH

3 March The Germans abandon operations at Anzio.

4 March The 1st Ukrainian Front opens offensive action in the Ukraine. The first American daylight raid on Berlin.

British units, who had been told that they would be working independently of one another, now found themselves attacking the same objective, the town of Enna. They took it, but Montgomery's action irritated Patton, since it meant that the role of the Americans in providing flank protection became more important, thus denying them the chance to participate in taking Messina.

Patton now personally asked General Alexander to order him to take Palermo – a request that verged on being a demand. He got his way, and the US 2nd Armoured and 3rd Infantry Divisions covered 160km (100 miles) in four days and entered the city on 22 July. There had been little resistance on the way, and the only enemy troops the Americans encountered in Palermo were Italians waiting to surrender. The Germans in the city had abandoned it some days before.

Patton, Bradley and Montgomery.

The drive on Palermo left Patton in a position to advance on Messina, and he was determined to arrive there before the British. Advancing on Messina would be more difficult than taking Palermo, since the terrain through which the Seventh Army had to pass was mountainous, with roads that could easily be blocked. The advance was indeed slow, and it stalled at Troina. An attack in divisional strength, supported by heavy air attacks, cleared out the defending Germans on 6 August.

By the middle of the month, British and American units were on the outskirts of Messina; on 17 August, an American patrol entered the city, to be joined a little later by British armour. The city was deserted, since the Germans had pulled back across the straits of Messina to the mainland. Kesselring had decided that the island was not worth the sacrifice of a large number of Germans. On 8 August, he ordered an evacuation, and by the time that Messina fell, 40,000 troops and their equipment had been withdrawn. After 38 days of fighting, Sicily was under Allied control.

Attention could now turn to mainland Italy, the scene of a dramatic development: Mussolini had been deposed.

1944

MARCH

5 March The 2nd Ukrainian Front joins the Ukrainian offensive.

6 March The 3rd Ukrainian Front begins offensive action.

10 March The 2nd Ukrainian Front captures Uman.

11/12 March Launch of Operation Diadem, a major Allied offensive designed to tie down German forces in Italy to prevent their removal to defend against the Normandy invasion.

13 March Kherson is liberated by the 3rd Ukrainian Front.

15 March The third offensive against Monte Cassino begins. Kesselring orders a withdrawal to the Dora Line.

17 March General Konev's 2nd Ukrainian Front reaches the River Dniester.

The End of Mussolini

By the middle of July 1943, as the Allies enjoyed success, discontent with Mussolini was mounting. An Allied bombing raid on 19 July not only destroyed the railway marshalling yards that were the target, but also killed and wounded 4000 civilians. Now came public complaints that further disasters would be inevitable as long as the war continued. Mussolini seemed the only obstacle to peace, so the Grand Council of the Fascist voted to replace their leader. Mussolini was amazed to find himself taken into captivity.

A new government, under Field Marshal Pietro Badoglio, was established. Hitler, certain that the Italians would surrender, ordered that Mussolini be rescued from captivity. He was recovered from a mountain-top fortress by commandos landing in gliders, and then taken to Berlin. Hitler was right to doubt the continuation of Italian support. Mussolini was deposed on 25 July; on the next day, Badoglio announced that Italy remained an unshakeable ally of Germany; and on the 31st, he sent emissaries to negotiate peace with the Allies.

Negotiations began, and the Allies planned

Mussolini is seen on his way to a Storch light aircraft that will fly him to freedom after his daring rescue from captivity by German commandos. The action was too late to stop the Italian people demanding peace, 1943.

19 March German troops enter Hungary to prevent the nation from concluding a separate armistice with the USSR.

21 March The Allies call off attacks on Monte Cassino.

24/25 March The Battle for Berlin ends.

25 March The 2nd Ukrainian Front reaches the Russian–Romanian border.

28 March Zhukov and Konev encircle the First Panzer Army.

30 March The First Panzer Army breaks out of encirclement.

30/31 March The RAF suffers the heaviest loss rate of the Bomber Offensive when more than 90 bombers are lost in the attack on Nuremberg.

APRIL

2 April Konev's forces enter Romania.

Men of the 2/6 Queens Regiment advancing in the Salerno area past a knocked-out German Mark IV 'Special' tank. The Germans put up stiff resistance at Salerno, but they no longer had the support of the Italians, 1943.

an invasion of the mainland with the complicity of the new government, which was anxious to ensure that the Germans could not install a government of their own. It was agreed that the Allies would land at Salerno on 9 September, just a few hours after an announcement of Italy's surrender. Anticipating this, the Germans chose to sacrifice most of Italy, and retire to a defensive line between Pisa and Rimini.

The Italian Campaign

The invasion of Italy began with a landing by the Eighth Army on the 'toe' of the country. The only Italian troops encountered offered to help unload the landing craft. A few hours later, Lieutenant- General Mark Clark's US Fifth Army (which included British troops as well as Americans) landed at Salerno, to meet much stiffer opposition from the Germans. Completing the invasion, the British 1st Airborne Division landed at Taranto and captured the port.

Kesselring's command put up stiff resistance. Counterattacks began on 11 September, driving British units from the Molina Pass the next day. Serious consideration was now given to

1944

APRIL		MAY		
8 April The 4th Ukrainian Front attacks into Crimea.	**17 April** Zhukov liberates Ternopol. The Finnish parliament rejects Soviet terms for an armistice.	**5 May** The Soviets begin an attack against Sevastopol.		**15 May** Final planning meeting for Operation Overlord.
10 April Odessa is liberated, isolating the German Seventeenth Army.			**12 May** The German Seventeenth Army surrenders. The Crimea is now cleared of German troops.	
		9 May Sevastopol falls under Soviet control.		

Soviet forces in Sevastopol.

abandoning the beachhead in the southern sector, a step that was avoided when Royal Navy gunfire prevented further German gains. The enemy had come to within 1.6km (1 mile) of the beaches by the time they were forced to stop. Allied reinforcements arrived, and between the 13th and 16th, the fighting was notably fierce. Once engineers built landing strips in the beachhead, air support could be provided, and the situation began to ease. The British 1st Airborne Division began to move out from Taranto to link up with the other Allied troops, which was achieved on 20 September.

Bren gun carrier passing through the streets of Salerno, 1943

The Allies then advanced on Naples, and on 1 October entered the city unopposed. Alexander ordered that armour from both the Fifth and Eighth Armies should pursue the enemy, and by 5 October the Allies were on the River Volturno. Notions of a quick victory were premature, however.

The Germans had a number of advantages in the defence of their positions. The mountain passes, which the Allies could not avoid if they were moving northwards, were relatively simple to defend, and their advance slowed. Early in October, about a month before it was normally due, heavy rainfall caused landslides, waterlogged the ground and made a rapid movement impossible. On 16 October, the Germans took the opportunity to conduct a fighting withdrawal to a new defensive position 24km (15 miles) north of the Volturno. Known as the 'Gustav Line', it became a major obstacle to the Allies, blocking the way towards Rome.

Alexander's plan for breaching the Gustav Line was for the British 46th Division to attack along a 16km (10 mile) front near Minturno, with other formations following up. The 46th Division went into battle on 4 January 1944.

17 May Eisenhower selects 5 June as the date for Overlord. The Poles attack Monte Cassino, taking the summit the following morning.

19 May The Americans take Gaeta and Itri.

22/23 May The Eighth Army attacks in Liri Valley.

23 May The US VI Corps breaks out from the Anzio beachhead.

25 May The Eighth Army crosses the River Melfa. The US VI Corps links up with II Corps.

30/31 May The American VI Corps breaks through defences in the Alban Hills.

JUNE

3 June Kesselring receives permission to abandon Rome.

4 June The last German troops leave Rome. Bad weather forces the postponement of Overlord for 24 hours.

Hard fighting continued for several days, and it was not until 17 January that the British managed to establish a bridgehead across the mouth of the River Garigliano. It took a further 10 days of struggle to expand the bridgehead to include Monte Juga and Minturno. An American attempt to cross the river ended in disaster, most of the US 36th Division being lost. Overall, the defenders still held the advantage.

Anzio and Cassino

On 22 January 1944, 36,000 men landed at Anzio, due south of Rome, with the aim of cutting the German lines of communication between the Italian capital and Cassino. The soldiers captured the port intact. The relative ease with which they did so was deceptive, however.

The struggle to take Cassino would be bitter. The fighting was

Field Marshal Albert Kesselring (left), the German Commander South, seen at Anzio. Kesselring headed the campaign in Italy that held of the Allies for some time, but he could not halt the later advance into Germany.

1944

JUNE

5 June The invasion fleet begins to cross the Channel; Allied airborne landings take place. The US Fifth Army enters Rome, ending Operation Diadem.

6 June The Allies land in Normandy.

7/8 June An attempt to seize Caen fails.

10 June A Soviet offensive begins against the Finns around Lake Lagoda.

11 June The second attempt to capture Caen is launched.

12 June Carentan falls. The beachheads at Omaha and Utah link up.

14 June The second attempt to take Caen ends.

intense and manoeuvre proved all but impossible. The Allies had to take Cassino in order to advance northwards. It had numerous fortifications, however, and was overlooked by a hill on which sat the famed medieval monastery, potentially a perfect defensive location.

The first fighting at Cassino occurred between January and February 1944. The Germans could not be dislodged, and the attack swiftly came to a halt. This set the pattern, as the Allies made attempts to advance but found the sheer face of Monte Cassino an impossible obstacle. Ground was regularly traded between the two sides, but never brought a benefit for the Allies. A new approach was required.

On 15 March 1944, a massive aerial bombardment was launched. The historic monastery was destroyed in the process, and it seemed that the way was now open for an advance. However, the Germans moved into the ruins of the monastery, which provided superb defensive positions. A third attempt to take Monte Cassino failed after a week.

It was not until early May 1944 that a fourth attempt was made. On this occasion, the better weather and the fact that the Allies had massed an overwhelming number of troops meant that they were able to carry the hill. The remains of the monastery fell on 18 May, and the Gustav Line had finally been unlocked. The advance on

Landing ships unloading supplies and men on the beach at Anzio, at the start of the drive to Rome, May 1944.

20 June Viipuri falls to the Soviets.

21 June The Karelian Front attacks Finnish positions between Lake Lagoda and Lake Onega.

22 June Beginning of Operation Bagration, the Soviet main offensive against the Germans. The Battle for Cherbourg begins.

23 June The 3rd Byelorussian Front attacks down the Minsk Highway, joined the next day by the 1st Byelorussian Front.

26 June Attempt to break through German lines west of Caen – Operation Epsom.

28 June Soviet troops cross the Beresina.

JULY

3 July The Americans attack towards St Lô.

4 July Minsk is liberated. A pocket of German forces is trapped to the east of the city.

Above: German paratroopers in defensive positions in the ruins of the monastery at Cassino, 1944.

Right: The air attack on Cassino, which destroyed the medieval monastery.

Rome could now continue, after five months of savage fighting. It was hardly the swift advance that had been predicted when news of the Italian surrender came through eight months before.

The Anzio Beachhead

The landings at Anzio met with similar difficulties. The Germans made determined efforts to reach the beaches and drive the Allies back into the sea. On 19 February, they came

1944

JULY

8 July The British make a further attempt to take Caen.

11 July The Minsk pocket is reduced. The way to Poland and Lithuania is now open to the Soviets.

13 July The 1st Ukrainian Front and left wing of the 1st Belorussian Front attack Army Group North. More than 40,000 German troops are trapped in a pocket around Brody.

17 July Rommel is wounded in an air attack.

18 July Operation Goodwood begins, with the aim of facilitating an American break-out, Operation Cobra. St Lô falls to the Americans.

19 July Livorno falls to the Allies.

20 July The 1st Belorussian Front reaches the River Bug. An assassination attempt against Hitler fails.

22 July The Brody pocket is destroyed.

perilously close to doing just that, and were driven off with some difficulty. Further attacks followed, but without success. The stalemate persisted at Anzio until 23 May, when the Allies broke out from the beachhead. Within two days, the US 1st Armoured and 3rd Infantry Divisions had linked up with the US 2nd Corps, which was heading for Rome. General Clark had decided that he was going to take Rome, and duly entered it on 4 June 1944. This was despite orders to the contrary from Alexander, who (rightly) considered that seizing the capital was irrelevant. Clark's move also caused resentment amongst the troops who had fought at Cassino, since their efforts – essential to the taking of Rome – were overshadowed, while Clark gained the glory.

To the Gothic Line

There was still much fighting to do to dislodge the Germans from the north of Italy. Several Allied formations had been withdrawn to support the Normandy campaign, making Alexander's task more difficult. He had to break through the Gothic Line, the last German defensive line, just to the south of the Lombardy

A German mortar team in action amongst the ruins of the monastery at Monte Cassino, exploiting the protection offered by the rubble.

plains. Success would offer access to Austria and the Balkan states.

The offensive began on 25 August. The Eighth Army, now under Lieutenant General Sir Oliver Leese after Montgomery's appointment to command the 21st Army Group in Normandy, carried out the attack, and initially progressed well. However, bad weather and supply problems slowed the offensive. A series of attacks along the length of the Gothic Line during September gained some ground, but this was insignificant. By early November,

23 July The 1st Belorussian Front enters Lublin. The extermination camp at Maidenek is liberated.

25 July The Americans launch Operation Cobra.

26 July The 1st Belorussian Front reaches the River Vistula. The Leningrad Front takes the Estonian town of Narva.

27 July The 1st Ukrainian Front liberates Lvov. Dvinsk in Lithuania is taken by the 2nd Baltic Front.

30 July The British launch Operation Bluecoat to tie up German forces.

31 July The 3rd Ukrainian Front enters Kanunas.

AUGUST

1 August The Warsaw rising begins.

3 August The Americans attack Rennes.

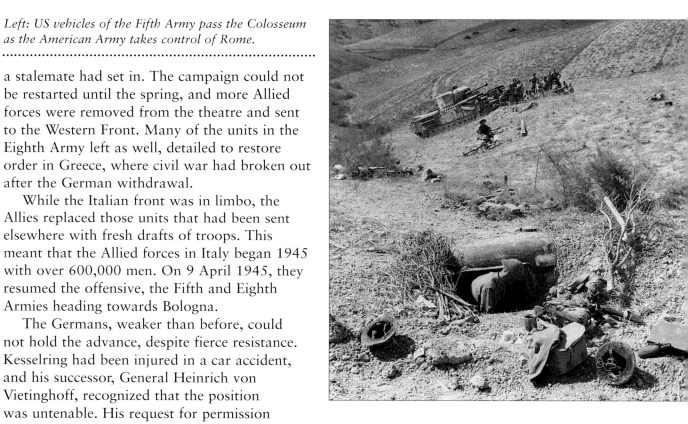

Left: US vehicles of the Fifth Army pass the Colosseum as the American Army takes control of Rome.

a stalemate had set in. The campaign could not be restarted until the spring, and more Allied forces were removed from the theatre and sent to the Western Front. Many of the units in the Eighth Army left as well, detailed to restore order in Greece, where civil war had broken out after the German withdrawal.

While the Italian front was in limbo, the Allies replaced those units that had been sent elsewhere with fresh drafts of troops. This meant that the Allied forces in Italy began 1945 with over 600,000 men. On 9 April 1945, they resumed the offensive, the Fifth and Eighth Armies heading towards Bologna.

The Germans, weaker than before, could not hold the advance, despite fierce resistance. Kesselring had been injured in a car accident, and his successor, General Heinrich von Vietinghoff, recognized that the position was untenable. His request for permission

Right: Allied troops examine a defensive position on the approach to the Gothic Line, June 1944.

to fall back to the River Po was refused, but he told his men to withdraw anyway. The German position collapsed.

AUGUST

6 August Patton's Third Army reaches Lorient.

6/7 August The Germans launch a counterattack at Mortain.

7/8 August Operation Totalize is launched against Falaise.

8 August Patton liberates Le Mans.

15 August The Allies land in the south of France. A German attack at Mortain ends in failure.

19 August An uprising in Paris begins.

20 August The 2nd and 3rd Ukrainian Fronts attack in Romania.

21 August The Falaise gap is closed.

British paratroops took Milan and Genoa, while a band of partisans found Mussolini and his mistress near Lake Como. Nominally reinstalled as Italian dictator after the rescue mission by German commandos, Mussolini had been little more than Hitler's puppet ever since. The partisans executed Mussolini, his mistress and other members of his entourage, and hung the corpses in the town square.

Lake Garda, Verona, Trieste and Turin all fell, and the Germans were pushed to the point of surrender. Negotiations between the head of the SS in Italy and the US Office of Strategic Services had begun as early as February, but Hitler's refusal to accept reality had meant that no conclusion could be reached. Finally, the German commanders decided to ignore Hitler, since it was clear that the lives of German soldiers were being sacrificed for no purpose. Negotiations were renewed, and on 25 April 1945 orders were given for German and Italian Fascist forces to surrender at 1200 on 2 May. The war in Italy was over.

....

German prisoners, captured in the Po River area, are marched to the rear of Fifth Army lines.

23 August King Carol of Romania declares the end of war with Soviets and orders German troops to leave the country.

24 August German bombers attack King Carol's palace in a bid to assassinate him. The attack fails, but kills many civilians.

25 August The Finns request peace terms from the Soviets. Romania declares war on Germany. Paris is liberated. A new Allied offensive, Operation Olive, begins.

28 August Toulon and Marseilles are liberated.

30 August The Red Army occupies the Ploesti oil fields. British and Canadian forces attack the Gothic Line.

31 August Soviet forces enter Bucharest. The British cross the River Somme.

From D-Day to VE Day

Anglo-American planning for the invasion of France began after the Casablanca conference in January 1943. Two months later, it was decided that the landings would take place on 1 May 1944 under the codename 'Overlord'.

Planning responsibility was given to the British general Sir Frederick Morgan, appointed Chief of Staff to the Supreme Allied Commander (COSSAC). Actually, he reported to no one during the first months of planning, when Normandy was identified as the best invasion area. It was not until 7 December 1943 that General Dwight D. Eisenhower was appointed Supreme Allied Commander.

Eisenhower took the plans forward, and by early June 1944, everything was ready. The invasion was planned for 5 June, but bad weather led to a 24-hour delay. Despite only slightly better weather the next day, Eisenhower issued the orders to invade. During the night of 5/6 June 1944, more than 250,000 men launched one of the largest and most complex military operations in history.

Left: A DUKW 'Duck' amphibious transport is loaded aboard an American landing craft at Portland Harbor. Right: American personnel at an outdoor religious service before embarking for the invasion of Normandy.

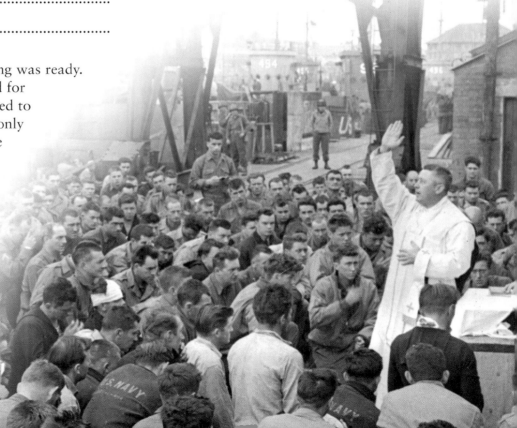

Allied troops head towards one of the Omaha landing beaches, 6 June 1944. As the ramps opened, the troops were exposed to fire from the beaches.

American wounded on Omaha Beach, which saw the heaviest Allied casualties on D-Day. The first wave of troops was hit the hardest, but subsequent waves also suffered.

D-Day

The airborne element of the assault ran into difficulties and many of the paratroopers ended up miles from their intended drop zones. Displaying the initiative expected from them, they set about attacking the Germans anyway.

The amphibious landings on the Normandy beaches a few hours later went relatively smoothly, with the significant exception of Omaha Beach. There, the Americans suffered heavy casualties before breaking through the defences and moving inland. The German response to the invasion was complicated by Hitler's initial refusal to accept that the Normandy landings were the main invasion. He was convinced that they were a small force intended to distract from a second, major landing in the Pas de Calais.

1944

SEPTEMBER

2 September The Canadians break through the Gothic Line and establish a bridgehead across the River Conca.

3 September Brussels is liberated.

4 September Heavy rain brings a halt to the offensive.

5 September A German–Hungarian counterattack in the southern Carpathians begins. The Soviet Union declares war on Bulgaria.

7 September The Hungarian Government demands additional forces from the Germans to protect against a Soviet attack, threatening to change sides should help not be forthcoming.

8 September The 3rd Ukrainian Front enters Bulgaria.

9 September Bulgaria declares war on Germany.

10 September Eisenhower approves Montgomery's plan for Operation Market Garden, an airborne assault to seize the Rhine bridges.

11 September The first Allied troops cross the German border.

The Breakout

Once ashore, the Allies had to break out to reach the countryside beyond. This was difficult because the topography of the Bocage country between Capriquet and the Cotentin peninsula was ideally suited to defensive operations. Attempts by the British and Canadians to take Caen were rebuffed until Operation Charnwood. This began with a massive aerial bombardment against the city on 8 July. By the 11th, British and Canadian troops had broken into Caen, although they could not dislodge the 12th SS Panzer Division from the southern sector of the city.

The resistance from the Germans meant that, by early July, the invasion forces were no more than 24km (15 miles) inland at any point. This represented just one-fifth of the ground that should have been taken by this date. On 10 July, General Bernard Montgomery, commanding the 21st Army Group, issued instructions for the breakout from Normandy. General Omar Bradley's First US Army would attack towards Avranches, and the lead element of the US Third Army (VIII Corps) would then strike into Brittany. To assist the advance, General Sir Miles

An American soldier walks through the streets of St Lô, July 1944. The town was virtually destroyed in the action, but its capture was a turning point for the Allies in their progress towards Germany.

12 September US troops attempt to break through West Wall defences. The US Fifth Army attacks east of Il Giorgo Pass.

12/13 September The Eighth Army resumes its attack.

14 September The Soviets reopen the offensive against Army Group North.

17 September The Leningrad Front launches a new attack in Estonia. The Bulgarian Army is placed under Soviet Command. Operation Market Garden begins.

21 September The Germans retake the bridge at Arnhem. Fiorenzuola is captured by the Americans.

22 September The Leningrad Front captures Estonian capital, Tallinn.

24 September Malinovsky's 2nd Ukrainian Front breaks through enemy positions in the Transylvanian Alps and closes on the Hungarian border.

Dempsey's British Second Army would attack
through the open countryside to the east of Caen.

This attack, Operation Goodwood, was
scheduled for 18 July, and Bradley's offensive,
Operation Cobra, for the next day. However,
Bradley could not start his attack until St Lô
was captured, and it took until 19 July before
the town fell. As a result, Cobra was put back

*Members of the French Resistance celebrate
the liberation of Rennes in August 1944.*

*American troops proudly display a captured German swastika flag after the taking of Chambois. Fierce fighting
had taken place around the villages of Chambois and St Lambert, an area that became known as 'Death Road'.*

1944

SEPTEMBER

26 September Market
Garden ends with the
evacuation of surviving
troops from Arnhem.

30 September Calais
is liberated.

28 September The 3rd
Ukrainian Front begins the
drive towards Belgrade.

OCTOBER

1 October A Hungarian
delegation arrives in Moscow to
seek armistice. Leese is sent to
Burma and replaced as
commander of the Eighth Army
by General Sir Richard McCreery.

2 October The
Americans resume
their attack on West
Wall defences.

4 October
German troops
seize key points
in Hungary.

5 October The 1st Baltic
Front attacks again.

6 October The Battle
of the Huertgen Forest.

until 24 July. Meanwhile, Goodwood had become bogged down after stiff resistance and heavy rains made the ground impassable. The attack had nonetheless achieved Montgomery's aim of drawing German armour away from the Americans. While the British faced 13 German divisions, there were only nine facing the Americans, and of these only two were armoured. The Americans thus had a considerable advantage for Cobra.

No one expected the operation to be easy, though – nor was it. The opening aerial bombardment had to be recalled because cloud cover made it impossible for the bombers to see the bomb line separating the American and German forces. Unfortunately, one bomber unit failed to receive the recall and released its bombs on elements of the 30th Division.

A Second Attempt

Cobra began again the next day with a massive air attack, in which more than 4000 tons of bombs were dropped. More than 1000 defenders were killed, and a similar number were wounded or so badly dazed that they were incapable of resistance.

The ground assault started at 1100, and ran into stiff resistance where bombing had not inflicted much damage. The first day proved disappointing for the Americans, who gained only about 1.6km (1 mile) rather than the 5km (3 miles) anticipated. However, armoured attacks over the course of the next three days reduced the German defences to disarray. Hitler now ordered a counterattack at Mortain.

The counterattack began on 7 August and penetrated

An American soldier takes the surrender of a German soldier. Most photographs were staged after fighting, the prisoner is probably 'surrendering' for the second time.

7 October The Karelian Front launches an attack against Petsamo.

11 October The Hungarians sign an armistice. The Eighth Army reaches the River Rubicon.

12 October The 3rd Ukrainian Front crosses the River Morava south of Belgrade.

14 October The Battle of Belgrade begins.

15 October The Germans install a puppet government in Budapest. The 2nd and 3rd Baltic Fronts capture Riga.

19 October The Eighth Army crosses the River Savio.

20 October Malinovsky's forces capture Debrecen.

21 October The Americans capture Aachen.

almost 16km (10 miles) into American lines. The Germans were assisted by the fact that bad weather kept the Allied air forces grounded. Good weather the next day, though, brought the full weight of air attack on to the Germans, and over the course of the next three days, their forces were steadily reduced by air attack and stiff American resistance. By 12 August, it was clear that the attack had failed.

The End in Normandy

On 17 August, Field Marshal Walther Model, a loyal Nazi willing to obey orders, was placed in command of operations in Normandy. His loyalty was not blind, however, and he appreciated that the position was hopeless. He was clever enough to conduct a withdrawal – expressly prohibited by Hitler – while using the remnants of his armour to make thrusts against both Falaise and Argentan. These, he knew, would fail, but they would also allow him to claim he had carried out Hitler's instructions to the letter, the withdrawal being forced upon him by circumstances. The Germans were now in a dire state.

Just a few weeks earlier, a bomb plot against Hitler on 20 July 1944 had failed. The deranged führer was now convinced that providence had saved him – and that his survival was a sign from divine authority. He believed that any operational plans he drew up would have the seal of approval 'from above'. Events in France suggested otherwise. On 25 August, French troops marched into Paris – largely to appease General De Gaulle, rather than for any military need. Still, it was a sign that the campaign for Normandy was over.

Operation Dragoon

An invasion of southern France began on 14 August, codenamed Operation Dragoon. On 17 August, orders for the abandonment of southern France (apart from the ports) were issued by the German High Command, and the forces there began to retreat.

American troops of the 28th infantry division march down the Champs Elysees to celebrate the liberation of Paris.

1944

OCTOBER

22 October Nyiregyhaza falls to Malinovsky, but is recaptured by a German counterattack.

27 October The US Fifth Army ends its offensive.

29 October Malinovsky begins an attack across the River Tisza towards Budapest.

31 October The Eighth Army crosses the River Ronco.

NOVEMBER

1 November British amphibious assault on Walcheren Island.

4 November Malinovsky's troops reach the outskirts of Budapest, but are unable to break into city itself.

8 November Walcheren is under British control. Patton begins an offensive in the Saarland.

20 November The British capture Castiglione.

24 November Alexander becomes Supreme Commander Mediterranean in succession to Maitland Wilson.

A mass airdrop by American forces between Nice and Marseilles during the campaign in the south of France. The Normandy campaign was all but over, with Marseilles surrendering to the Allies in August.

The Franco-American advance proceeded smoothly. Marseilles surrendered on 28 August, and leading elements of General Lucian K. Truscott's VI Corps entered Lyons on 3 September. By that time, Allied forces in the north had exploited their breakthrough. Montgomery launched Operation Kitten, an advance to the Seine on 16 August, forcing the Germans to carry out a phased withdrawal across the river. By the first week of September, the Allies had started to outrun their logistics, so they took the decision to pause.

The strained logistics system suggested that the Allies would be unable to sustain thrusts across a broad front, and that all efforts would have to go into one decisive offensive. The most ambitious of the Allied commanders, Montgomery and Patton, both wanted to be the man to conduct it, but limiting an offensive to one part of the front would inevitably deny one man his glory.

Market Garden

Montgomery thus proposed a plan to place his men across the River Rhine, putting them in a position to sweep towards Berlin, possibly even before the year was over. The plan was to land

DECEMBER

4 December Patton begins breaking through West Wall defences.

5 December Malinovsky begins a new attempt to take Budapest.

16 December The German offensive in the Ardennes begins.

22 December The German offensive in the Ardennes comes to a halt.

26 December American troops besieged in Bastogne since opening of the Ardennes offensive are relieved. The Germans launch a counterattack in the Serchio Valley.

29 December The Eighth Army ends offensive operations until spring.

31 December Operation Nordwind is launched by the Germans in an attempt to destroy Allied forces in Alsace.

30,000 British and American airborne troops at key river bridges while General Sir Brian Horrocks' XXX Corps drove north through Holland along the 96km (60 mile) corridor created by the landing, to take the Rhine crossing at Arnhem.

The operation began on 17 September 1944. After initial success, it became clear that the British troops in Arnhem – crucial to the success of the operation – were in trouble. This was largely because they were fighting against an SS Panzer Division that had not been identified by Allied intelligence. The British paratroopers' task was impossible, and the bridge at Arnhem (the 'bridge too far') was lost on 21 September.

The XXX Corps battled on towards Arnhem, and broke through German lines on 23 September. Their first attempt to cross the river failed, and Montgomery decided that the Airborne Division had to be withdrawn, since it had no chance of success. The surviving troops were evacuated from Arnhem across the river during the night of 25/26 September.

American paratroops prepare to board the C-47 transport aircraft as part of Operation Market Garden.

Back to Attrition

It was clear that the Germans were not yet prepared to accept defeat. They kept up a battle of attrition for the remainder of the year.

As December began, the Allies continued to advance, but they appeared to have lost momentum. The attritional nature of the struggle concerned the Allies, particularly Montgomery, who was well aware that there were relatively limited British reserves available. He sought to persuade Eisenhower that it was essential to find some means of forcing the Germans into mobile warfare. As Eisenhower pondered the problem, Hitler launched a massive offensive in the Ardennes.

1945

JANUARY

1 January Herbert Gille's IV SS Panzer Corps launches a counterattack towards Budapest, and gets within 24km (15 miles) of the city. The Germans launch Operation Bodenplatte in an attempt to destroy Allied air power, but suffer crippling losses in the process.

7 January III Panzer Corps attacks towards Budapest in an attempt to join up with IV SS Panzer Corps.

12 January Malinovsky's forces force IV SS Panzer Corps and III Panzer Corps to retreat to their start lines. Konev's 1st Ukrainian Front attacks the Fourth Panzer Army.

13 January The 3rd Byelorussian Front launches an offensive into East Prussia.

14 January Zhukov attacks south of Warsaw.

15 January Zhukov begins an attack against Warsaw from the north, with the aim of enveloping the city.

16/17 January The German garrison begins to withdraw from Warsaw.

17 January Gille launches a new counterattack towards Budapest. Soviet forces are taken by surprise.

19 January Konev's forces take Krakow. Zhukov's 1st Belorussian Front captures Lodz.

The Battle of the Bulge

Hitler's plan was an unrealistic bid to seize Antwerp. He was the only person not to see that this was beyond the capabilities of his forces in the West, and he refused to listen to any objections. Indeed, he believed that he could obtain a victory so decisive that the Anglo-American forces would be forced to sue for peace within a week. His generals – at least, those who had not already reached this view – concluded that he was mad.

Nonetheless, the attack began on 16 December 1944. The assault caught the Americans by surprise, but the pace of advance was nowhere near swift enough to allow Antwerp to be taken. The Germans were delayed at St Vith and a host of other places, and found that Bastogne, a key target because of its communications links, was far from easy to take. The 101st Airborne Division held out, despite being totally surrounded – a German offer of surrender was presented to the temporary commander of the division, Brigadier General Anthony McAuliffe. His reply was one word: 'Nuts!' His staff officers had to explain that this meant rejection.

Eisenhower ordered a counterattack. The Germans were slowed down, and then driven back in the face of a determined thrust by Patton. Bastogne was resupplied by air, and relieved on 26 December. The fighting continued until January 1945, including a German offensive against American troops in Alsace, but the Battle of the Bulge was over by the New Year. The Americans set about destroying the remaining German forces, and within exactly six weeks of the start of the offensive, the Americans had regained all the ground they had lost. The Germans had suffered heavy casualties for little return. The Allies could now make the final push – towards Berlin.

Members of the British 1st Airborne Division surrender to German soldiers at Arnhem after the failure in Operation Market Garden.

Germany Vanquished

By early 1945, Germany was on the verge of defeat. The Ardennes offensive had failed, and on the Eastern Front, the Red Army appeared unstoppable. The situation in Italy was slightly better, but it was just a matter of time before the Allies renewed their offensive. In the Balkans,

FEBRUARY

20 January Konev's troops cross the German frontier with Poland.

22 January The Soviet Fourth Tank and Fifth Guards Armies reach the River Oder.

27 January Gille's IV SS Panzer Corps comes within 19km (12 miles) of Budapest.

28 January The German salient in the Ardennes is finally destroyed.

31 January Zhukov's forces reach the Oder and establish bridgeheads in Kienitz and south of Kuestrin. The Americans begin advance to the Ruhr dams.

8 February Konev renews the offensive, with the aim of closing on the River Neisse. Launch of Operation Veritable, a massive Allied offensive to clear the way to the Rhine.

10 February The 1st Baltic and 2nd and 3rd Byelorussian Fronts begin an offensive to take East Prussia and Pomerania.

13 February Budapest falls to Malinovsky's forces.

13/14 February Bombing of Dresden.

the Germans had been forced out of Greece, Yugoslavia, Hungary and Romania. The war at sea was lost, and although the Luftwaffe was still flying, Allied bomber formations could attack anywhere in Germany, and at any time of day.

Hitler's misguided optimism remained, however, and it would not be until the very last days of the war that the reality of the situation became clear to him.

German troops participating in the Ardennes offensive re-enact an attack on an American convoy for the benefit of a German news photographer.

The War in the West
The Allies were now preparing to cross the Rhine and enter Germany. However, the combination of bad weather, the formidable natural obstacle of the Rhine and the West Wall defensive line meant that the Allies had to plan carefully.

The plan for crossing the Rhine involved two phases. In Operation Veritable, the 21st Army Group would clear the approaches to the Rhine, and 30 Corps would advance to the Reichswald. Once complete, Operation Grenade would take effect, Lieutenant General William H. Simpson's

US Ninth Army pushing through Münchengladbach to link up with the rest of Montgomery's forces. Once the forces were consolidated, the 21st Army Group would cross the Rhine, with the aim of outflanking the Ruhr from the north. Montgomery would then drive on to the North German plain, placing his armour in a position to move on towards Berlin.

In the American sector, Bradley's Twelfth Army Group would conduct Operation Lumberjack, clearing the approaches to the Rhine between Cologne and Koblenz. Patton's Third Army would then head for Mainz and Mannheim, linking with American forces advancing from the Saarland as part of Operation Undertone by the 6th Army Group. These various operations would conclude with the seizure of bridgeheads over the Rhine.

Veritable and Grenade
Montgomery's plans for Veritable and Grenade were thorough – and they needed to be, since the defences were well-prepared. The enemy held the high ground, and waterlogged conditions in much of the region would compel the use of the roads through the Reichwald – an

1945

FEBRUARY	MARCH

23 February The Soviets capture Posen.

24 February Rokossovsky's 2nd Byelorussian Front launches a new offensive into Pomerania.

1 March Zhukov's forces join the Pomerania offensive.

3 March The German counterattack aiming to reopen the railway link between Berlin and Silesia fails.

5/6 March Operation Spring Awakening – German counter-attacks across the Drava and south of Lake Balaton against the 3rd Ukrainian Front – become bogged down.

13 March The 3rd Byelorussian Front begins attack to capture Köenigsberg.

16 March Kolberg falls to Zhukov.

23 March Patton crosses the Rhine at Oppenheim.

23/24 March Montgomery's forces cross the Rhine.

area densely forested and difficult to fight through. At 0500 on 8 February, Veritable began with a bombardment lasting two and a half hours. Yet when it stopped, the Germans returned fire. The British and Canadian artillery therefore resumed their barrage, for another three hours. Only then did the infantry moved forward.

The waterlogged ground made the advance slow, and it was the last week of February before the objectives were obtained. The Germans destroyed all the

A German soldier during the 'Battle of the Bulge'.

bridges over the Rhine, and opened the gates to the Ruhr dam. This delayed Operation Grenade until the waters had subsided, on 23 February. When the advance began, the Ninth Army faced little opposition. A link with Anglo-Canadian forces was made at Geldorn on 3 March, leaving the approaches to the Rhine from Nijmegen and Düsseldorf clear of German forces. Montgomery began planning the crossing of the Rhine, to occur on 23/24 March. The lack of bridges meant that an assault crossing would be required, and this would be very difficult if opposition was stiff.

In the American sector, Bradley's attack went far more smoothly. Cologne fell into American hands on 6 March 1945. The 9th Armoured Division moved down the Ahr river valley, covered by Combat Command B, which was instructed to close the Rhine at Remagen. When the lead elements of the Command reached Remagen, they found the

bridge across the Rhine still intact. Crossing it, they reached the east bank of the Rhine at 1600 on 7 March. Meanwhile, Patton secured the Rhine as far as Koblenz, and sent the 11th Infantry Regiment across the river by boat at Nietstein on 22 March in the face of negligible opposition.

American infantry from the 7th Infantry Regiment leave their assault boat after crossing the Rhine.

24/25 March American forces cross the Rhine.

25 March Rokossovsky reaches the Gulf of Danzig.

28 March Hitler sacks Guderian as Army Chief of Staff. The British Second Army attacks out of the bridgehead at Wesel.

29 March The German bridgehead over the Oder at Kuestrin is destroyed.

30 March Danzig falls to the Soviets.

31 March Knoev captures Ratibor, leaving him on the east bank of the Neisse, having overrun almost all of Silesia.

APRIL

1 April The Soviet High Command orders that the capture of Vienna is to be the top priority for the 2nd and 3rd Ukrainian Fronts.

5 April The US Seventh Army crosses the River Main.

6 April The Soviets reach the outskirts of Vienna. The final assault on Königsberg begins.

The British Cross the Rhine

Montgomery's plan to cross the Rhine, Operation Plunder, took place on the night of 23/24 March. It was preceded by a massive bombardment, combined with air attacks on German positions.

A dense smokescreen was put across the river, and at 1800 on 23 March, more than 5000 guns bombarded the opposite bank of the Rhine and beyond. Assault troops crossed the river and gained a foothold on the far bank. After a pre-arranged bomber attack on Wesel, they moved forward into the town. By dawn on 24 March, it was clear that the crossings had been a major success, five bridgeheads having been established.

The momentum of the attack was maintained by Operation Varsity, a huge airborne assault by the US 17th and British 6th Airborne Divisions. Air supremacy allowed a daylight drop. Unlike the drop at Arnhem that was part of Operation Market Garden, all the troops were to be landed in one lift, almost on top of their objectives and within range of friendly artillery. The landings began at 1000 on 24 March. Some landed in the wrong place, and the Germans managed to destroy more than 100 gliders and transport aircraft. Despite this, the paratroops took their objectives. By the end of the day, the 21st Army Group was established on the German side of the Rhine.

Supplies cross the Rhine on a pontoon bridge. The soldiers on the pontoons keep a look out.

British 'Ducks' ferry supplies across the Rhine. These amphibious cars were indispensable during the campaign.

Changing Plans

At this point, Eisenhower changed the focus of operations. The 12th Army Group was instructed to conduct operations around the Elbe and Mulde rivers, cutting the German

1945

APRIL

7 April The Battle for Vienna begins.

9 April The Allied spring offensive opens.

10 April Königsberg falls to the Soviets. The landing at Menate on Lake Comacchio.

11 April American troops reach the River Elbe. A bridgehead is established over the River Santerno.

12 April –President Roosevelt dies and is replaced by Vice-President Harry S. Truman. Zhukov begins small-scale probing operations from the Kuestrin bridgehead.

13 April The Soviets complete the taking of Vienna.

14 April The US Fifth Army launches attacks, having been delayed for two days by poor weather.

Army in two and then linking with the Red Army. The 21st Army Group was to drive towards the Baltic coast, clearing Holland, seizing the north German ports and cutting off Denmark from Germany. Meanwhile, the US Sixth Army was to drive into Austria and defeat German forces remaining there.

The British Second Army broke out of its bridgehead on 28 March, crossed the Weser River, gaining 322km (200 miles) over the next three weeks. By 18 April, 1 Corps had reached the Zuider Zee; 12 Corps was well on the way to Hamburg; 30 Corps had reached Bremen; and 8 Corps had taken Lüneburg and was closing in on the Elbe. The 12th Army Group encircled the Ruhr, while the US Ninth and First Armies met at Lippstadt on 1 April. The Americans reached Essen by 12 April, and it was clear that German resistance was faltering. Organized resistance in the West soon collapsed in the American sector, and was extremely limited in the British sector as the 21st Army Group drove through the Netherlands and on towards the Baltic coast. Attention now turned to the east, where the Soviets had closed in on Berlin.

The Russian Advance to Berlin

In March 1945, Hitler gave orders for the defence of the capital, but his confidence that Germany would ultimately triumph despite all setbacks meant that plans to turn Berlin into a fortress had not been implemented. German units were also short of ammunition, and a shortage of fuel meant that tanks were immobile, supplies could not be transported, and what was left of the *Luftwaffe* was grounded. The Berlin garrison had a strength of one million, but many of the troops were boys beneath military age or men who had been too old or unfit to serve with the army before. Lacking in experience, they had only their determination to defend their capital against the Soviets.

Hitler moved to a fortified bunker underneath the Chancellory building. Becoming ever further detached from reality, he produced grand plans for defeating the Soviets. Cheered by the news on 12 April that Roosevelt had died, he suggested that this would allow him to negotiate an armistice.

He seemed oblivious to the fact that the

Soviet armies were about to attack, having been building up their strength since February. Nor would negotiations with the Western powers prevent the attack. More than 2.5 million men, 45,000 guns and rocket launchers, and 6000 tanks and armoured fighting vehicles were in place by the second week in April. On 16 April, the attack against Berlin began.

Boy soldiers from the Volksturm, the German home guard enjoying their lunch.

15 April The British liberate the concentration camp at Bergen-Belsen.

16 April The Soviet advance on Berlin begins. Zhukov's forces are stopped at Seelow Heights, while Konev's forces end the day on the verge of breaking through the Fourth Panzer Army.

17 April Seelow Heights fall to Zhukov. Konev breaks though the Fourth Panzer Army.

18 April Rokossovsky's 2nd Byelorussian Front attacks north of Berlin, preventing the Third Panzer Army from deploying to aid the defence of the capital.

21 April The Second Guards Tank Army crosses the autobahn to the northeast of Berlin and begins to shell the city centre. Bologna falls.

24 April Hitler strips Goering of his office and orders him to be placed under arrest.

25 April Berlin is encircled as Zhukov and Konev make contact with each other east of Ketzin. Fighting in suburbs of Berlin begins. American and Soviet troops meet at Torgau on the Elbe.

26 April The Soviets approach Berlin city centre.

The Soviet plan was brutally simple: to launch a number of attacks along a wide front, thereby encircling the German forces. Zhukov's 1st Byelorussian Front was to attack Berlin directly, while Koniev's 1st Ukranian Front crossed the Neisse to attack southwest of the enemy capital. Rokossovsky's 2nd Byelorussian Front was to attack around Stettin, to ensure that Third Panzer Army could not be used to reinforce Berlin.

Russian tanks move through Berlin, April 1945. Armour proved extremely useful in the bitter street fighting.

Zhukov attacked at 0300 on 16 April, aiming to take the Seelow Heights. More than one million shells fell on the German positions, and the bombardment was accompanied by a heavy bombing raid. Despite this, the Germans fought hard, and Zhukov did not break through that day. Koniev enjoyed some success, and the pattern was repeated the next day. To encourage Zhukov, Stalin told him that he that he might allow the 1st Ukranian Front to seize Berlin if the Seelow Heights could not be captured.

Zhukov could not bear the thought of being denied the final victory. Energizing his subordinates through a mixture of flattery, fear, cajoling and coercion, he broke through on

Refugees displaced from their homes by the fighting in Berlin pass through the Brandenburg Gate.

1945

APRIL

27 April The Americans reach Genoa.

28 April Mussolini is executed by Italian partisans. Hitler discovers that Himmler has opened armistice negotiations with the Allies and dismisses him.

29 April The Battle for the Reichstag begins. The Germans sign an unconditional surrender.

30 April Hitler commits suicide. The Reichstag falls to the Soviets.

MAY

1 May Goebbels commits suicide.

2 May The Berlin garrison surrenders. The 21st Army Group secures the base of the Schleswig-Holstein peninsula. The armistice comes into effect, ending the war in Italy.

3 May A German delegation arrives at Montgomery's headquarters at Lüneberg Heath to offer the surrender of forces trapped between the 21st Army Group and the 2nd Byelorussian Front. Montgomery demands the surrender of all German forces in northwest Germany.

19 April. On 21 April, the Third and Fifth Shock Armies entered the Berlin suburbs of Berlin, advancing towards the city centre. Koniev's troops reached the Tetlow canal by the end of 22 April, and began to push on towards Zhukov's forces. The 1st Ukrainian and 1st Byelorussian Fronts met on the River Havel on 24 April, encircling Berlin. The Battle for Berlin was now fought street by street, the Soviet tanks and artillery blasting through German positions.

By 27 April, the Germans were left in a small corridor about 16km (10 miles) long and no more than 4.8km (3 miles) wide. The defensive perimeter broke the next day, and the last pockets of resistance were reduced to fighting isolated but vicious skirmishes with the Soviets. On 30 April Hitler shot himself. The Reichstag fell on the same day. Finally, on 2 May, the Berlin garrison surrendered.

Meanwhile, fighting around the city continued. On the Western Front, Bremen was taken on 27 April, while Lübeck and Hamburg fell on 2 May. The 12th Army Group captured Hale and Leipzig on 19 April, and Dessau three days later. Finally, on 24 April, the US First Army reached its stop line on the River Mulde.

The Soviet forces not engaged in Berlin had driven on towards their advancing allies in the West, and on 25 April they linked up with American forces on the Elbe.

The US Third Army crossed the Danube on the same day, took Regensburg and headed into Austria, where Linz fell on 5 May. The US Seventh Army had taken Nuremberg on 20 April, and then had crossed the Danube along with the First French Army. By 4 May, almost all German resistance had ceased. At Montgomery's headquarters on Lüneburg Heath, the Germans surrendered all their forces in Holland, Denmark and North Germany; the next day, emissaries arrived at Eisenhower's headquarters and after some attempts to delay the process, signed on 7 May at 0240. The Soviets demanded a proper ceremony in Berlin at which they were present, and this met in the Soviet sector of the city. The final act of surrender thus came early in the morning of 8 May. The war in Europe was over.

A Russian soldier raises the Soviet flag over the Reichstag, one of the final acts in the Battle of Berlin, as the war in Europe draws to a close.

4 May Montgomery accepts the surrender of all German forces in northwest Germany, Denmark and Holland.

5 May Hostilities in northwest Germany cease. Eisenhower rejects the German proposal for a separate armistice between Germany and the Western allies.

6 May General Jodl arrives at Eisenhower's headquarters to conduct surrender negotiations.

7 May The Germans sign an unconditional surrender at Reims. The Soviets demand a second surrender ceremony in Berlin.

8 May The surrender ceremony in Berlin. VE Day is declared.

9 May Fighting continues in Czechoslovakia, Croatia and Austria.

11 May Army Group Centre surrenders to the Soviets in Czechoslovakia.

14 May The remaining German forces in Yugoslavia surrender.

PART 2:
The Pacific Theatre 1939–1945

Left: A cruiser of the Imperial Japanese Navy under air attack in Kure Harbour, Honshu, Japan.
Right: Japanese Kamikaze pilots are briefed the night before a sortie.

Japanese Expansion

The origins of the war in the Pacific lay in the volatile situation in Asia by 1918. A combination of national ambition, revolutions and American isolationism from Asian affairs created a situation that led inexorably to conflict. The Pacific became a battleground for Japan and the United States.

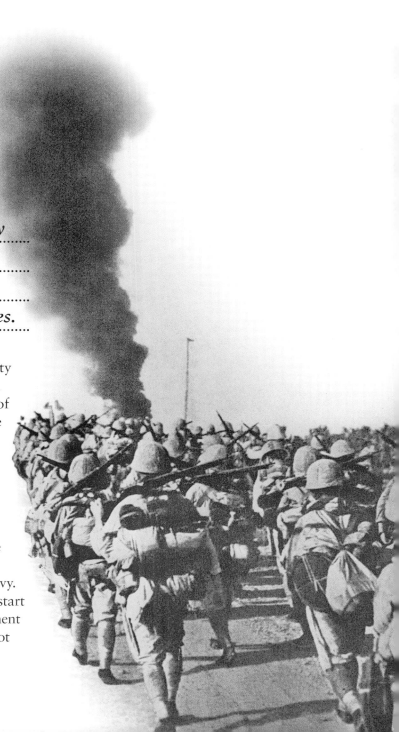

The Japanese had hoped that their support for the Allied powers during the war would bring them territorial gains as Germany was stripped of her colonies. However, their contribution had been relatively small, so the possibility of a reward proved controversial. Japan clearly had ambitions to become a major world power and to dominate China – a threat to the United States, which had adopted an 'open-door approach' to China as a means for

increasing trade. Nonetheless, the peace treaty gave Japanese control of the former German trading concessions in Shantung in the face of Chinese protests and American disquiet. The Americans now feared that the Japanese presented a long-term threat to US interests in the Pacific.

In an effort to control the Japanese, they were invited to the Washington Naval Conference of 1921–22. This defined the size of the navies of the Allied powers, limiting the size of certain vessels and the overall numbers of different types of ship possessed by each navy. The Americans hoped this would prevent the start of a naval race with the Japanese – an assessment that would prove optimistic, but which was not unreasonable at the time.

Left: A firefighting tug tackles the blazing USS West Virginia, *hit by six Japanese torpedoes and several bombs during the Pearl Harbor attack.*
Right: Japanese troops advance on Manila 1941.

Chiang Kai-Shek, defeated by Mao Zedong's Red Army, arrives in Taipei at his new headquarters.

The domestic situation in Japan, however, began to deteriorate. The feudal system appeared increasingly outmoded, and universal suffrage was introduced in 1924. This move towards representative democracy was welcomed abroad, but it created fearful problems. Moving rapidly to democratic government from a traditional system of governance, which was underpinned by centuries of tradition and had a firmly rooted political culture, caused considerable instability. The old way of conducting political business proved incompatible with democratic ideals. Corruption proved to be a major problem, and a host of political scandals tainted the promise of reform.

Many Japanese now turned to extreme parties, which offered either a return to the days of the Shogun or a new world based on socialist principles. The right-wing, traditionally oriented parties believed that Japan's destiny lay in controlling China, a step that would increase Japan's position in the world – and also secure economic benefits to address current problems. Population growth had pushed Japan's economy to the brink of crisis, with rising unemployment

and poverty the result. Looking for a solution, nationalists turned their eyes to Manchuria, an area rich in natural resources. The region was already heavily influenced by Japan, having been divided between Russian and Japanese control after the 1904–05 Russo–Japanese War. The Nationalists now concluded that by expanding her influence and exploiting resources further, Japan would enhance her international position and end her economic difficulties. And they were in a unique position to achieve this. Many were junior and middle-ranking army officers, and they began to immerse themselves in politics, believing that military power was the way to realize their vision of a great Japan.

Crises in Manchuria

The Japanese were fully aware that any attempt to impose direct control on Manchuria would be an affront to the Western powers, and they now adopted a cautious approach – initially, at least. Much of Manchuria was dominated by a Chinese warlord, Marshal Chang. Since 1927, central government, always patchy, had broken down entirely following the outbreak of civil

1937

JULY

7 July The Sino–Japanese war begins.

26 July Japanese troops move into northern China.

NOVEMBER

9 November The Japanese capture Shanghai.

DECEMBER

12 December The Japanese attack British and American shipping.

14 December The Japanese capture Nanking.

war between the Chinese Nationalists led by Chiang Kai-Shek and the Communists of Mao Zedong. Elements of the Japanese Kwantung Army, which garrisoned southern Manchuria, set out to eliminate Chang. On 4 June 1928, Chang was killed when his train was mined. The mine was planted on the orders of two Nationalist officers, Colonels Kanji Ishihari and Seishiro Itagaki – the first notable occasion when elements of the Army chose to enact their own policy rather than that of the Government. The politicization of the Army now grew as a number of secret, nationalist societies were established, all aiming to further the cause of Japanese nationalism.

In the three years after the death of Marshal Chang, Manchuria came under increased Japanese influence. Then, in September 1931, Japanese troops from the Kwantung Army laid an explosive charge on the railway line near a Chinese army barracks at the town of Mukden. Blaming Chinese 'terrorists' for the act, they now seized Mukden, on the pretext of

Japanese infantry move into the hills of northern Manchuria, during the invasion of 1932.

1940

JULY

27 July The Japanese proclaim the creation of the Greater East Asia Co-Prosperity Sphere.

AUGUST

29 August The Vichy French Government permits the Japanese to station troops in Indo-China.

SEPTEMBER

27 September Japan signs the Tripartite Pact with Germany and Italy.

1941

JANUARY

16 January Clashes occur between French and Thai forces over disputed border areas.

31 January The Japanese impose a ceasefire on French and Thai forces.

re-establishing law and order. The Government in Japan was outraged at this unilateral act, but could do nothing. Senior army officers supported the action, and attempts by the Government to quell the fighting and bring the Kwantung Army to heel failed. Moreover, Japanese officers now began to regard civilian government as an obstacle to their political aims.

The 'threat' presented by the Government was clarified by the arrest of several members of the Cherry Society, a secret society that had been plotting a coup against the Government. A general lack of public confidence in the Government meant that there was much public sympathy for their cause, and the plotters received only nominal sentences after their convictions. This emboldened the secret societies, and over the course of the next year a number of prominent politicians and public figures considered obstacles to nationalism were murdered. Then, on 15 May 1932, nine army officers went to the residence of Prime Minister Tsuyoshi Inukai to confront him. Inukai naively

A Japanese reconnaissance aircraft circles above an advancing column during the war in Manchuria.

1941			
MARCH	APRIL	MAY	JUNE
8 March The Lend-Lease Act is signed.	**13 April** Japanese–Soviet non-aggression treaty.	**11 May** The Japanese make proposals to the United States to improve relations between the two nations. Negotiations begin.	**29 June** The Germans demand the Japanese attack the Soviets; the Japanese decline.

offered his guests cigarettes, and invited them in for a chat. At this point, the leader of the group shouted, 'No use talking!' Drawing his pistol, he shot the prime minister, and his eight accomplices followed suit. To their disappointment, their other target, the actor/comedian Charlie Chaplain (a symbol of American decadence), was not having tea with the prime minister that day. The nine men were tried for murder, and received only derisory sentences, which they never served. Militant, militarist nationalism was now in the ascendant.

The League of Nations finally protested about Japan's behaviour in Manchuria. The Japanese response was to walk out of the organization on 27 March 1933. There was nothing the League could do, and the member states were forced to sit and watch as the Japanese created Manchukuo, a puppet state in the occupied territory. From this point, Japanese foreign policy became a cause of international concern. In April 1934, the Japanese Government issued a statement that Japan alone was responsible for the conduct of international relations and military security in the Far East, staking out its sphere of influence in much the

The cover of Time magazine, 28 December 1931, shows the newly elected Japanese premier Inukai.

same way as the United States had done with the Monroe Doctrine in 1823. This was followed at the end of the year with the announcement by the Tokyo Government that it intended to abrogate its observance of the Washington Treaty in 1936, and to build as many ships of whatever size it chose.

Despite these decidedly nationalistic actions, the Japanese Government was still mistrusted by militant army officers. On 26 February 1935, a large faction of army officers attempted a coup. A number of prominent politicians were murdered, and the Government was forced to call on the Navy to suppress the uprising. To their surprise, the coup leaders did not enjoy the same lenient treatment that their predecessors had experienced, but were tried in secret and then executed by firing squad. Firm action indeed, but actually it concealed the weakness of the Government. It was clear that many naval officers shared sympathies with their brother officers in the army, and also that the only way of preventing further coup attempts was to rely on the Army to keep its officers under control. This could be achieved only by appeasing the younger, nationalist

JULY

18 July Japanese foreign minister Matsuoka is sacked.

23 July The Vichy French Government agrees to Japanese demands to station troops in southern Indo-China.

26 July All Japanese assets in America are frozen in response to a Japanese move into southern Indo-China.

officers, which meant that military influence over the Government increased.

The Drift to War

Having alienated the Western democracies with its actions in China, the Japanese sought new allies. On 25 November 1936, the Anti-Comintern Pact was signed between Japan and Germany. Its explicit aim was to protect the aspirations of both nations from the threat of Communism, whether from the USSR or Mao Zedong's Communist guerrillas fighting the Chinese Government.

Tension between the Chinese and the Japanese increased, and on 7 July 1937 came a clash between Chinese soldiers and members of the Kwantung Army at the Marco Polo bridge in Peking. The Army now ignored efforts by less hawkish members of the Japanese Government to impose a ceasefire.

Japanese artillery shells the gateway and walls of Nanking during the Sino–Japanese War, while infantrymen with fixed bayonets await the order to storm the city.

Soldiers crossed from Manchukuo into northern China, a step that began the Sino–Japanese War. The first major clash came on 25 July, and the Japanese embarked upon a run of successes. Shanghai fell under their control on 9 November 1937, and just over a month later Nanking followed. There the Japanese troops embarked upon an orgy of looting, murder and rape over the next six weeks – provoking international outrage. To make matters worse, the Japanese attacked British and American shipping near Nanking. The Americans proposed a naval blockade, but the British feared that this might lead to war. While the two powers debated their response, the Japanese decided to apologize, fearful that a blockade would cut off their vital supplies of raw materials. This closed the matter, but both Britain and the United States began to make contingency plans for dealing with a possible future conflict with Japan.

1941

SEPTEMBER

6 September The Japanese Government decides that it needs to be fully prepared for war with the US by the end of October.

10 September The Japanese begin a planning exercise to determine strategy in the event of a war with the US.

NOVEMBER

3 November The US ambassador to Tokyo warns Washington that the Japanese may be about to start a war, either against the US or the USSR.

20 November Attack orders for a raid on Pearl Harbor are issued to the Japanese fleet.

By 1939, the Japanese had increased their gains in China, but suffered their first setback when they clashed with the Soviets in the Nomonhan area of the border between Outer Mongolia and Manchukuo. Fighting began in May, and ended after the General Georgi Zhukov launched a major offensive on 20 August 1939. The defeat persuaded the Japanese to turn their attention back to the war with the Chinese, rather than to press their ambitions towards Outer Mongolia.

This setback was only temporary, however.

The year 1940 brought the collapse of France, a major colonial power in Southeast Asia, and of the Netherlands, the imperial rulers of the East Indies. Meanwhile, the other major colonial power – Britain – was hard-pressed in Europe, unprepared for war in the Far East and unlikely to be able to reinforce the theatre for the foreseeable future.

The Co-Prosperity Sphere

The Japanese Army began to agitate for action. The cautious attitude of the Government incensed the officers, and on 16 July 1940, Admiral Yonai's moderate administration was usurped and replaced by a more aggressively minded one led by Prince Konoye. The nationalist fervour was articulated most clearly on 27 July, when the Konoye government declared the Greater East Asia Co-Prosperity Sphere. This was intended to reduce Japan's reliance upon resources imported from the Western powers. Instead, these would be obtained from the Dutch East Indies, Malaya,

Japanese howitzers prepare to open fire on Chinese defences during the Sino–Japanese War.

24 November US garrisons overseas warned that the risk of hostilities with Japan is high.

26 November The US Government demands that Japan withdraws all forces from China. The Japanese fleet sets sail.

27 November A further warning is issued to US forces that war with Japan appears likely, as Japanese reject the US demand for withdrawal from China.

30 November The Japanese Government commits to an attack on Pearl Harbor.

Siam, Burma and the Philippines – by the simple expedient of placing the territories under Japanese control. It was clear that such an approach ran the risk of war against Britain and, possibly, the United States, prompting the Japanese to begin plans for war.

One of the first moves was to pressurize the French colonial authorities in Indo-China to allow the stationing of Japanese troops in the north of the country. The French were too weak to refuse, and troops began moving in at the end of August 1940. A month later, the Tripartite Pact was signed between Japan, Germany and Italy, with the aim of deterring the US from intervening to prevent Japanese moves against territory in east and southeast Asia. The move backfired, however, hardening the attitudes of the Western powers, particularly the United States. By mid-1941, Prince Konoye was so concerned by the deterioration of relations that he sacked his hawkish foreign minister, Matsuoka, replacing him with a moderate. This might have assuaged American concerns had not Japan demanded that France allow troops to occupy southern Indo-China, effectively placing the whole area under Japanese rule.

Germany, Italy and Japan sign the Tripartite Pact in Berlin, 27 September 1940.

1941

DECEMBER

1 December The Japanese fix the date for attack: 7 December.

4 December Japan begins to evacuate its Washington embassy.

6 December Roosevelt issues an appeal for peace to Emperor Hirohito. British reconnaissance aircraft locate Japanese transports off Cape Cambodia.

7 December Japanese naval aircraft strike Pearl Harbor.

The USS Arizona *sinks beneath the waves.*

In response, Britain, America and the exiled Dutch Government imposed sanctions. This step cut off three-quarters of Japanese trade and more than 90 per cent of its oil supplies. There were now only two options available to Japan: to compromise so that the sanctions would be lifted, or to go to war before resources ran out. The first option was too humiliating to contemplate, the second required the seizure of the Dutch East Indies to alleviate oil shortages.

Konoye was painfully aware that the military was now in favour of war rather than seeking compromise. Nonetheless, he sought to negotiate in the hope that an agreement that was acceptable to both nations could be reached. However, he became an increasingly isolated figure, barely tolerated by his own military and unable to make headway with the Americans. He resigned on 16 October 1941, and was replaced by the nationalist war minister, General Hideki Tojo. The option of compromising disappeared.

A fuel storage tank on Ford Island, Pearl Harbor, explodes after being hit by a Japanese bomb.

Attacking the United States

It was clear to the Japanese that the major threat to their ambitions was presented by the US fleet. This prompted the decision that the first step of the war would be an attack by Japanese navy aircraft on the Pacific anchorage at Pearl Harbor. The Japanese had invested heavily in carrier aviation

8 December The Japanese bomb Singapore. Japanese forces land in Malaya and Siam.

9 December Tarawa and Makin in the Gilbert Islands are invaded by Japan.

10 December The British warships HMS *Repulse* and *Prince of Wales* are sunk in a Japanese air attack. The first Japanese troops land in the Philippines.

12 December British troops in Malaya are forced to withdraw to Alor Star.

The USS Arizona *blows up as her forward magazine explodes after being hit by a Japanese bomb.*

during the interwar era, and the success of the Royal Navy's air attack on the Italian fleet at Taranto in 1940 suggested that a similar assault at Pearl Harbor might work. If it did, it would instantly remove the Americans' ability to respond to Japanese action in the Pacific.

The plan, drawn up by Admiral Yamamoto, involved the use of six aircraft carriers with 400

aircraft. On 26 November 1941, after training was completed, the carrier force set sail from its anchorage in the Kurile Islands. Meanwhile, Japanese submarines made their way towards Hawaii, with the aim of providing intelligence and attacking targets of opportunity at Pearl Harbor.

As the Japanese approached the point for launching their aircraft, the submarines

reconnoitred the area around Pearl Harbor. Their reports and those from Japanese spies in Hawaii brought news that there were no US aircraft carriers at Pearl Harbor (they were on exercise at sea). There were, though, more than 80 ships at anchor, providing a tempting target. Just after 0600 on 7 December 1941, the first wave of Japanese aircraft left the decks of the carriers.

At about 0755, the first aircraft arrived at Pearl Harbor, splitting into separate formations. Some of the attack force targeted nearby airfields to prevent American fighters from taking off to intercept, while others began their bombing and torpedo runs against the American ships.

The airfield attacks were an outstanding success. About 200 American aircraft were destroyed, and another 160 damaged. A few surviving aircraft were able to take off, but there was little they could do to change the outcome.

The attack aircraft found an array of targets situated below them. At the centre of the anchorage sat Ford Island, off which was

1941

DECEMBER

16 December The Japanese invade Borneo. Penang is evacuated.

14 December Siam allies itself with Japan.

13 December The British governor of Hong Kong rejects a Japanese ultimatum demanding surrender.

15 December Japanese troops enter Burmese territory.

'Battleship Row'. High-level bombers attacked first, followed by strikes by torpedo aircraft approaching from the opposite direction at low level. With the anchorage so full, it was not difficult for the Japanese airmen to score hits on the ships.

Within 10 minutes of the start of the attack, the USS *Arizona* was struck by a bomb that penetrated her forward magazine. The ship was blown apart. USS *West Virginia*, next to *Arizona*, took six torpedo hits and sank to the bottom, while *California* was hit by torpedoes and began to flood. The captain of the USS *Nevada* got under way to attempt escape, but had made little progress before the second wave of aircraft attacked. The *California* was hit again and sank, while the *Nevada* was beached, to prevent it from sinking in the middle of the channel and blocking it.

The commander of the Japanese carrier force, Admiral Nagumo, decided against launching the planned third wave of aircraft, since American defences were on full alert by this point. The last Japanese aircraft was recovered aboard the carriers by midday. Nagumo then began a high-speed withdrawal.

The Consequences

The attack on Pearl Harbor was devastating – but not decisive. The failure to sink any of the American aircraft carriers meant that the US Navy, although weakened, remained in a position to make a strong response. The Japanese also missed the chance to prevent enemy naval operations in the months to come by failing to target the shore facilities; had they done so, American operations in the Pacific would have been badly hindered.

The attack was a gamble. If it had succeeded in destroying the aircraft carriers and the shore facilities at Pearl Harbor, the United States would have been unable to fight back for a considerable amount of time, even allowing for the nation's prodigious industrial capacity. Indeed, American warships would go on to be produced in timescales that would have been regarded as almost impossibly short before the war.

As it was, the gamble failed. The Americans were roused to anger, articulated by President Roosevelt's description of 7 December as a 'day of infamy'. As Yamamoto feared, Japan had aroused a sleeping giant. Yet this would not be apparent for some time to come. Pearl Harbor

President Roosevelt signs the congressional declaration of war against Japan, 22 December 1941.

17 December British and Commonwealth forces withdraw to the River Perak.

18 December The Japanese land on Hong Kong island.

20 December Japanese forces land on Mindanao Island.

22 December Launch of a full-scale invasion of the Philippines by Japanese forces.

was followed by a run of Japanese success that presented the Western allies with a major crisis in the Pacific Theatre.

Crisis in the Pacific

Even as Admiral Nagumo's aircraft were returning to the carriers following the raid on Pearl Harbor, other Japanese units were on the move. An attack on Luzon was the opening move in the conquest of the Philippines; troops were moving from their positions in China towards Hong Kong; and Japanese ships were ferrying an army towards Siam and Malaya, to land on the Siamese coast for the drive into Malaya.

Everywhere the Japanese attacked, they enjoyed success. A mixture of contempt for a supposedly backward and inferior military power meant that the British, American and Dutch forces had not been equipped to the required standard. Moreover, the notion that the Japanese would prove skilled jungle fighters had simply not been considered. The results were

Japanese troops rush Kuala Lumpur railway station during the invasion of Malaya.

disastrous for the Allies. Within eight months, the Japanese had driven the British from Malaya, Singapore and Burma; the Americans had been ejected from the Philippines and their Pacific territories;

and the Dutch had been utterly defeated in the Dutch East Indies. India and Australia now seemed to be at risk.

By June 1942, it seemed impossible that the Japanese could be prevented from becoming the dominant power in the Pacific. The Japanese advance also included many small islands and atolls, which were significant only for their position in the Pacific Ocean. From these, the Japanese could operate

1941

DECEMBER

23 December The Japanese capture Wake Island.

24 December General MacArthur begins the withdrawal of forces to Bataan.

25 December Hong Kong falls to the Japanese.

ships and aircraft to maintain their power. By the middle of 1942, the Allies seemed in crisis, unable to offer a response.

Malaya and Singapore

Burma and Malaya were the main objectives for Japan's planners at the end of 1941. Capturing Malaya would give the Japanese control of 38 per cent of the world's rubber production and nearly 60 per cent of tin output.

The Japanese invasion convoy had set sail before the raid on Pearl Harbor, and was sighted by a British reconnaissance aircraft on 6 December 1941. Bad weather prevented any further investigation by the British, and the invasion fleet continued unmolested, landing its troops in Thailand and on the northeast coast of Malaya shortly after 0100 on 8 December. The Japanese encountered heavy resistance, many of their troops drowning as they scrambled to the beach. Nonetheless, they took the British positions and then established a foothold.

After the Japanese 5th Division took Singoran (Songkhla), an airfield became available. The Japanese now set about gaining air superiority against the poorly equipped and under-strength Royal Air Force squadrons protecting Malaya. The RAF had estimated that it required more than 500 aircraft to successfully defend Malaya and Singapore against Japanese attack, and its strength was well below this. Worse still, Japanese capabilities had been underestimated, meaning that RAF Malaya had been provided with aircraft that were obsolescent. The most extreme example was the Vickers Vildebeest biplane, which had been obsolete for years but was now being used as a torpedo bomber, providing the

Victorious Japanese troops enter Moulmein after heavy fighting with the 17th Indian Division during the Japanese invasion of Burma.

26 December The Japanese cross the River Perak. Manila is declared an open city.

28 December General Sir Archibald Wavell is appointed to command the defence of Burma.

31 December Admiral Chester Nimitz is appointed as commander of the US Asiatic Fleet.

Japanese troops enter Mandalay following the withdrawal of the defenders during the invasion of Burma.

RAF's only anti-shipping capability. The Royal Australian Air Force provided a few Lockheed Hudson patrol aircraft, while the American Brewster F2A Buffalo was the RAF's main fighter in the region, and no match for the Japanese fighters. Squadrons of the superior Hawker Hurricane and the American-built P-40 were despatched to the Far East, but even these were hard-pressed to match the best Japanese fighters. The Hurricane units had only just arrived when the Japanese attack began, while the P-40s would eventually be diverted elsewhere. A further difficulty facing the air force was that Churchill's promise to send aircraft to the USSR prevented more Hurricanes from being sent to boost the defences on the Malayan peninsula.

With air superiority established, the Japanese advance continued swiftly. The 5th Division began a drive from Signora across to the west coast of Malaya, and then turned south. By midday on 11 December, they were breaking through towards the town of Jitra, the main base in Kedah province. They reached the outskirts of Jitra in darkness, and spent the night trying to break through, without success.

1942

JANUARY

2 January British and Commonwealth forces in Malaya withdraw to the River Slim. Japanese forces enter Manila.

3 January South West Pacific Command is established by the Allies.

5 January American forces complete the withdrawal to Bataan.

7 January In Malaya, the Japanese cross the River Slim. Sarawak is occupied.

Japanese troops of the Fifteenth Army cross the Chindwin River on a pontoon ferry.

the main element of the Navy's Force Z, were sent to intercept the shipping supporting the Japanese landings on the Siamese and Malayan coasts. They did so without any air cover – despite the fact that Admiral Tom Phillips, the commander of Force Z, had warned his friend Air Marshal Sir Arthur Harris never to leave without 'the air umbrella', or tragedy would ensue. On 10 December, Harris' prophecy came true. The *Prince of Wales* and *Repulse* were both sunk by Japanese bombers, a bitter blow for the British.

By 15 December, the Japanese had reached Gurun, and Penang Island was evacuated the next day. The British army commander General Sir Arthur Percival made attempts to establish a new defence line behind the River Perak, but to no avail. British morale declined as the Japanese pressed forward, until by early January 1942, Percival realized that the situation was untenable. General Sir Archibald Wavell, the recently arrived Commander-in-Chief, India, was astonished to discover that no one had drawn up plans for defending the island from attack or for the withdrawal of forces from Malaya to Singapore. Churchill's vision of a

However, when day broke, they realized that the British were positioned in front of the town, and thus vulnerable to a flanking attack. The position was hopeless, and the British withdrew, heading for Alor Star.

The loss of Jita, leaving the west coast of Malaya open for a swift Japanese advance towards Singapore, was not the only disaster to befall the British. On 8 December, the Royal Navy battleships *Prince of Wales* and *Repulse*,

11 January The Japanese make landings in the Celebes. Kuala Lumpur is occupied.

12 January Japan declares war on the Dutch East Indies.

15 January The Japanese invade Burma.

19 January The Japanese capture British North Borneo.

22 January The first reinforcements reach Singapore. American troops pull back to final defence lines in the Bataan peninsula.

'fortress Singapore' serving as a last, near-invincible redoubt against an attacker proved to be an illusion. The situation in Malaya became so bad that by 31 January Percival had ordered British forces to withdraw to Singapore.

The Japanese found it a relatively simple task to cross the Straits of Johore on to the island on the night of 7/8 February, and the British were swiftly pushed back. By 13 February, some 80,000 men were trapped around the city, while Percival contemplated surrender. Two days later, he hoisted a white flag – one of the greatest humiliations in British military history.

The Fall of Burma

With Malaya under their control, the Japanese turned their attentions to taking Burma, which was rich in oil. The difficult terrain of the country would also serve as a useful defence against any attempt to attack the Co-Prosperity Sphere from India. The Japanese Fifteenth Army landed in Siam, and headed for Bangkok, reaching it on 8 December. This gave the Japanese effective control of Siam, and access to airfields from which Burma could be attacked. Having control of Siamese railways also offered

Japanese troops parade near Battery Road, Singapore, following their capture of the British colony.

considerable logistics benefits for the invasion of neighbouring Burma, making the transportation of supplies a relatively simple task.

Japanese aircraft attacked Rangoon on 23 and 25 December 1941, and on 15 January 1942 the first Japanese land operations against Burma commenced when units advanced up the Kra Isthmus. Victoria Point and its airfield were occupied the next day, while Tavoy, some 400km (250 miles) to the north, had been taken by the 19th. Within a week of fighting, the Japanese had secured three Burmese airfields,

1942

JANUARY

23 January The Japanese land at Rabaul, Kavient, Bougainville and Kendari.

24 January Landings by Japanese forces in Dutch Borneo.

25 January Siam declares war on Britain and the United States. The Japanese land in New Guinea.

30 January The Japanese capture Ambonia. Moulmein falls.

31 January The British complete an evacuation of forces from Malaya to Singapore.

giving them the ability to bomb Rangoon. It was a stunning success, and one achieved from a subsidiary operation only.

The main Japanese attack was in the north, where the Fifteenth Army invaded Burma from Raheng in Siam. The attack faced light resistance at first, the British finding themselves in a weak position. The Commander-in-Chief, Burma, Lieutenant-General Thomas Hutton had only recently arrived in Burma, and did not yet know his subordinates. The commander of British forces in the field was Acting Major General Sir John Smyth. Famed for his courage, having won the Victoria Cross in World War I, he was well-regarded by his contemporaries. By 1942, though, he was in poor health, which may have adversely affected his ability to command. Worse still, none of his troops was trained in the art of jungle-fighting, and many of the best leaders had been transferred to units in North Africa.

Smyth's assessment of the problem facing his troops was sound, and he asked Hutton for permission to defend behind the Sittang River, a formidable natural obstacle. Permission, however, was denied, forcing him to concentrate his forces to face the Japanese assault. He met with little success. Finally, on 19 February, Hutton granted permission for Smyth to pull back behind the Sittang – which meant that the British had spent a month taking casualties, only to pull back to the very spot Smyth had chosen at the outset. Then, on 21 February, he was forced to fall back across the Sittang Bridge. One brigade managed to cross, but by the early morning of 23 February, the Japanese were on the verge of capturing the bridge. Smyth gave orders that it be destroyed to prevent the Japanese from crossing it, giving them a straight run on Rangoon. Two British brigades had not yet crossed the bridge, and the men were forced to swim across, leaving behind the most seriously wounded of their colleagues – and most of their arms and equipment. The position of the British was now even weaker than before.

The Fall of Rangoon

By this stage, the situation in Rangoon was appalling. Many key workers had fled their posts under the bombing, many policemen had deserted, and the ethnic tensions between the native Burmese and Indians spilled into

Japanese naval parachutists land in the Dutch East Indies, presaging the arrival of larger forces.

FEBRUARY

8 February The Japanese land on the west coast of Singapore.

11 February The Japanese cross the River Salween.

14 February Japanese airborne landing at Palembang, Sumatra.

15 February The surrender of British and Commonwealth forces at Singapore.

violence. Non-native inhabitants began to be evacuated, while command changes were imposed. Smyth was too ill to remain in command and was relieved, while Hutton was replaced by Lieutenant-General Harold Alexander. Alexander quickly realized that there was no hope of holding Rangoon, and that it was necessary to withdraw to the Irrawaddy Valley. Three days later, the Japanese entered Rangoon.

Alexander reorganized his forces, placing Lieutenant General Bill Slim in charge of 1 Burma Corps (known as 'Burcorps'). Slim now controlled all the troops in Burma, leaving Alexander to oversee cooperation with the Chinese. Burcorps was tasked to attack the Japanese at Paungde and Prome in the Irrawaddy valley, to relieve the Chinese forces under Brigadier-General 'Vinegar' Joe Stilwell. The attacks proved unsuccessful: the Chinese forces holding Toungoo abandoned it on 30 March, and Burcorps was left exposed. Slim began a withdrawal to the Yenangyaung oil fields. When it was clear that the Japanese were in a position to attack Burcorps, he gave orders on 15 April that his troops were to withdraw,

Japanese troops advance during the invasion of the Dutch East Indies in December 1941.

destroying the oil fields as they went, denying them to the Japanese. On 29 April, the Japanese advance reached Lashio, cutting the Burma Road. The following day, Burcorps withdrew across the Irrawaddy. Over the next three weeks, Burcorps retreated towards India, reaching the frontier on 20 May. The Japanese were now in complete control of Burma. Was there anything that could stand in the way of Japanese ambitions in the Pacific?

The Dutch East Indies

With their array of natural resources, notably oil reserves, the Dutch East Indies were a prime target. The Japanese landed on the Sarawak coast on 16 December 1941, and by early January it was clear to the American, British, Dutch and Australian command (ABDA) that an invasion of the vast territories making up the East Indies was imminent.

The Japanese divided their troops into Eastern, Western and Central Forces, to attack the east and west sides of the Dutch East Indies respectively. The concept behind the plan was simple: to seize ground, consolidate and then move on to their next objectives. The Eastern

---

1940

FEBRUARY

19 February The Japanese bomb Darwin.

20 February The Japanese land on Portuguese Timor. President Quezon of the Philippines is evacuated by American submarine.

27 February Battle of the Java Sea.

MARCH

1 March Battle of the Sunda Strait.

Force attacked first, seizing Celebes, Ambon, Timor and Bali. The defenders on Timor dispersed, conducting a guerrilla campaign against the invaders for over a year before the last of them was killed; it was the most notable resistance the Japanese faced. An Allied naval effort in the Lombok Straits on the night of 19/20 February caught the Japanese by surprise, but was beaten off and delayed the Japanese offensive by no more than a few hours.

Eastern Force landed on Java on 1 March, along with Western Force, which had taken Sumatra on the way, and Central Force, which had taken key coastal areas on Borneo. The landings were preceded by the Battle of the Java Sea, in which an Allied force was comprehensively defeated, with the loss of all but four of its ships. The Allied forces left in Java, including survivors from the Malayan and Singapore campaigns, were heavily outnumbered, and their position was obviously hopeless. The Japanese demanded talks with the Dutch on 7 March. The Dutch felt compelled to

....

Japanese marines pass through burning caba, *following their landings during the invasion of the Philippines.*

accept, and were offered a stark choice: either to surrender, or to watch the Javanese capital of Bandung be razed to the ground. Reluctantly, but feeling they had no choice, the Dutch agreed to an unconditional surrender.

The Invasion of the Philippines

American and Filipino forces had been brought under a unified command structure in July 1941, led by General Douglas MacArthur. Their main duty was to deal with internal unrest, so it

Japanese infantry take cover in a Philippine farm during the advance from Lingayen Gulf.

came as something of a surprise when information about the attack on Pearl Harbor filtered through in the early morning of 9 December 1941. The commander of the American air forces in the Philippines, General Lewis Brereton, requested permission from MacArthur to bomb Japanese airfields in Formosa.

MacArthur gave his consent, and Brereton's B-17s returned to the airbase at Clark Field to be armed – just as the Japanese airforce arrived to attack. More than 200 aircraft attacked the base field, rendering it useless in the space of two hours. The freshly armed B-17s, neatly lined up in the open, were easy targets. By the afternoon of 9 December, more than 100 American aircraft had been written off.

This was a particularly serious blow, since MacArthur's plans for defending the Philippines were based upon the premise that his forces would hold out until the American Pacific Fleet came to the rescue. With the fleet's ships destroyed or damaged at Pearl Harbor and a much-reduced air force to hand, the plan was hampered from the outset.

The first Japanese landings on Luzon took place on 10 December, with the objective of

1942

MARCH

11 March MacArthur leaves the Philippines, handing the command to General Jonathan Wainwright.

12 March British forces in the Andaman Islands are evacuated. The Americans occupy New Caledonia.

19 March General William Slim is appointed as commander of I Burma Corps (Burcorps).

23 March The Japanese occupy the Andaman Islands and attack Port Moresby.

American prisoners on Corregidor pass down to boats for transfer to Bataan, where they will be subjected to the 'Bataan Death March' to their prison camp.

seizing airfields to enable close air support for the army. The troops then pushed to the south, to join up with the units that were to carry out the main Japanese attack. These landings took place on 22 December, and by the next day, the invasion forces were well-established and moving forward. On 24 December, a landing occurred on the isthmus south of Manila, around Siain and Mauban. MacArthur realized that his forces were now in serious difficulty. Declaring Manila an open city, MacArthur moved to Corregidor Island, to defend the Bataan Peninsula, as the American and Filipino position collapsed.

However, Japanese victory was not imminent. Tropical disease took a heavy toll, and coupled with strong American defensive positions, this caused a lull in the fighting until April. By this time, MacArthur had been ordered to leave for the United States. He left on 11 March, promising 'I shall return'. General Jonathan M. Wainwright was left to continue the defence in the face of the renewed Japanese onslaught, but all he could do was to delay the inevitable.

The Japanese resumed their offensive, against Bataan, on 5 April 1942, using bombers and heavy artillery to pound the American defences

24 March The Japanese begin a bombardment of Bataan and Corregidor.

30 March The Allies form the South West Pacific Command under MacArthur and the Pacific Ocean Zone under Nimitz.

APRIL

3 April The Japanese launch an offensive in Bataan. Heavy air attacks against Mandalay.

on the Bagac-Orion defensive line. They broke through on 7 April, beating off American attempts to counterattack. General Wainwright knew the position was hopeless: he could not be reinforced or evacuated, and it was only a matter of time before his forces were completely overrun. On 9 April, he ordered that Bataan should surrender. He might not have done so had he appreciated that the subsequent behaviour of the Japanese would be so brutal: a notable percentage of his 78,000 men would die within a month on the infamous 'Bataan Death March', and yet more would die in captivity. Some survivors, including Wainwright himself, were able to flee to Corregidor. The Japanese now took their time to reduce the defensive positions with artillery. After nearly a week, they attacked on 5 May. On the next day, they were ashore, and Wainwright felt compelled to surrender.

US Army B-25B Mitchell bombers aboard the USS Hornet en route to the launching point for the Doolittle Raid on Tokyo.

1942

APRIL

5 April The Japanese bomb Colombo. The British cruisers HMS *Dorsetshire* and *Southampton* are sunk.

9 April American forces on Bataan surrender. The British aircraft carrier HMS *Hermes* is sunk.

10 April The Japanese land on Cebu Island.

15 April Burcorps begins the destruction of Yenangyaung oil wells to deny them to the Japanese.

The Doolittle Raid and the Coral Sea

The Japanese success in the Pacific represented a serious blow to the morale of the Allies. By the spring of 1942, the possibility of Japanese victory in the Pacific seemed extremely plausible. In fact, the Japanese campaign had already reached its zenith.

The first setback suffered by the Japanese came from a propaganda victory for the United States. This came in the form of an air raid on Tokyo, led by Lieutenant-Colonel James Doolittle. The plan was particularly audacious, since the only way of putting American bombers over the Japanese capital was by flying them from an aircraft carrier. The US Army Air Force's bombers were not designed to operate from ships, and there was considerable doubt as to whether any of them would be able to do so. After some consideration, the North American B-25 Mitchell medium bomber was chosen for the task.

The selected pilots and their aircraft were put aboard the carrier USS *Hornet*, which conveyed the bombers to within 998km (620 miles) of Japan. The B-25s then lumbered into the air from the *Hornet*'s deck and headed for their targets. To the consternation of the Japanese,

Yokosuka naval base, photographed from a B-25 on the famous Doolittle raid.

16 April The Japanese land on the Panay Islands.

18 April The 'Doolittle raid' on Tokyo by US bombers.

29 April The Japanese reinforce Minadnao. Lashio is captured by the Japanese, allowing them to cut the Burma Road.

30 April Burcorps withdraws across the River Irrawaddy.

the B-25s bombed Tokyo with relative ease. Some of the aircraft were lost to the defences; the survivors could not return to the carriers because they were unable to land back aboard, and made for bases in China. Difficulties with navigation meant that the aircraft force landed in a variety of locations. Nonetheless, the raid was a huge success, and a considerable boost to morale in the United States, which had been the aim.

The attack also had an effect on the Japanese. They moved to improve the quality of their air defences, meaning that resources had to be diverted from elsewhere, and also sought to extend their defensive perimeter further, denying bases to the Americans for any future raids.

Grumman F4F Wildcat fighters aboard the damaged carrier USS Lexington, *during the Battle of Midway.*

1942

MAY

1 May The Japanese capture Monywa and Mandalay.

3 May The Japanese land on Tulagi.

4 May The British evacuate Akyab.

5 May The Japanese land on Corregidor. British troops land on Madagascar.

As a result, the Japanese High Command concluded that Papua New Guinea should be taken, to provide a base from which they could patrol further into the Pacific. The first step would involve an amphibious assault against Port Moresby.

This led directly to the Battle of the Coral Sea. Forewarned after the successful decryption of Japanese naval codes, the Americans sent two aircraft carriers and their accompanying escorts against the Japanese invasion force. The first action came on 4 May, as an attack on a Japanese seaplane base by aircraft from USS *Yorktown*. Three days later, the Japanese carrier *Shoho* was sunk by American naval aircraft. With both sides now aware of the other's position, a major battle followed on 8 May 1942. The Americans lost the carrier *Lexington* and the destroyer *Sims*, while the Japanese lost a number of aircraft, forcing them to call off the invasion of Port Moresby. The battle was the first strategic victory won by the Americans in the Pacific, even if the

exchange of losses between the combatants did mean that the result looked like a tie at the time. What the Americans did not realize was that the Japanese had lost a number of their most experienced naval aviators. Their training system had not kept pace with the great

demands of war, and the losses at the Battle of the Coral Sea were keenly felt, since there were no ready-made replacements for the men lost. This failure to sustain a proper cadre of naval aviators was to have serious implications.

The wreck of a Japanese Zero beached on a coral reef after being shot down by fighters.

7 May The Corregidor garrison surrenders. The Battle of the Coral Sea begins.

8 May The Japanese capture Myitkynia. The Battle of the Coral Sea ends.

10 May The remaining Allied forces in Philippines surrender to the Japanese.

20 May Burcorps crosses into India.

Japan Challenged

Although the Battle of the Coral Sea thwarted Japanese plans to invade Port Moresby, the Japanese were not unduly concerned. The Americans had lost the carrier Lexington *and the* Yorktown *had been badly damaged. Admiral Yamamato assumed, not unreasonably, that the extent of the damage inflicted on the* Yorktown *would put the carrier out of action for many months.*

He also knew that the remaining two US carriers, *Enterprise* and *Hornet*, were likely to be in the south Pacific. He now concluded that it might be possible to provide a secure and decisive naval victory. The US fleet was now so weak that drawing its remaining ships into battle could, to all intents and purposes, end the war in the Pacific in Japan's favour. Yamamoto proposed to invade Midway Island, calculating that the Americans would have to respond to

such an action. He could then send his aircraft and battleships to destroy what remained of US naval power in the Pacific.

Unfortunately for Yamamoto, the *Yorktown* was less badly damaged than had been thought. In addition, he had underestimated the sheer determination of the dockyard workers at Pearl Harbor. They worked around the clock to repair the damage, and *Yorktown* was ready to return

Left: An F6F Hellcat prepares for launch aboard the USS Lexington *during Marianas air strikes, June 1944. Right: View of damage on Midway Island following Japanese air attacks.*

to sea in a far shorter time than anyone might have thought possible. Yamamoto had a further difficulty of which he was blissfully ignorant: the codebreaking efforts of the US Navy had provided the American commander, Admiral Chester Nimitz, with advanced warning of the plan. He now despatched Task Force 16, under Rear Admiral Raymond Spruance, and Task Force 17, under Rear Admiral Frank Fletcher, to the north of Midway. Also waiting there for the opportunity to strike were *Hornet* and *Enterprise,* specifically despatched there to confront the Japanese, and the recently restored (though still slightly battered) *Yorktown.* They now waited for an opportunity to strike.

Yamamoto assembled four fleets to conduct the Midway battle. One was the invasion force to draw the Americans into battle; the other three were heavy support forces.

Douglas SBD Dauntless dive-bombers, the aircraft that won the Battle of Midway for the US Navy, destroying the Japanese aircraft carriers.

At his disposal were five carriers (*Akagi, Kaga, Soryu, Junyo* and *Hiryu*), three light carriers, 11 battleships and more than 100 other vessels.

On 3 June 1942, American aircraft from Midway conducted largely ineffectual bombing raids against the Japanese ships. Little damage was inflicted, but the constant raid kept the Japanese fighters busy, and prevented Yamamoto from launching strikes against the US naval force, which he now believed to include an aircraft carrier.

The next day, the Japanese began their assault on Midway with a series of bombing raids on the island. These inflicted serious damage, but the Japanese were alarmed to be attacked by carrier aircraft from the two US Task Forces. The Americans had discovered the location of part of the Japanese fleet thanks to a PBY

1942

JUNE

4 June The Battle of Midway begins.

5 June All four Japanese aircraft carriers at Midway are sunk by the end of the day.

6 June The Japanese withdraw ships from Midway.

7 June A Japanese submarine sinks carrier USS *Yorktown.* The Battle of Midway ends.

JULY

2 July The Americans begin planning the recapture of the Solomon Islands.

Catalina flying boat. The first attacks by the Americans were relatively limited in scope, for Admiral Fletcher was convinced that there was a larger Japanese force in the area, and he was anxious to conserve aircraft for further strikes against the rest of the Japanese fleet when it was finally found. The two limited strikes were ineffective. The first, from the *Hornet*, failed to find the Japanese, and the aircraft had to land at Midway since they were too short of fuel to return to their carriers. The other strike, by torpedo bomber squadrons using the ageing Douglas TBD Devastator, met with disaster. Some 37 out of 41 aircraft were lost, and not a single torpedo hit the target, the carrier *Kaga*. However, the position of four of the Japanese carriers was now known.

As the Americans prepared for another strike, Japanese scout planes located some of their ships. Plans were now made to launch an attack against them once Japanese aircraft had returned from another raid on Midway. At just before 1000, while the Japanese were refuelling and rearming their aircraft, 35 dive-bombers appeared overhead, beginning a series of strikes against the main body of the Japanese fleet.

The Japanese aircraft carrier Hiryu *burns during Battle of Midway, the last of the carriers to be hit.*

Hit by air attack, a Japanese cruiser burns uncontrollably.

The carriers *Akagi*, *Kaga* and *Soryu* were all hit, to devastating effect. *Akagi* was hit amidships by a bomb, which detonated the torpedo store. The ship blew up as fuel and ordnance on the main deck exploded in a series of secondary detonations caused by the first blast. *Soryu* was ablaze within 20 minutes, struck by three bombs that set off explosions amongst the ordnance on deck and the freshly refuelled strike aircraft. Aboard the *Kaga*, a bomb hit on a refuelling truck sent a sheet of

7 July The Australians create the Maroubra Force at Port Moresby.

15 July The Maroubra Force reaches Kokoda.

21 July The Japanese land at Gona, Papua New Guinea.

23 July The Maroubra Force skirmishes with the Japanese before withdrawing from Kokoda.

AUGUST

7 August The Americans land on Guadalcanal.

Damage-control parties attempt to save the USS Yorktown after it has received five direct hits by Japanese bombs and torpedoes.

flame towards the bridge, killing everyone there, while three other hits set the carrier's aircraft park on fire. Within a matter of minutes, the ship was consumed by an inferno that would prove impossible for damage-control parties to extinguish.

Within the space of 20 minutes, the balance of power in the Pacific had been altered irrevocably.

This left only the *Hiryu,* which launched a strike against the Americans by sending its dive-bombers to follow the departing aircraft back to their own carriers. This led them to the *Yorktown,* and they now inflicted heavy damage on the recently repaired carrier.

Japanese dive-bombers attack the USS Yorktown, *patched up from an earlier onslaught, during the Battle of Midway.*

At 1705, another strike by American SBD Dauntless dive-bombers descended on *Hiryu.* The carrier was hit by several bombs, and was left burning uncontrollably by the time the American strike aircraft departed. Meanwhile, it became clear that the blaze aboard *Kaga* could not be put out, and she was abandoned. For the same reason, the order to abandon the *Akagi* was given. Over the course of the next two hours, the fire-fighting efforts aboard *Soryu* ended, and the

1942

AUGUST

8 August The Maroubra Force retakes Kokoda, but is forced to evacuate as a result of lack of supplies.

8/9 August The Battle of Savo Island.

18 August The Japanese land at Buna, Papua New Guinea.

21 August The Japanese counterattack on Guadalcanal.

23 August The Battle of the Eastern Solomons begins.

The destroyer USS Hammann *sinks after being torpedoed on 6 June 1942.*

ship sank at 1913. Just 12 minutes later, the abandoned hulk of the *Kaga* blew up and sank. Later, the *Hiryu* succumbed to the damage sustained, foundering in the early hours of 5 June.

On 6 June, the Americans added insult to injury by sinking the cruiser *Mikuma* and badly damaging the *Mogami*, removing another two major Japanese surface units from the order of battle. The last act of the battle came when the *Yorktown* was hit by a torpedo from a submarine on 7 June as she was under tow. Damage-control parties did their best, but by the morning of 8 June, it was clear that the *Yorktown* could not be saved, as she was listing to port. The ship was abandoned, and just before 0600, she rolled over and sank. The Battle of Midway was over.

For the Japanese, the battle was an unmitigated disaster. It marked a turning point in the war, and was the first in a series of blows from which Japan was never to fully recover. The loss of four carriers meant that Japanese power in the Pacific had been dramatically reduced, and despite efforts to build more carriers it never recovered. Japanese naval aviation had also suffered a mortal blow, losing many experienced aviators, who could not be replaced. While the Japanese struggled to recover from such losses, the Americans went from strength to strength. Within a month of the ending of the battle, there were 131 new aircraft carriers either being built or on order in American shipyards.

Guadalcanal

Guadalcanal and the Solomon Islands became a key strategic objective in the South Pacific in the course of 1942. Taking them would give the Japanese a base from which to attack Allied supply lines between the United States and Australia. However, if they fell to Allied control, the islands would be a key base from which to launch offensive action, as well as providing a barrier against Japanese attacks towards Australia.

In early May 1942, the Japanese landed on Guadalcanal and the neighbouring island of Tulagi. Teams of coast-watchers, operating covertly around the Solomon Islands, subsequently reported that the Japanese had begun to build an airfield on Guadalcanal, and the Americans realized that they had to act.

25 August The Battle of the Eastern Solmons ends after Japanese ships are forced to withdraw.

26 August The Japanese land at Milne Bay, Papua New Guinea.

27 August The Australians counterattack at Milne Bay.

29 August The Australians are forced to withdraw along the Kokoda Trail.

SEPTEMBER

4 September The Australians withdraw from Myola to Efogi.

An airfield on Guadalcanal would allow Japanese bombers to operate against shipping in the region, and possibly against Australia.

A force of 19,000 US Marines landed on Guadalcanal on 7 August 1942. There, the first 24 hours of the invasion were strangely calm, with no fighting. The same could not be said for the landings of Tulagi and Gavutu, which were cleared of Japanese only after considerable effort. Back on Guadalcanal, the Americans pushed on towards the half-finished airfield, taking it late on the afternoon of 8 August. The airfield was renamed 'Henderson Field' and completed by US engineers.

The Japanese responded immediately, sending a force of cruisers to Guadalcanal through the passage between New Georgia and Santa Isabel, known as 'the Slot'. They engaged the Allied naval force off Savo Island on the night of 8/9 August, and sank four Allied cruisers. The transports being escorted by the naval force had to pull back hurriedly, and were saved from pursuit only because the Japanese feared that they would come under air attack from American carriers if they did not withdraw before daylight.

US Marines land at Guadalcanal. The island was already occupied by the Japanese, but by seizing the airfield, the Americans gained a significant advantage, as they had a landing base in the region.

1942

SEPTEMBER

7 September The US Marine Corps raids Taivu.

6 September The Japanese are forced to evacuate from Milne Bay.

8 September The Japanese infiltrate Efogi.

12 September The Japanese attack begins the Battle of Bloody Ridge, Guadalcanal.

14 September Japanese troops are repulsed, ending the Battle of Bloody Ridge. The Australians on Papua New Guinea launch a counterattack to recover Kokoda, but are rebuffed.

The departure of the transports left the Marines at a disadvantage. With limited supplies, they now had to hold an enclave on the occupied island, surrounded by waters that were also under Japanese control. Henderson Field was bombarded from the sea, and air attacks around the clock fell upon the American positions. The Japanese now launched a series of attacks against the Marines. The first attack on 18 August across the Tenaru River was beaten back with heavy casualties on the Japanese side: the Marines discovered that the enemy preferred to fight to the death rather than surrender, and only a handful of Japanese troops escaped to Taivu.

A further attack by the Japanese, on 12/13 September, came close to success. The Battle of

US Marines search for snipers in a pine grove on Guadalcanal.

Light tanks from the United States Marine Corps patrol on Guadalcanal.

15 September American troops land at Port Moresby.

17 September The British begin planning for an offensive in Arakan, Burma.

27 September The Australians resume the attack along the Kokoda Trail.

OCTOBER

11 October The Battle of Cape Esperance.

24–26 October The Battle of Santa Cruz.

Bloody Ridge saw some of the most ferocious fighting on the island, but the Japanese were beaten back by the weight of American fire, boosted by the provision of air support from Henderson Field. The battle for control of the island raged on for two more months. On 23 October 1942, the Japanese managed to break into a small part of the perimeter of Henderson Field, but were soon dislodged with heavy casualties. On the next day came the naval Battle of Santa Cruz. The Japanese combined fleet moved into position to fly aircraft to Henderson Field, and two American Task Forces, under Admiral William 'Bull' Halsey, were sent to intercept. The Japanese fleet was located on 25 October, but the air strike sent to tackle it failed to locate its target and returned to the carriers *Enterprise* and *Hornet*. The following day brought an exchange of air strikes. The Japanese managed to sink the *Hornet*, but their carriers *Zuiho* and *Shokaku* were damaged, and more than 100 of their aircraft and many of their irreplaceable crews were lost – a pyrrhic victory.

Marine reinforcements come ashore at Guadalcanal, September 1942.

The Final Phases
The final phase in the battle for Guadalcanal began in November 1942. The Japanese decided to make one last effort, landing their entire 38th Division on Guadalcanal, supported by all the

ships in the Combined Fleet. However, the Americans' ability to read the Japanese signals code meant that the plan was known in advance.

The 38th Division was to be landed by Admiral Tanaka's 'Tokyo Express', which also kept the Japanese troops on the island supplied. Meanwhile, other naval forces would prevent the Americans interfering with the landings. On the night of 12/13 November, a fleet of two battleships, a cruiser and six destroyers under the command of Admiral Hiroaki Abe made its way along the Slot. The Americans sent five cruisers and eight destroyers commanded by Admiral Daniel Callaghan against them. The two forces met off Savo Island, and within minutes of fire being opened, Callaghan had been killed by a shell that hit the bridge of his ship, the *San Francisco*. The Americans concentrated their fire on the enemy battleships, but could do little to prevent the loss of three cruisers and two destroyers before Abe withdrew to the north.

1942

NOVEMBER

2 November The Australians capture Kokoda.

12 November The Battle of Guadalcanal, resulting in the loss of the American carrier USS *Hornet*.

14 November The Second Battle of Guadalcanal. The Americans begin the advance on Burma.

30 November The Battle of Tassafaronga, Guadalcanal.

DECEMBER

10 December The Australians capture Gona.

The Japanese had won the sea battle, but had not landed at Henderson Field. The next day, aircraft from the base found that the Japanese battleship *Hiei* had been damaged in the fighting, and they sent it to the bottom.

During the next day, American pilots located the Japanese troop transports and their escorts and mauled them. Four cruisers were sunk or disabled, and six troop transports were sent to the bottom. Thousands of soldiers died in the process. Despite this defeat, Tanaka was ordered to make a final effort to overcome Henderson Field, by shelling the airbase with a battleship and four cruisers. This time, the US Navy was ready. Two new battleships, the *Washington* and the *South Dakota*, were waiting, along with a force of destroyers. The *South Dakota* suffered a systems failure and took more than 40 shell hits, but the *Washington* used its radar-guided guns to put 54 shells into the Japanese *Kirishima*, leaving it a blazing wreck.

The Japanese withdrew, leaving Tanaka with the task of landing the 38th Division in daylight against an alerted enemy. The end result was a slaughter, with the convoy under constant air attack. At the end of the day, only 2000 men

Japanese torpedo aircraft and dive-bombers attack the USS Hornet *during the battle of the Santa Cruz islands. It succumbed to the attack, but the Japanese lost two vital carriers in the same action.*

from the 38th Division were left alive to link up with their colleagues in the jungle.

The Americans enjoyed yet more success on 30 November at the Battle of Tassafaronga. Coast-watchers reported that eight Japanese destroyers were heading for the Slot, and these were promptly intercepted. Again, the Japanese secured a slight victory, sinking one American ship and damaging three others for the loss of one destroyer, but they had failed in their mission of supplying the garrison on Guadalcanal.

It was clear that the crisis was over for the Americans, but the island was not yet secure. After months of hard fighting, the 1st Marine

17 December The Americans attack Mount Austen, Guadalcanal. British forces begin an advance in Arakan.

18 December The Allies launch an offensive against the remaining Japanese positions on Papua New Guinea.

22 December The Japanese withdraw from the Buthiduang–Maungdaw Line in Burma.

28 December The British advance in Arakan reaches Rathedaung, but they are unable to take the town.

Division was relieved, replaced by General Alexander Patch's XIV Corps, made up of the 23rd and 25th Divisions from the Army and the 2nd Marine Division. The newly arrived units started to patrol aggressively beyond Henderson Field, intending to launch a major offensive in January 1943. A preparatory operation to clear Mount Austin began on 17 December, but was not complete by 10 January, when the offensive began. By this point, the Japanese had decided that they could not afford the continuing casualties. The order for withdrawal came on 4 January, although it did not begin until 1 February. Within a week, the last Japanese soldier had left. General Patch signalled Halsey: 'Tokyo Express no longer has terminus on Guadalcanal.' The Americans had won their first, and possibly most important, land victory in the Pacific war.

New Guinea

The fighting on Guadalcanal has to some extent overshadowed the fighting that took place at the same time on New Guinea. The island occupied a key strategic position in the Pacific, which prompted the Japanese to make plans for occupying it. Their first attempt was thwarted

An Australian position on the Mubo track during the Allied attack on New Guinea.

1943

JANUARY

2 January Buna Station is captured.

4 January Japanese troops are ordered to prepare for the gradual evacuation of Guadalcanal.

7 January The British attack Donbaik in Burma, but are rebuffed.

9/10 January Further British attempts to take Rathedaung are unsuccessful.

12 January The Americans occupy Amchitka in the Aleutian Islands.

by the Battle of the Coral Sea, and in the aftermath of the disaster of Midway, the Japanese were forced to delay a second attempt until July 1942.

On 21 July, the South Seas Detachment under Major General Tomatoro Horii was put ashore to the East of Gona. The plan was that it should advance down the Kokoda Trail to Port Moresby and seize the area. Unfortunately, the plan was based on the assumption that the Kokoda Trail was a trafficable road across the Owen Stanley Mountains. It was, in fact, little more than a narrow jungle track, and difficult to traverse.

Nonetheless, the Japanese managed to take Kokoda within a week, and by mid-September they were some 48km (30 miles) from Port Moresby itself. At this point, Horii halted the advance, since he had been ordered to await reinforcements and was also aware that his supply lines were dangerously extended. However, the fighting on Guadalcanal persuaded the Japanese High Command to redirect Horii's reinforcements to that campaign, along with many of the supplies.

An attempt to aid Horii was made, but it failed, the Japanese reinforcements being driven back and then evacuated to Rabaul. This left Horii in a perilous position. The Australian and American forces on New Guinea simply waited, appreciating that Horii had neither the men nor material to advance, and that any attempt to remove him from the island could wait until his supply position was even less favourable. On 24 September, Horii was ordered to withdraw to Buna and the surrounding area. Two days later, the Australians launched their counterattack. Horii was killed in the retreat, but survivors from his force joined up with their colleagues holding Buna, Gona and Sanananda.

Assessing the situation, General Douglas MacArthur sent the US 32nd Division to New Guinea to assist with the offensive. The 32nd Division was tasked with capturing Buna, while the Australians dealt with the other two

Australian troops and an M3 light tank at Giropa Point, New Guinea, January 1943. The men in the foreground are armed with Bren light machine guns.

FEBRUARY

23 January Mount Austen is captured by the Americans.

1 February British attempts to take Donbaik and Rathedaung fail.

8/9 February The last Japanese troops leave Guadalcanal.

22 January The last Japanese forces on Papua New Guinea are destroyed.

1/2 February The Japanese start the evacuation of Guadalcanal.

13/14 February British Chindit expedition crosses the River Chindwin.

18 February The US Navy bombards Japanese positions at Attu in the Aleutians.

Japanese garrisons. A lack of armour and heavy weapons meant that the initial attacks were thrown back with heavy losses. MacArthur responded by sending General Robert Eichenberger to take over command. Eichenberger launched one attack, which failed, prompting him to wait until he had more men and armour. Once these became available, he resumed his attacks, and enjoyed rather more success. The Australians took Gona on 9 December; 10 days later, the Americans launched the attack that finally removed the Japanese from Buna. The Japanese began to evacuate the garrison at Sanananda, but not all had left when the town was taken on 22 January 1943.

From this point, the Allies advanced throughout New Guinea, and by September 1943 had removed the Japanese from a large proportion of the island. They would not be entirely removed until late in the war, but from this point they were never in a position to take the island, and were a strategic irrelevance, albeit a difficult and tenacious one. New possibilities for the Allied campaign in the Pacific now opened up.

US troops board a truck to move up to the front lines after landing near Port Moresby, New Guinea. Despite Allied success in the area, the Japanese remained a presence on the island almost until the end of the war.

1943

MARCH

1 March The main body of Chindits reaches Pinbon, in Japanese-held Burma.

3 March The Chindits cut the Mandalay–Myitkyina railway. The Battle of the Bismarck Sea begins.

4 March No. 4 Column of the Chindit force is ambushed, and disperses to withdraw to the Chindwin.

Chindits preparing to fire a mortar.

Japan on the Defensive

The run of victories following the Battle of Midway led the Allies to move on to their next phase of operations, a projected push towards Rabaul. The plan encountered its first difficulty when MacArthur and Nimitz disagreed, not just about the command and control of the operation but also its intended outcome. The solution was a compromise, a smaller attack codenamed 'Operation Cartwheel'. Admiral William 'Bull' Halsey's naval force would undertake a series of amphibious landings to advance along the Solomon Island chain to Bougainville, while MacArthur's forces would conduct an offensive along the New Guinea coast.

The Japanese made determined efforts to bolster their position. They despatched the 51st Division from Rabaul, but their convoy was spotted by US reconnaissance aircraft on 1 March 1943. B-25 bombers were sent out to attack the ships the next day, in what became known as the Battle of the Bismarck Sea. The attacks picked off the landing craft, and out of a complete Japanese division sent from Rabaul only 100 Japanese soldiers made the shore.

Japanese armed merchant ships on fire and sinking during the Battle of the Bismarck Sea.

Wounded American soldiers aboard a landing craft taking them to a hospital ship during fighting in New Georgia.

6 March American ships bombard Wila and Munda in the Solomons.

7 March The Japanese begin a counterattack in Burma, forcing British troops opposite Rathedaung to withdraw.

18 March A British attempt to take Donbaik fails.

24 March The Japanese troops cross the River Mayu, forcing a British withdrawal.

26 March The Battle of the Bering Sea.

5 March The Battle of the Bismarck Sea ends.

Marines of the 4th US Marine Division move through deserted Japanese installations near Target Hill during the occupation of Majuro Atoll in the Marshall Islands.

Part of the US Navy task force that assaulted the Marshall Islands, April 1944. This formidable fleet eventually won control of the Pacific from the Japanese.

Responding to the run of alarming failures since the end of 1942, the Japanese planned an air offensive, codenamed 'I-Go'. This was to be launched against a number of Allied bases, inflicting serious damage on both naval and air forces. The offensive began on 2 April 1943, and the Japanese conducted it with considerable vigour. However, their pilots were inexperienced and incapable of achieving the decisive blows anticipated by the High Command. To make matters worse, the pilots returned from their missions confident that they had inflicted grievous damage. It is true that about 30 Allied aircraft were destroyed, along with a destroyer, a corvette and two merchant ships. But Japanese aircraft losses were at least the same as those of the Allies, and probably higher.

More damaging still, Admiral Yamamoto now decided to visit his airmen to congratulate them on their apparent success. American signals intercepts revealed his plan, providing an opportunity to target the man who had

1943

MARCH

27 March The Chindits begin to withdraw towards British-held territory.

28 March The Japanese prevent an attempt by the Chindits to cross the Irrawaddy.

APRIL

7 April The Japanese launch air attacks against American bases in the Solomons.

14 April The Chindits begin crossing the Chindwin in small groups.

planned the Pearl Harbor attack. On 18 April 1943, 18 Lightnings left Henderson Field and flew 700km (435 miles) to rendezvous with their target. Thanks to impressive timing and navigation, they reached the place exactly as planned, finding two G4M 'Betty' bombers transporting Yamamoto and his entourage, and their fighter escorts. The Lightnings fought their way through the escort and shot down both bombers. Yamamato was killed.

At the end of June, MacArthur's forces landed at Nassau Bay in New Guinea, while Halsey's men landed in New Georgia on 21 June. A series of further landings took place over the next two weeks, and after the landings at Rice Anchorage on 4 July, the Japanese began to respond from their main base at Munda, New Georgia. They defended with some vigour, and it took a month to remove them, even

Japanese ships in Truk harbour in the Caroline Islands under attack by American aircraft. Planes from US carriers targeted the Japanese naval base in February 1944.

though they were heavily out-numbered. Not until 5 August was the airfield at Munda was taken.

In New Guinea, MacArthur's troops landed east of Lae on 4 September, and a week later, the pressure on the Japanese was such that they decided to withdraw from Salamaua. On 15 September, they pulled back from Lae, leaving these two crucial positions in Allied hands. Back in the Solomons, the Japanese concentrated their forces on Kolombangara, but Halsey simply bypassed it, taking Vell Lavella instead. The Americans promptly opened an airfield, thus making Kolombangara vulnerable to attack.

The final part of the operation in the Solomons was the seizure of Bougainville, which could then be used as a base for air attacks against Rabaul.

Landings on Bougainville began on 1 November, and met little

MAY

15 April General Slim is appointed to command all troops in Arakan.

18 April Admiral Yamamoto, mastermind of the attack on Pearl Harbor, is shot down and killed by American fighters.

29 April The last of the surviving Chindits reaches British territory.

4 May The Japanese cut the Buthidaung–Maungdaw Road.

11 May The Americans land on Attu.

14 May The Japanese capture Maungdaw, bringing the Arakan campaign to a conclusion.

30 May The last Japanese forces are evicted from Attu.

resistance. Construction of the airstrip began almost as soon as the beachhead was secured. The Japanese sent a force of 10 ships to destroy the beachhead, but this was intercepted by the US Navy. On 5 November, Halsey conducted a daring carrier-borne air strike against another Japanese naval thrust. This risked the loss of both the *Saratoga* and the *Independence,* but his luck held. The Japanese realized that they were outmanoeuvred, and the battle for Rabaul was slipping from their grasp, as they withdrew their ships and aircraft to Truk. There, they were 'left to wither on the vine', bypassed as part of the strategy of 'island hopping' – landing on islands of strategic significance on the way to the Japanese home islands and ignoring those locations where the Japanese troops could be safely ignored. Here, they posed little threat, unable to have any significant influence upon the overall campaign.

The tide was now turning in favour of the Allies, both in the Pacific campaign and in Burma. While the Americans had been engaged in the south and southwest Pacific, the British had taken the first steps towards victory in Burma after an unpromising start.

Burma – The First Arakan Campaign and the Chindits

Plans to retake Burma began to be made within weeks of the Japanese expelling the last British forces from the country. On 17 September 1942, Sir Archibald Wavell, Commander-in-Chief India, ordered General Noel Irwin's Eastern

Destroyer Squadron 21 en route to the landings on Vella Lavella in the Solomon Islands, August 1943.

1943

JUNE		JULY	
		6 July The Americans begin air attacks on Japanese positions in Bougainville.	
	21 June The Americans begin operations against New Georgia.		
15 June Churchill proposes the creation of a Southeast Asia Command to improve command arrangements in the Far East.			**12/13 July** The Battle of Kolombangara.
			17/18 July Japanese counterattacks in New Georgia.

Troops from the US 37th Division, supported by a Sherman tank, mop up Japanese resistance after a skirmish on Bougainville. This was a key strategic point for the Allies, providing them with a Pacific airbase.

Army to conduct an offensive in the Arakan. A series of delays and modifications to the plan followed as Irwin struggled to compensate for the lack of amphibious vessels, and heavy rains interfered with the build-up of supplies. Finally, on 17 December, the 14th Indian Division began to advance. The Japanese withdrew from the Buthidaung-Maungdaw Line on 22 December, and the British reached Rathedaung six days later. The Japanese repulsed two attempts to take the town, and began an advance of their own on 4 January 1943, taking Donibak. Four British attacks between 7 and 11 January failed to dislodge the enemy, as did renewed efforts between 1 and 3 February.

The situation deteriorated for the British and Indian forces as the Japanese 55th Division entered the line in early March. On 7 March, the division attacked the British forces facing Rathedaung, then moved into a position to cut them off, compelling them to withdraw to India. A further British attack on Donibak on 18 March failed, and when the Japanese crossed the River Mayu six days later, the British withdrew from their positions on the Mayu Peninsula.

AUGUST

25 August New Georgia is cleared of Japanese troops.

SEPTEMBER

4 September Amphibious landings at Lae.

5 September Nadzab airfield, northwest of Lae, is seized by American paratroops.

11 September The Japanese evacuate Salamua.

22 September The Australians land at Finschhafen, New Guinea.

Above: British troops move through a village in Burma, checking for any remaining Japanese troops.

....

A marine officer is hoisted up a tree to observe the fall of shot from artillery on Bougainville.

On 15 April, Lieutenant-General Bill Slim was appointed to command all the troops in the Arakan, but was unable to stem the Japanese advance. His troops were exhausted and weak from malaria, and the only option was to continue to withdraw. The Japanese cut the Buthidaung–Maungdaw road on 4 May, and by 14 May had captured Maungdaw itself. The monsoon brought action to an end. The Arakan

1943

SEPTEMBER

28 September The Japanese begin the evacuation of the Kolombangra garrison, Solomon Islands.

OCTOBER

2 October Finschhafen falls to the Australians.

5 October A US Navy task force bombards Wake Island.

6 October Admiral Lord Louis Mountbatten takes over the Southeast Asia Command.

campaign cost the British 5000 casualties and brought almost no gains at all. However, the experiences gained would be particularly useful for training other formations in the art of jungle warfare, and the first Chindit campaign further north in Burma had enjoyed pleasing, albeit limited, success.

The British Chindit formations owed their existence to Brigadier Orde Wingate. Wingate proposed a Long Range Penetration Group, designed to operate deep behind Japanese lines, supported from the air. By early 1943, the 77th Indian Brigade, the official designation of the Chindits, was ready for action.

It crossed the Chindwin River into Burma on 8 February 1943, catching the Japanese by surprise. Attacks on supply lines were very successful, tying down large numbers of Japanese troops. The advantage shifted, however, when Wingate sent his men across the Irrawaddy on 19 March, which took them into more open country. If they had stayed in the jungle, it would have been more difficult for the Japanese to attack their lightly armed opponents. Furthermore, the Chindits had advanced to a depth where the air supply on

which they were so reliant was much more difficult.

A series of hard-fought contacts with the Japanese in mid-March suggested that further success was unlikely, and a withdrawal began. The Japanese managed to block the route back to India, however, forcing the Chindit columns to split into a series of small groups, to live off the land while moving slowly through the jungle to reach safety. Eventually, about two-thirds of the force returned to India. Many of the troops were so badly affected by tropical diseases that a number were no longer fit for service, and many more were out of action for months. Nonetheless, the raid was good for British morale, demonstrating that the British

Chindits carry one of their wounded through the jungle.

NOVEMBER

27 October Preparatory operations for Allied landings in Bougainville begin.

1 November Allied landings in Bougainville begin.

5 November US Navy carrier aircraft attack the Japanese naval task force at Rabaul.

1/2 November The Battle of Empress Augusta Bay.

7 November The Japanese counterattack the American beachhead on Bougainville.

could fight just as proficiently in the jungle as the Japanese, and disproving the belief that the Japanese were superior jungle fighters to those from Western backgrounds – as American and Australian forces had discovered for themselves on Guadalcanal and New Guinea.

The Second Arakan Campaign

After the disappointments of the first Arakan campaign, the British command structure in the Far East was altered. General Sir Archibald Wavell was made Viscount Wavell and appointed Viceroy of India, handing his role as Supreme Commander of British forces to General Sir Claude Auchinleck. Auchinleck's command was now part of Lord Louis Mountbatten's Southeast Asia Command, and substantial reorganization took place within this new structure to prepare for future operations. The 11th Army Group was formed, including the Fourteenth Army, commanded by Lieutenant-General William Slim. He nominated Lieutenant-General Philip Christison's XV Corps for a second campaign in the Arakan.

The plan for Burma in 1944 involved reoccupying the north of the country, and re-establishing communications with China along the Burma Road to enable supplies to be sent to the Chinese. Lines of communication in India were improved, with a major logistics base being established at Kohima, ready for the forthcoming offensive. As a preliminary step, the second Arakan campaign opened in early January 1944. The 5th and 7th Indian Divisions of XV Corps drove down into the Arakan, one on each side of the Mayu Range,

Members of the Mars Task Force, which worked with the Chinese to open up the Burma Road.

1943

NOVEMBER

10 November The Gilbert Islands invasion fleet leaves Pearl Harbor.

20 November Launch of Operation Galvanic, the invasion of the Gilbert Islands.

23 November Tarawa and Makin are secured.

24/25 November The Battle of Cape St George.

26 November The Americans land on Abemama Atoll, Gilbert Islands.

intending to take Maungdaw and Buthidaung. In response, the Japanese launched a counteroffensive into India, with the aim of drawing as many British units as possible into the Arakan. Operations to this end began in February 1944.

British manoeuvres were supported by a reinvigorated Chindit campaign. Although the First Chindit Campaign had not been a success, it had made heroes in Britiain of Wingate and the survivors, and also showed that the concept of long-range raids was possible. When the

plans to take northern Burma were drawn up, Wingate argued that a long-range penetration would facilitate the invasion. The Chindits were reformed into six brigades, referred to as Long Range Penetration Groups (LRPGs), each divided into fighting columns of 400 men, and provided with fire support and an air liaison officer to call in air support where required.

Wingate envisioned using half his force for the opening stages of the operation, the other half relieving them in place after two months. As they went across the border into Burma, they had no idea that the Japanese were heading the other way, to launch their own attack in the Arakan.

By 6 February, the 5th Indian Division had been outflanked by the Japanese, who then attacked XV Corps's administrative area at Sinzweya. Since this was the Corps' forward administrative area, the fighting became known as the Battle of the Admin Box. Air supply by the RAF and USAAF ensured that the British and Indian troops held their ground, until the

British Sherman tanks in Arakan, Burma hills. Shermans were much superior to their enemy counterparts.

1944

DECEMBER

4 December US carrier aircraft attack Kwajalein and Wotje in the Marshall Islands.

9 December The airfield on Bougainville is opened by the Americans.

15 December The Americans make a preliminary landing on New Britain.

JANUARY

2 January The Americans land at Saidor, New Guinea.

9 January Indian troops occupy Maundaw, Burma.

30 January Launch of Operation Flintlock, landings on the Marshall Islands.

26th Indian and 36th British Divisions were sent to raise the siege. By the middle of February, the Japanese withdrew, to concentrate upon an attack on Imphal. As this began, the 5th Indian Division captured Razabil, while the 7th Indian Division took Buthidaung.

This was the last action for both divisions in the second Arakan campaign, for they were withdrawn to assist at Imphal on 22 March. They were replaced by the 26th Indian and 36th British Divisions, which moved forward to capture Maungdaw and Point 551. With this ground taken, the second campaign effectively ended; a combination of conventional fighting and the work of the Chindits had achieved notable success.

It had caused serious problems in the Japanese rear areas, impeding their offensive; the Chindits had even taken some key areas behind the lines. Sadly, Brigadier Wingate did not live to see this, being killed in an air crash on 25 March 1944 on his way back to India. The 77th and 111th Brigades were withdrawn after constant operations left them heavily depleted, but the remaining units captured Sahmaw and Taugni, contributing to wider operations.

Japanese Invasion of India

The British operations persuaded Lieutenant-General Renya Mutaguchi, commander of the Japanese 15th Army, to use similar tactics to invade India. Plans were already in place for an offensive against the border towns of Imphal and Kohima, with the aim of fermenting revolution that could be exploited by the pro-Japanese Indian National Army. As the Second Arakan Campaign developed, the importance of Kohima as a military target increased, and Mutagachi argued that an invasion of India was now an extremely attractive proposition. The Japanese High Command had been unconvinced to this point, but events in the Arakan prompted them to give permission for the attack.

On 7 March 1944, Mutagachi launched operation U-Go, sending his forces across the Chindwin River. The first phase of the operation was to be the capture of Imphal. This demanded that the settlement at Kohima be captured first, since it commanded the approach to Imphal. Taking it would also enable the Japanese to prevent the arrival of British reinforcements.

The Japanese arrived at Kohima on 5 April, but encountered improvised defences thrown up

Japanese troops make use of elephants to cross the Chindwin River, in preparation for the attack on Imphal.

1944

FEBRUARY

1 February The Americans land on the Kwajalein Atoll.

5 February The new Chindit expedition in Burma begins as lead elements depart from Ledo on foot.

6 February The Japanese launch a counterattack in Arakan.

17 February The Battle of Eniwetok Atoll begins.

23 February The Battle of Eniwetok Atoll ends.

26 February The Japanese call off attacks in Arakan.

A British mortar team prepares to fire during the bitter fighting at Kohima. Support weapons such as mortars played a vital part in blunting the Japanese assault, and the British were able to relieve Kohima.

by the 161st Indian Brigade, supported by a battery of howitzers. Fighting was fierce from the outset. The Japanese had assumed they would take the settlement in two days, but the resistance was stubborn. An initial penetration of the defensive perimeter was pushed back on 6 April. The British were resupplied from the air, while the battle raged around the district commissioner's bungalow and his tennis court. Both sides took heavy casualties. On 18 April, British reinforcements broke through and relieved Kohima. The next day, the Japanese went on the defensive, running short of supplies. Lieutenant-General Sir Montagu Stopford, commanding XXXIII Corps, then moved to clear the Japanese from Kohima and reopen the Kohima–Imphal Road.

A similar pattern was followed at Imphal, where the Japanese and their allies from the Indian National Army found it impossible to break the British lines. Although surrounded, the defenders were supported from the air, a benefit denied to the Japanese. They continued the offensive until early June, but the defence was tenacious and it became clear that continuing the battle was pointless. On 22 June, Stopford

MARCH

29 February The Americans land at Los Negros, Admiralty Islands.

5 March Chindit brigades make successful landings in Burma as the second stage of Chindit expedition begins.

7 March The Japanese 'U-Go' offensive begins in Burma.

8 March The Japanese attack the American beachhead on Bougainville.

11 March The British capture Buthidaung in the Arakan.

succeeded in opening the Kohima–Imphal road, and permission was granted for the Fifteenth Japanese Army to retire to Burma. The offensive had cost more than 30,000 Japanese fatalities, and another 25,000 were wounded or evacuated with disease, rendering the Fifteenth Japanese Army almost totally ineffective. The final blow came on 3 August, when Myitkyina fell to the Allies. From this point onwards, the Japanese were firmly on the defensive in Burma, facing a defeat that had appeared improbable just 18 months previously.

Central Pacific Operations

American campaigns in 1944 were marked by a new development in the use of carrier-based aircraft, with the formation of Task Force 58 (TF58), equipped with around a dozen 'Fast Carriers'. This came under the overall command of Admiral Marc T. Mitscher, who assumed control on 13 January 1944. After two weeks' preparation, the Task

Gurkhas in the Imphal area prepare their positions to meet a possible Japanese attack. The British succeeded in opening up the Kohima–Imphal road.

Force left Hawaii at the end of the month.

Japanese reconnaissance aircraft revealed the sortie, prompting the Japanese to pull back a number of their more important units from Truk to Palau. This was not, in fact, the intended destination of the US carriers; TF58

had been tasked with supporting landings on Kwajalien on 29 January 1944. Once these had been completed, the carriers headed for Majuro, then moved off on 13 February to strike Truk, aiming to neutralize its threat to operations.

The first strike was launched just before dawn on 14 February, with a fighter sweep. They were met by heavy anti-aircraft fire and about 80 Japanese aircraft, but the American pilots had little difficulty in asserting their dominance. Some 50 Japanese aircraft had been destroyed by the middle of the afternoon, giving the Americans air superiority. They now attacked the Japanese airfields, and more than 150 enemy aircraft were put out of action. Meanwhile, anti-shipping strikes from the carriers sank more than 100,000 tons of Japanese shipping around the island. After a final attack on 18 February, the Task Force withdrew, having destroyed over 250 Japanese aircraft and nearly 200,000 tons of shipping.

1944

MARCH

14 March The Japanese advance in Burma reaches the Tamu–Imphal Road.

15 March The Americans land at Manus, Admiralty Islands.

19 March The Japanese attack northeast of Imphal.

20 March US Marines occupy Emirau Island.

24 March The Japanese counterattack at Bougainville is beaten off. Chindit leader Orde Wingate is killed in an air crash.

The Task Force refuelled, and then headed west towards the Marianas. Japanese aircraft found it on the night of 21/22 February, and an attack followed. None of the aircraft was hit, which allowed TF58 to launch a full strike the next morning. Airfields were strafed and bombed, along with any shipping. Some Japanese ships escaped from their anchorages into the open sea, only to run into US submarines sent to intercept them. Once the strikes were completed, the Task Force retired to Majuro on 23 February. There was then a break of a month before an attack against Palau was launched.

The assault began on 30 March, with the opening fighter sweep shooting down more than 30 Japanese aircraft sent to intercept them. Merchant shipping was attacked, while mines were laid to confine some vessels to harbour, where they were easier targets. A further sortie by TF58 occurred on 13 April, in

....

US Marines storm ashore at Tarawa. The Americans won control of the Pacific island in November 1943.

support of the landings on the New Guinea coast. These took place on 21 April, and Japanese resistance was light. TF58 provided air support to the landings, and then withdrew to replenish. Once this was complete, it headed back to Truk.

There, the Japanese had repaired much of the damage, and flown in replacement aircraft. TF58 conducted air strikes against the island on 29 April, and rapidly gained control of the air. The airfields were then attacked, and about 90 Japanese aircraft written off. The threat now

neutralized, TF58 headed for a new anchorage at Eniwetok, its accompanying force of cruisers shelling Ponape on the way.

The three carrier raids provided a clear demonstration of how aircraft had become a major maritime weapon, enabling the US Navy to remove the threat posed by Japanese strongholds. And even if the Japanese managed to restore their previous position, the carriers could easily return to undo the repair work.

APRIL

3 April The Japanese offensive in Burma closes on Kohima and cuts off the British forces.

17 April The Japanese begin an offensive in southern China.

18 April The Kohima garrison is relieved.

22 April The British begin to clear Japanese forces around Kohima. The Americans land at Hollandia, New Guinea.

24 April The Australians occupy Madan, New Guinea.

29 April American carrier-based aircraft destroy the Japanese base at Truk in the Caroline Islands.

Operation Galvanic

In addition to operations in the Central Pacific, the Americans focused on taking the Gilbert Islands. Operation Galvanic was led by Rear-Admiral Raymond A. Spruance. He aimed to

seize the two most westerly islands of Makin and Tarawa, which would neutralize the other islands by removing their source of supply. Makin was attacked on 20 November 1943, and taken after three days of bitter fighting,

in which only one of the 800-strong Japanese garrison surrendered – the rest were either killed or committed suicide. Tarawa would prove even a far more difficult proposition.

One of the major issues for the attack on Tarawa was the presence of a submerged coral reef, which prevented landing craft from getting directly on to the beaches when the tide was low. When the assault began on 20 November, the landing craft were trapped on the coral reef, since the water was even lower than anticipated. The entire landing effort now depended on amphibious armoured tractors (AMTRACs) to ferry supplies and men ashore, while many of the troops were forced to wade to the beach, often under heavy fire. At one stage, the Americans feared they would not make it ashore in sufficient strength, but they eventually did so. The Japanese defenders fought to the death – out of a garrison of 4750, only 17 men surrendered. The fighting lasted for three days, and cost the lives of more than 1000 US Marines.

Marines take cover in the face of heavy Japanese fire during the operation to capture Tarawa.

1944

MAY

11 May The Chinese begin an offensive on the Salween Front.

13 May Fighting begins again around Imphal.

14 May Japanese forces start to evacuate New Britain.

27 May American landings on Biak Island, New Guinea.

JUNE

11 June The Americans begin a preliminary aerial bombardment of Saipan in preparation for an invasion of the Marianas Islands.

15 June US Marines land on Saipan.

The Americans next moved on to Roi, Namur and Kwajalien in the Marshall Islands, as part of Operation Flintlock. Roi and Namur were attacked by the 4th Marine Division and Kwajalien by the 7th Infantry Division on 1 February 1944. At Roi, the Marines found that the defenders had been stunned by the preparatory bombardment, and offered little resistance. By the evening, Roi was in American hands.

Namur proved less easy, since the terrain reduced the efficacy of the bombardment. The Japanese had strong defensive positions, and defended them with great tenacity. It was only when tanks came ashore that the Marines were able to advance. But they were then checked for several hours after an ammunition bunker exploded, killing and wounding the attacking men. The momentum was lost for the rest of the day, and it was not until more tanks and men from Roi arrived that the remaining Japanese positions were carried.

Kwajalien had similarly awkward terrain, and the fighting was hard until nightfall, when the Americans finally reached the airfield in the centre of the island. Fighting over the next three

The Stars and Stripes is raised on Roi in the Marshall Islands shortly after the capture of the island.

days was particularly ferocious, the Americans forced to make liberal use of tanks and flamethrowers to dislodge the defenders. Not one of the Japanese garrison survived.

The fighting in the Gilbert and Marshall Island chains provided many valuable lessons for future operations against Japanese-held islands. With the fall of the entire Marshall group on 23 February 1944, the scene was set for the Americans to close on the Philippines.

Battle of the Philippine Sea

Attention turned to the Mariana Islands. As a first step, the Americans landed on Los Negros and Manus in the Admiralty Islands between 29 February and 15 March, before moving to Emirau Island in the Saint Matthias group. This closed the ring around Rabaul, giving control to the Americans. The Japanese made a final attempt to destroy the Bougainville bridgehead on 24 March, but were defeated and then allowed to retreat inland, where they did not pose anything more than a nuisance.

The attack on the Marianas began with the invasion of Saipan. On 11 June, carrier-borne aircraft attacked positions on the island, a

17 June The US Army's 27th Division joins the Marines on Saipan.

18 June The Japanese capture Changsha in southern China.

19/20 June The Battle of the Philippine Sea.

22 June The British reopen the Kohima–Imphal road.

25 June Mount Tapotchau, Saipan, is captured.

26 June The Chindits capture Mogaung.

A Japanese aircraft falls in flames after being brought down during operations off Saipan.

'softening up' process prior to the invasion. The Japanese still aspired to destroy the US carrier fleet, and intended to use aircraft based in the Marianas. The arrival of the fleet off Saipan prompted the launch of Operation A-Go, a combined naval and aerial assault to destroy the Americans.

The theory behind their plan was sound, but in practice the operation went badly wrong. The Japanese sent nine carriers (six light and three fleet), five battleships, 12 cruisers, 27 destroyers and 24 submarines. It seemed an impressive force, but TF58 had 15 carriers (eight light and seven fleet), seven battleships, 21 cruisers, 62 destroyers and 25 submarines.

On 19 June, two days after the landings on Saipan began, the main Japanese force launched its first attack on the US carriers. The anti-aircraft fire and defending fighters shot down 42 of the 69 aircraft, however, and the Japanese managed only to inflict slight damage on the battleship *South Dakota*. A second strike followed, but only minutes after its launch,

one of the Japanese carriers was torpedoed by a US submarine, and sank. The attacking Japanese aircraft were shot to pieces by the defenders, losing 79 from a total of 110. A third strike by 47 aircraft evaded the defences of the forward battle line, but found few targets. The final strike of the day, by 82 aircraft, lost its way, and the bombers that found Task Force 58 suffered heavy losses.

At 1222, the carrier *Shokaku* was torpedoed and blew up, sinking just under three hours later. The Japanese commander, Admiral Ozawa, believed reports that his aircraft had inflicted serious damage, and resolved to continue the assault the next day – a fatal error. The Americans discovered the position of the Japanese fleet late on the afternoon of 20 June, and despite the risks to air crew returning to carriers at night, Admiral Spruance ordered Mitscher to launch an air strike. More than 200 aircraft participated, and the attack overwhelmed the Japanese. One carrier was sunk, and three others badly damaged, along with several other ships. The US aircraft returned to the fleet in darkness; in a move that endeared him to his pilots, Mitscher ordered every ship in

1944

JUNE	JULY

11 July The Japanese call off their offensive in Burma.

21 July American landings on Guam.

30 June Biak Island falls to the Americans.

18 July General Tojo resigns as Japanese prime minister, and is replaced by General Kuniaki Koiso.

24 July The Americans land on Tinian.

his force to turn on its lights. One hundred and sixteen US aircraft landed safely as a result, and the remaining 80 survivors ditched nearby, allowing the majority of the crews to be saved. By the end of 20 June, the Battle of the Philippine Sea was over. At least 219 Japanese aircraft had been shot down, and more were destroyed on the ground, prompting the US naval aviators to dub the action 'The Great Marianas Turkey Shoot'.

The Battle of the Philippine Sea marked the effective end of Japanese carrier aviation. The failure to defeat the landings in the Marianas also ensured that American bombers would soon be seen over Japan in large numbers. Prime Minister Tojo was forced to resign on 18 July, and was replaced by General Kunaki Koiso. Within a week, American troops landed on Guam and Tinian. Attempted counterattacks failed, and the Americans had complete control of Tinian by 1 August, and of Guam by 10 August. Japan now faced defeat. The only question left was how long and how bloody the final struggle for victory would be.

A Japanese Kamikaze aircraft narrowly misses an American warship, shot down by anti-aircraft fire.

AUGUST

25 July The Japanese begin two days of unsuccessful counterattacks on Guam.

1 August Organized Japanese resistance on Tinian ends.

3 August Myitkyina falls to Allied forces under General Stillwell. Chindits are flown back to India.

8 August Japanese forces in southern China capture Hengyang.

10 August Organized Japanese resistance on Guam ends.

The End in the Far East

By late 1944, the Japanese Empire still covered a large geographical area, but this was steadily being reduced in size as the Allies advanced. The Japanese position was not helped by the fact that Allied submarines and aircraft interdicted the lines of communication linking the disparate territories.

Increasing attacks on Japan itself would further hamper the war effort as a run of failures left the authorities facing defeat.

The Americans planned to seize islands near Japan, and use them to launch an invasion of the home islands. Planning was well under way, but concern over the casualties that would be sustained by both sides had begun to mount. The Japanese troops had shown that they were prepared to fight for every inch of their homeland, while civilians had demonstrated that they were willing to commit mass suicide rather than live in occupied territory.

The most significant operation in the Pacific between September 1944 and January 1945 was in the Philippines. The islands would be liberated after particularly bitter fighting, allowing General MacArthur to fulfil his promise to return.

Left: Douglas MacArthur fulfils his promise to return to the Philippines.
Right: Commonwealth troops fighting their way into Mandalay as the Japanese are driven from the city.

Meanwhile, in south Asia, British and Indian forces regrouped after the Second Arakan campaign to launch a new drive through Burma. Plans were drawn up for the reconquest of Malaya and Singapore, in the summer or autumn of 1945.

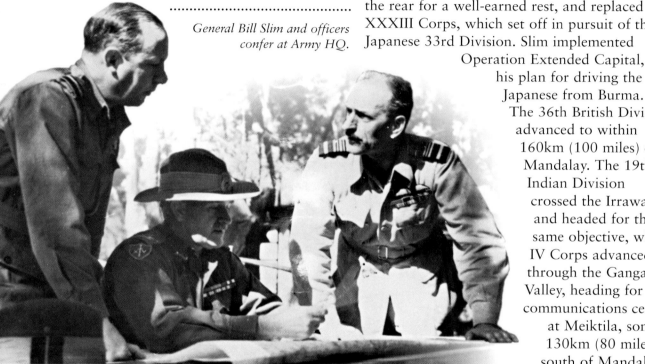

General Bill Slim and officers confer at Army HQ.

The Retaking of Burma

The British were ready to return to the offensive. Imphal had been relieved, and General Slim reorganized his forces. IV Corps and the 50th Parachute Brigade were sent to the rear for a well-earned rest, and replaced by XXXIII Corps, which set off in pursuit of the Japanese 33rd Division. Slim implemented Operation Extended Capital, his plan for driving the Japanese from Burma.

The 36th British Division advanced to within 160km (100 miles) of Mandalay. The 19th Indian Division crossed the Irrawaddy and headed for the same objective, while IV Corps advanced through the Gangaw Valley, heading for the communications centre at Meiktila, some 130km (80 miles) south of Mandalay.

The advance risked overstretching the supply lines from Imphal to the forward units, so Slim set XV Corps the task of seizing airfields for use by RAF transports. An amphibious assault by 3 Commando Brigade on the island of Akyab was followed by another by 71st Brigade (25th Division) on Myebon. The 71st Brigade seized the north of Ramree Island, and once the bridgehead was established, the rest of the division arrived. With the Japanese expelled, the RAF established an airfield, from which supply missions could be flown to the troops in the front line.

Further inland, XV Corps blocked the Japanese Twenty-Eighth Army from assisting with the defence of Mandalay, but this did not prevent heavy fighting when the 20th Division and Japanese Fifteenth Army met at Myinmu, on 12 February 1945. The battle stopped the advance 48km (30 miles) short of its target, although IV Corps was able to continue its advance on Meiktila. On 1 March, the 17th Division attacked and took the town in 48 hours. Japanese counterattacks, were rebuffed with heavy losses. To the north, XXXIII Corps assaulted Mandalay, prompting a Japanese

1944

SEPTEMBER

4 September
Lingling airbase in southern China falls to the Japanese.

OCTOBER

3 October
US Joint Chiefs of Staff directive to MacArthur and Nimitz sets the date of invasion of Luzon as 20 December.

12 October The US Third Fleet begins four days of air attacks on Formosa and Luzon as a preparatory step before landing at Leyte. The first B-29 bomber arrives in Marianas Islands.

14 October An American invasion force for Leyte sets sail.

17 October US Rangers seize Suluan Island in the mouth of the Leyte Gulf.

20 October
American landings on Leyte.

23 October The naval Battle of Leyte Gulf begins. The Japanese use Kamikaze attacks for first time.

evacuation on 20 March. Stillwell's Northern Combat Area Command took Hsenwi and Lashio, removing the last significant opposition from the north of Burma. Slim now prepared to move on Rangoon, the Burmese capital.

On 30 April, a naval bombardment preceded the attack. The next day, an airborne battalion landed at Elephant Point, creating a bridgehead for the 26th Indian Division. On 3 May, the division marched into Rangoon without opposition. XXXIII Corps captured Prome, which meant that all major towns in Burma were under Allied control. The Japanese Burma Area Army had now ceased to exist as a viable fighting force, leaving the British and Indians with nothing more to do than mop up. Burma had been reconquered.

Leyte Gulf and the Philippines

American military planners spent much of 1944 debating the correct course of action for future operations. The point of contention was the Phillipines. Some within the US Navy saw little point in attacking the islands, believing they presented little threat to the Allied advance. Bypassing the islands would allow an attack

on Formosa. General MacArthur argued against this, pointing out that retaking the islands would cut Japanese communications with Southeast Asia and the Dutch East Indies.

The debate was settled once the Navy decided that the Japanese would be compelled to use the bulk of their remaining naval strength to thwart an invasion of the Philippines. Initially, the Americans planned to invade the Philippines in December 1944. However, the date was brought forwards by two months when a sortie by Task Force 38 met with little resistance, suggesting that the Japanese naval forces in the area were weak.

A large invasion fleet was assembled. As it approached the Philippines, Task Force 38 launched air attacks on targets ranging from Okinawa to the Philippine Sea. On 12 October, Halsey's Third Fleet launched heavy air attacks on Formosa and Luzon. Admiral Toyoda, commanding the Japanese Combined Fleet, believed that the strikes were a sign that landings on Formosa and Luzon were imminent. He therefore committed all his aircraft, with disastrous results. The 6th Base Air Force lost more than 500 aircraft over the course of the

A B-25 medium bomber 'skip bombs' Japanese shipping. American air attacks of this kind caused carnage.

next four days. While the air battle was raging, the Leyte invasion force left its anchorage, reaching its destination on 17 October.

Suluan Island at the mouth of Leyte Gulf was shelled. US Rangers landed, overwhelming the garrison, although not in time to prevent them from sending a warning that an American

---

NOVEMBER

11/12 November The Americans carry out a naval bombardment against Iwo Jima.

24 November The first air raid on Japan from the Marianas is launched.

26 October The Battle of Leyte Gulf ends in defeat for the Japanese.

DECEMBER

3 December The British begin Operation Captial, the advance on Mandalay.

8 December General Frank Messervy takes command of IV Corps in Burma. The Americans begin 'softening up' air raids against Iwo Jima.

15 December The Americans land on Mindoro.

25 December Leyte is cleared of Japanese troops

invasion fleet was in the vicinity. Admiral Takeo Kurita's First Striking Force, the surviving elements of Vice-Admiral Jisaburo Ozawa's Mobile Fleet and Admiral Teiji Nishimura's Second Striking Force, were sent to Leyte Gulf to engage the American invasion force. They had not reached Leyte Gulf when Leyte itself was invaded, on 20 October 1944. The invasion was a considerable success – for the loss of only 49 men, the Americans seized control of a sizeable amount of Leyte.

First Striking Force lost two cruisers to American submarines on 23 October, reaching the San Bernardino Strait the next day. A series of air attacks by Task Force 38 sank the battleship *Musashi* and crippled an accompanying cruiser, forcing the entire Japanese force to slow to the speed of the damaged ship. A further American attack proved fatal, the vessel sinking slowly during the course of the afternoon as First Striking Force withdrew. The Mobile Fleet's ships approached Luzon the same afternoon, tempting Admiral Thomas Kinkaid's Seventh Fleet into pursuing it. This left the landing beaches protected by escort carriers only, potentially leaving them at the

American tanks fighting their way through Manila walled city, during the liberation of the Filipino capital.

mercy of First Striking Force: Kurita had altered direction under cover of darkness, and was heading back to the invasion beaches.

Nishimura approached the Surigao Strait, but

his ships were mauled by the US Seventh Fleet destroyer force. A battleship and three destroyers were lost, and the battleship *Yamashiro* damaged, which left the ship vulnerable to fire from battleships and cruisers. Kurita, meanwhile, had emerged from the San Bernardino Strait, and surprised the escort carrier force. He might have caused havoc among the carriers, the but the American resistance was so stiff that Kurita withdrew.

Meanwhile, the rest of Task Force 38 headed north to finish off Ozawa's forces. The ships were helpless against the American air attack, and four Japanese carriers and a destroyer were sunk before Admiral Halsey headed back towards Samar, to protect the escort fleet. The remaining American ships sank another enemy carrier, two destroyers and a light cruiser before the Japanese survivors withdrew. The battle of Leyte Gulf was one of the largest naval battles in history, and a decisive victory for the Americans. It was marked, however, by a new Japanese weapon, the Kamikaze suicide air attack. The American carrier *St Lo* was sunk by this form of attack on 25 October, and would not be the last American vessel to succumb.

1945

JANUARY

2 January British forces reach Yeu, Burma.

7 January British XXXIII Corps reaches Schwegu, prompting the Japanese to withdraw behind the Irrawaddy River.

9 January US landings in Lungayen Gulf, Luzon.

14 January The 19th Indian Division begins to establish bridgeheads across Irrawaddy.

20 January The Japanese issue directives for the defence of the Japanese mainland.

21 January US XIV Corps reaches San Miguel, Luzon.

26 January XIV Corps reaches Clark Field airbase. In Burma, the 7th Indian Division captures Pauk.

27 January The Burma and Ledo roads are joined at Monguyu.

29 January US XI Corps lands at San Antonio, to the north of Bataan Peninsula.

The immediate aftermath of a Kamikaze hitting an American aircraft carrier.

Leyte

After initial success here, fierce resistance by the Japanese Thirty-Fifth Army slowed the American offensive considerably. As a result, the invasion of Luzon was put back to 9 January 1945. The impasse was broken when a division from Lieutenant General Walter Krueger's Sixth Army landed on the western side of the island on 7 December, cutting the Japanese forces in two. Badly dislocated, Japanese resistance foundered before collapsing on 25 December, although isolated pockets of resistance were encountered for several more weeks.

The assault on Luzon could now take place. A week before the intended invasion, a naval force under Admiral Jesse B. Oldendorf set out to bombard the island. Heavy Kamikaze attack cost the force an escort carrier and three minesweepers. Oldendorf responded by launching a series of air attacks against the Kamikaze airfields. The strength of the strikes was such that the few surviving Japanese aircraft were forced to withdraw.

The landing on 9 January met little opposition, bar Kamikaze attacks, and a beachhead 6km (4 miles) deep and 27km (17 miles) wide was established within a day. Resistance stiffened, however, and an attempt to take Rosario on 16 January slowed considerably when American I Corps encountered the Japanese Shibu Group, a force of some 150,000 men.

MacArthur ordered the US XIV Corps to push forward to Manila, sending two divisions to aid I Corps in driving the Shibu Group away from XIV Corp's line of advance. This finally overcame resistance, and XIV Corps moved forwards. It met with the Japanese Kembu Group on 23 January 1945, and fierce fighting between the two formations lasted for more than a week before the Americans managed to push the enemy back.

On 31 January, the US 11th Airborne Division landed at Nasugbu at the entrance to Manila Bay, heading for the centre of the city. Vicious fighting broke out, made worse by the

A mortally damaged Kamikaze aircraft falls blazing into the sea.

FEBRUARY

31 January The 11th Airborne Division lands at the entrance to Manila Bay.

3 February The US XIV Corps reaches the outskirts of Manila.

4 February American I Corps captures San Jose.

12 February The 20th Indian Division crosses the Irrawaddy at Myinmn.

14 February The 7th Indian Division crosses the Irrawaddy at Nyaungu.

15 February Americans land on the Bataan Peninsula.

16 February Airborne landings on Corregidor.

19 February The American invasion of Iwo Jima begins.

21 February The Bataan Peninsula is secured. US forces off Iwo Jima are subjected to heavy Kamikaze attacks. The British 36th Division captures Myitson in Burma.

fact that the Japanese had refused to allow the civilian population to leave. The fighting continued bitterly throughout February, while landings were made on the Bataan Peninsula on 15 February, and on Corregidor the next day. The Bataan Peninsula was secured within a week, but it took until 2 March for resistance on Corregidor to be overcome. Finally, on 3 March, Manila was cleared of all Japanese troops. The cost had been high, for more than 100,000 Filipinos had died – many as the result of Japanese atrocities that would prompt trials for war crimes. On both Luzon and Mindanao, fighting continued until the end of the war, but the Japanese forces remaining were a strategic irrelevance. The prize of Japan itself was now close at hand.

Iwo Jima and Okinawa

The next phase of operations was carried out against the Japanese island of Iwo Jima. The island offered a number of benefits, most notably for enabling increased air attacks against the Japanese homeland. Its proximity to the home islands made it an ideal base for fighters escorting raids by B-29 bombers, while any damaged bombers would be able to make emergency landings on one of the island's two airfields. Another key consideration was that the loss of Japanese territory was likely to have a devastating effect on Japanese morale.

The Japanese made major efforts to establish effective defensive positions, sending experienced reinforcements to Iwo Jima in the latter part of 1944. By the end of the year, the defenders had dug an extensive complex of tunnels to protect them from air and sea bombardment. This began on 11 November with naval gunfire, while air attacks struck from 8 December.

On 19 February 1945, the invasion force landed, and met little resistance. As the Marines made their way a little further inshore, however, they came under heavy fire. A sharp engagement

US Marines consolidate their position on the beaches of Iwo Jima, facing surprisingly light enemy resistance.

1945

FEBRUARY

22 February The 17th Indian Division advances on Meiktila.

23 February Mount Suribachi, Iwo Jima, is captured.

24 February The 17th Indian Division captures the Burmese town of Taungtha while the 2nd British Division crosses the Irrawaddy at Ngazun.

26 February The 19th Indian Division advances on Mandalay.

27 February The British IV Corps reaches the outskirts of Meiktila.

28 February The British IV Corps begins an attack on Meiktila.

MARCH

2 March Corregidor is brought under US control.

3 March The Japanese are cleared from Manila. In Burma, Meiktila falls to the 17th Indian Division.

4 March The first B-29 lands on Iwo Jima. The Japanese counterattack in Burma retakes Taungtha.

followed, but by nightfall, some 30,000 Marines were ashore. On 23 February, Mount Suribachi, the highest point on the island, fell – but still the fighting continued. The first B-29s landed on Iwo Jima on 4 March; 10 days later, the island was declared secure. Some 23,000 Japanese had died in the fighting, and only 216 survived. As for the US Marine Corps, it was the bloodiest operation in their history: 6281 were killed and another 18,000 wounded.

The way was clear for an attack on Okinawa. The US Tenth Army invaded on 1 April 1945, and met only light opposition at first. However, massive Kamikaze attacks were launched against the invasion fleet on 6/7 April. On the second day, a Japanese naval raid, headed by the massive battleship *Yamato*, was intercepted by American carrier aircraft. The *Yamato*, three destroyers and a light cruiser were sunk. The five surviving destroyers escaped, but the loss of *Yamato* after losses at Leyte meant that the Japanese Navy was now irrelevant.

From 9 April until the end of the month, the Americans continued to attack against the Shuri defence line on the south of the island,

encountering fanatical resistance as they advanced. The Japanese garrison was gradually split into three pockets, and was destroyed by the end of June. For the first time, Japanese soldiers began surrendering, suggesting that morale was suffering. Nonetheless, the number of troops who fought to the death, as well as the scale of American casualties in taking Iwo and Okinawa, raised the question of how costly the final assault on Japan might prove.

'Ruin From the Air'

Bombing raids brought the war direct to the heart of the empire from 24 November 1944, when B-29s attacked industry outside Tokyo. Only 24 out of the B-29 force of 100 aircraft found the factory that was their target. After similarly poor results from a

Marines toss sticks of dynamite into an enemy position during the fighting on Okinawa.

9 March The 19th Indian Division reaches the outskirts of Mandalay.

9/10 March American bombers carry out a major incendiary attack against Tokyo.

11 March British forces capture Mandalay Hill, allowing the swift clearance of most Japanese forces from the city.

11/12 March B-29s conduct fire raid on Nagoya.

13 March The 19th Indian Division captures Maymyo, Burma.

13/14 March B-29 fire raid against Osaka.

14 March Iwo Jima is declared secure despite some remaining Japanese resistance.

17 March The 2nd British Division captures Fort Ava, Burma.

18/19 March Kobe and Nagoya suffer further fire raids.

Yokohama is subjected to an air raid by American B-29 bombers.

further nine attacks, it was clear that the use of the bombers had to be reassessed.

On 20 January 1945 Major General Curtis E. LeMay took over XXI Bomber Command. LeMay was a pugnacious commander, and made notable tactical changes. He abandoned high-level daylight bombing in favour of low-level night attacks with incendiary bombs. Many buildings in Japanese cities were made of inflammable material, and LeMay exploited this to the full.

On the night of 9/10 March, 300 aircraft attacked Tokyo and Yawata. Some 40 square kilometres (16 square miles) of Tokyo was burned to the ground. A series of similarly destructive raids on Nagoya, Osaka and Kobe followed. LeMay then made a further modification to tactics, combining high-level daylight bombing and low-level night incendiary attacks against targets throughout Japan.

On 25/26 May, a major attack on Tokyo destroyed more of the city. On 29 May, an attack on Yokohama destroyed more than 85 per cent of the city. By July, more than half a million Japanese civilians had been killed and 13 million made homeless.

Devastating though the fire raids were, it was by no means clear that they would be enough to force the Japanese to surrender. At this point, politics came into play. On 5 April 1945, the USSR informed the Japanese that it intended to renounce the 1941 non-aggression pact. This indicated that the Soviets were considering war with Japan, and the Japanese Council for the Supreme Conduct of War now began to discuss peace. On 28 May, Stalin informed the United States that the USSR would declare war in mid-August, and expected to participate in the occupation of the defeated country.

This was a cause for some concern to the United States, since relations with Moscow had declined following a series of disagreements over the nature of the postwar settlement. Following Roosevelt's death, President Truman took a more aggressive attitude towards the USSR. He recognized that the possibility of Soviet interference in Japan and Manchuria would give Stalin the means to support Mao Zedong's Communist revolutionaries in China – something he wished to avoid.

Truman now faced the prospect of immense casualties when the Japanese home islands were

1945

MARCH

20 March The 19th Indian Division captures Fort Dufferin, the last major source of Japanese resistance in Mandalay.

24 March The start of operations against Okinawa as the Americans capture the Kerama Islands for use as an anchorage. The Bombardment of Okinawa begins.

US Marines lay down fire against Japanese defences blocking their advance.

26 March The Japanese launch the last major attack on Americans in Iwo Jima.

28 March Japanese counterattacks against Meiktila end.

30 March The Allied advance from Meiktila begins.

31 March The 36th British Division reaches the Burma Road.

APRIL

1 April Landings on Okinawa begin.

5 April The USSR informs Japan of its intention to renounce the 1941 non-aggression pact between the two nations.

Large areas of Tokyo destroyed by American fire raids. The fire raids killed more people than even the atomic bomb attacks on Hiroshima and Nagasaki.

invaded, and of a Soviet Union with an uncomfortable amount of influence in postwar Asia. In such circumstances, it is perhaps not surprising that he looked for a new weapon to bring a quick victory: the atomic bomb.

Debate about the atomic bomb – and how to use it – was under way by the time that the Japanese began to consider peace talks. After failing to make any headway with the Soviets, the Japanese made an approach to the

Americans via Switzerland. This news reached Truman while he was attending the Potsdam Conference with Stalin and Churchill. He decided the bomb had to be used, and a test at Alamogordo, New Mexico was carried out

6 April The Japanese begin two days of heavy Kamikaze attacks on the Okinawa invasion fleet. In Burma, the 17th Indian Division captures Yindaw, blocking the line of retreat for the Japanese Thirty-Third Army.

7 April The Americans sink the Japanese battleship *Yamato*, an event that marks the effective destruction of the Japanese Navy as a major combat force.

9 April The Americans attack the Shuri defence line in southern Okinawa.

16 April American landings on Ie Shima, west of Okinawa.

23 April The 19th Indian Division reaches Toungoo in Burma.

25 April The British capture Yenangyaung and its oil fields.

29 April The 17th Indian Division reaches Pegu, Burma.

MAY

1 May Operation Dracula, a combined airborne and amphibious assault on Rangoon, begins with an air assault on Elephant Point to secure the approaches to Rangoon. The Japanese begin the withdrawal from Rangoon.

successfully on 16 July 1945. He now felt confident enough to inform Stalin that the Americans had a bomb of 'unusual power', which might have a decisive effect – little realizing that an effective spy network meant that Stalin understood exactly what he meant.

The Potsdam Conference issued a demand for unconditional Japanese surrender on 26 July. This was rejected two days later, largely because no mention was made of allowing Emperor Hirohito to remain on the throne. As a result, Truman issued the order that the atom bomb should be employed 'as soon as weather will permit visual bombing on or after about 3 August 1945'. A target list was provided and a city chosen: Hiroshima.

Hiroshima, Nagasaki and Surrender

Colonel Paul Tibbets was the commanding officer of the 509th Composite Group, the cover name for the unit formed to conduct the atomic raids. On 6 August 1945, he took off from Tinian in a B-29 bearing the name of his mother,

Hiroshima fire station, which was around 4000 feet from ground zero, seen following the atom-bomb attack.

1945

MAY

2 May The amphibious element of Operation Dracula is launched by the 26th Indian Division.

3 May Rangoon is entered by the 26th Indian Division. XXXIII Corps takes Prome, cutting off the Japanese Twenty-Eighth Army in the Arakan.

7 May General Slim is temporarily replaced in command of the Fourteenth Army by General Sir Philip Christison. Slim is appointed commander of the Twelfth Army with effect from 28 May 1945. The decision is reversed and Slim is appointed Commander in Chief Allied Land Forces, Southeast Asia.

12 May The Japanese Supreme War Council has first discussions about seeking peace with the US.

25 May US Joint Chiefs of Staff issue a directive for the invasion of Japan, scheduled for 1 December 1945.

27 May Naha, the capital of Okinawa, is captured by the Americans.

28 May Stalin informs the Americans that he intends to go to war with Japan in mid-August.

Left: The mushroom cloud caused by the detonation of the 'Fat Man' atom bomb over Nagasaki.

Enola Gay. The aircraft reached Hiroshima to find perfect visibility beneath. At 0815, the *Enola Gay* released its weapon, the prosaically codenamed 'Little Boy' uranium bomb. It detonated with a blinding flash, and within seconds, the city was flattened by the heat and blast. Some 80,000 people died in the attack, and many more wounded, perhaps up to 100,000.

Members of the Japanese Government now fought amongst themselves to determine whether or not to surrender. The pressure increased when Soviet forces crossed the border at dawn on 9 August 1945. Stalin was eager to take control of Manchuria, Sakhalin and the Kurile Islands, which he realized would be more difficult to achieve if the USSR played no part in the fighting. As a result, 76 Soviet Divisions drove into Manchuria. The campaign went exactly to plan, the Japanese being unable to

Right: The main street in Nagasaki, 1000 feet north east of ground zero from the atom-bomb explosion.

offer much resistance. Khorokhon Pass was taken in two days, Changchung and Mukden fell on 21 August, and finally the Soviets captured Matuankiang.

Still the Japanese Government equivocated. As a result, the Americans conducted another

JUNE

29 May Shuri Castle, the main point of resistance of the Shuri defence line, falls to US Marines.

3 June The Japanese make a peace approach to the USSR.

6 June The Japanese Supreme War Council passes a resolution that Japan will fight until total destruction.

19 June On Okinawa, the first voluntary surrenders by Japanese troops take place.

22 June Japanese commander on Okinawa, General Ushijima, commits suicide. Emperor Hirohito instructs the Supreme Council that it must take steps towards peace, the decision of 6 June notwithstanding.

JULY

3 July Remnants of the Japanese Thirty-Third Army make an attempt to break through Allied lines.

12 July The Japanese attempt to arrange the visit of an envoy to Moscow, but the Soviets refuse to make a decision.

16 July The Americans detonate the nuclear test weapon 'Trinity' at Alamogordo, New Mexico.

1945

19 July The Japanese launch an attack against the 17th Indian Division south of Toungoo in an attempt to allow the remnants of Japanese Twenty-Eighth Army to break out and withdraw to Malaya.

26 July At the Potsdam Conference, the US, Britain and China make demand for the Japanese surrender.

28 July The Japanese announce that they intend to ignore the Potsdam Declaration.

4 August The last surviving Japanese troops in Burma reach the east bank of Sittang River.

6 August The atomic bomb is dropped on Hiroshima.

The Enola Gay

9 August The atomic bomb is dropped on Nagasaki. The USSR declares war on Japan.

10 August Emperor Hirohito instructs the Supreme Council that the Potsdam Declaration is to be accepted. The Supreme Council signals acceptance of the Declaration to the Americans with caveat that the emperor is to be retained as ruler of Japan.

atomic raid. Kokura was spared by bad weather, and the B-29 *Bockscar,* flown by Major Charles Sweeny, dropped the bomb codenamed 'Fat Man' at 1058 on Nagasaki instead.

Finally, on 10 August, Emperor Hirohito issued instructions that the demands made at Potsdam should be accepted. The Government obeyed, sending a reply to the Americans that it agreed to surrender, but with the provision that 'unconditional' did not imply that the emperor would be replaced. After some debate, the US administration accepted this, and conveyed the message to the Japanese on 11 August. Nonetheless, hardline elements within the Government opposed the notion of surrender. The debate continued for another day as the Government split into factions – one for surrender, the other for a fight to the death.

The emperor made the Government's decision for it. On 14 August 1945, he told the Government that he would prepare a recording to be broadcast to the Japanese people the next day. A coup attempt by militant officers failed

Left: The Japanese surrender delegation arrives on the deck of the USS Missouri, *2 September 1945.*

to locate the recording, and the next morning, at 11.15 a.m., the Japanese public heard their emperor announce their defeat.

This was not, in fact, quite the end. The Soviet assault in Manchuria, led by Marshal Malinovsky's Trans-Baikal Front and Marshal Meretskov's 1st Far Eastern Front, continued. The two fronts punched through the Japanese lines, and linked up on 21 August – seven days after the Japanese had announced their capitulation, and six days after the British and Americans had celebrated VJ-Day. The Soviet success was completed by the seizure of the Kurile Islands by the Navy.

Once news of the emperor's decision reached Japanese forces, they began to lay down their arms. The different outposts surrendered at different times. Japanese units on the Palau Islands and the Carolines surrendered on 2 September, at the same time as the signing of the peace treaty between Japan and the Allies. The remaining outposts gave up over the next few weeks. Indo-China was the last place where the Japanese occupying forces laid down their arms, their surrender being taken on 30 November 1945.

After six years, a period that Churchill had predicted would call for 'blood, toil, tears and sweat', World War II was over. The world would never be the same again.

General Yoshira Umeza signs the surrender document on behalf of the Imperial Japanese Army.

11 August The Americans send a reply to the Japanese surrender document, signalling willingness to permit Hirohito to remain as emperor.

12 August The Japanese debate the American reply to the surrender, while hardline members of the Army endeavour to organize a coup to prevent capitulation.

14 August Hirohito issues orders that the Allied terms are to be accepted.

15 August Hirohito makes a radio broadcast to the Japanese people announcing their surrender.

28 August The first American forces land in Japan.

SEPTEMBER

2 September The Japanese sign a formal surrender.

8 September General MacArthur arrives in Tokyo to assume command of the occupation forces.

9 September Allied landings on the Malayan coast are conducted unopposed.

12 September Mountbatten takes the formal surrender of the Japanese in Southeast Asia.

Index